DATE DUE   *18717*

ALL KIDS ARE OUR KIDS

ALL KIDS ARE OUR KIDS

What Communities Must Do
to Raise Caring and Responsible
Children and Adolescents

Peter L. Benson

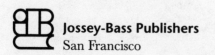

Jossey-Bass Publishers
San Francisco

Chapter One excerpt from Barbara Kingsolver *High Tide in Tucson* originally from *The New York Times Magazine,* February 9, 1992. Reprinted with permission.

Chapter One excerpt from William Raspberry, *A National Movement for Children* © 1994 *Washington Post* Writers Group. Reprinted with permission.

Substantial discounts on bulk quantities of Jossey-Bass books are available to corporations, professional associations, and other organizations. For details and discount information, contact the special sales department at Jossey-Bass Inc., Publishers (415) 433–1740; Fax (800) 605–2665.

For sales outside the United States, please contact your local Simon & Schuster International office.

Jossey-Bass Web address: http://www.josseybass.com

TCF Manufactured in the United States of America on Lyons Falls Turin Book. This paper is acid-free and 100 percent totally chlorine-free.

Library of Congress Cataloging-in-Publication Data

Benson, Peter L.
    All kids are our kids : what communities must do to raise caring and responsible children and adolescents / Peter L. Benson. — 1st ed.
        p. cm.
    Includes index.
    ISBN 0–7879–1068–6 (cloth : acid-free paper)
    1. Child rearing—United States. 2. Child development—United States. 3. Adolescent psychology—United States. 4. Community life—United States. I. Title.
HQ769.B51177 1997
649'.1'0973—dc21   97–21092

FIRST EDITION
HB Printing   10 9 8 7 6 5 4 3

CONTENTS

APPENDIXES

LIST OF FIGURES AND TABLES

Figures

Tables

To
Tunie, Liv, Kai
Dorothy, John, Bob, Ann
Vi, Swede, Ken
and all the other asset-builders in my journey

PREFACE

The measure of the health of a society is how well it takes care of its youngest generation. By this standard, we fail. This conclusion hardly needs more empirical justification. When it comes to paying attention to one's most precious resource, ours is a society losing its way.

The February 1997 report on firearm-related deaths among children is one somber reminder. As tabulated by the Centers for Disease Control and Prevention, the U.S. rates for gun-related homicide, suicide, and unintentional death for children fourteen and under is higher here than the *combined* rates for twenty-five other industrialized nations. Tragic. Alarming. No surprise. U.S. rates of many indicators of young people's health status—alcohol, tobacco, too-early sexual activity, too-early pregnancy, violence, school dropout, percentage of children raised in poverty, achievement test scores—are unsavory, whether you take them in absolute terms or in comparison to other nations.

The critical issue before us is: How do we as a nation respond collectively and individually?

Three interlocking strategies are needed. The first is the "meeting basic human needs" strategy, through which we dramatically enhance our national capacity to ensure economic security, food, shelter, good and useful work, and safety for all residents. The second strategy is to target and reduce—if not eliminate—the risks and deficits that diminish or thwart the healthy development of children and adolescents. Guns, unsafe streets, predatory adults, abuse, family violence, exclusion, alcohol and other drugs, racism, and sexism are among the threats.

Both of these familiar strategies are essential and necessary if we are to raise healthy children and adolescents. But by themselves, even if they are successfully implemented and achieved, these two approaches are not enough. *All Kids Are Our Kids* articulates a third way. It is no more important than the first two, but without diligent pursuit and achievement of this third strategy, we will make only insufficient progress in growing healthy, vibrant, attached, engaged, and competent citizens.

The third way is largely about language, vision, and community. Chapter One presents the vision and the challenges we face. In Chapters Two through Four, I define the concept of *developmental assets*: forty building blocks of human development, each of which enhances the health and well-being of children and adolescents. The language of developmental assets is one of positive development, of good things that must be named and promoted in the dailiness of life. It is a framework grounded in decades of scientific research, reminding us of the "molecules" of healthy development—the gestures, relationships, opportunities, and symbols—that must coalesce to shape lives of hope and possibility.

Based on studies in 460 urban, suburban, and rural communities, I document that these powerful molecules, these developmental assets, are in short supply in communities of all sizes. Furthermore, this rupture in the developmental structure, this failure to pay attention to the development of our young, goes a long way toward explaining the proliferation of health-compromising and future-jeopardizing behaviors among young people that unnerve all of us.

Language is consciousness. One primary goal of *All Kids Are Our Kids* is to shift the language about children and adolescents from a preoccupation with problems, deficits, and risks to a vocabulary of what we need to promote. It is an important first step in unleashing the power of community.

In Chapters Five and Six, I explore a vision of what an asset-building culture and asset-building communities look like. In this vision of child-friendly, child-nurturing, children-and-youth-first places, the actors shift. The prime actors are you and me and our neighbors, coworkers, employers, congregation members, teachers, coaches, and youth group leaders—and our children and adolescents. Professionals, experts, policy makers, and politicians also matter. But the power, the action, and often the leadership is most deeply grounded in the people. In this third way, in this intentional effort to pay attention to healthy development, no resident of a community is on the sidelines. All of us are on the team.

Chapters Eight through Eleven provide strategy, story, and technique for growing healthy, asset-promoting communities. These chapters mix theory with the experiential savvy of people devoted to social change. They are informed equally by knowledge generated by experts and wisdom gleaned from people and communities engaged in and committed to building developmental assets. These chapters present a way of thinking about organizing and implementing asset-building community movements. As importantly, they define the specific capacities and responsibilities of individual citizens, parents, neighborhoods, caregivers, schools, congregations, youth organizations, businesses, health care providers, the media, and local government.

All Kids Are Our Kids is targeted to all who seek to bring about positive change for the sake of children and adolescents in our society. It is designed to prompt action in anyone who knows, sees, lives with, lives next to, works with, or passes by children and adolescents. It is a call to action that seeks to unleash the extra-ordinary power of community when communities unite around a widely shared vision of healthy child and adolescent development.

The third strategy, building asset-promoting communities, is also a long-term one. This emphasis cannot be overstated. Long-term means forever, permanent, a change in normative behavior in which symbols, policies, resource allocation, dialogues, decision making, and the self-definition of what it means to be human incorporate deep commitment to human development in the first two decades of life.

The third way also requires (in the parlance of contemporary social change ideologies) the simultaneous process of grassroots and top-down change, of residents taking individual action, and leaders altering systems. *All Kids Are Our Kids* weaves stories both of processes and of the synergy among them.

Finally, the third way advocated in this book is not the end point. At some point, a fourth way merges and integrates the three approaches of meeting basic human needs for food and shelter, reducing threats to human development, and promoting the atoms and molecules of healthy development. It is my hope that the work on furthering the third strategy so raises the profile of America's young that it functions to unleash sustained energy in addressing the first two.

The jury is still out on how such change-making occurs. We learn from the close to two hundred communities now working with these ideas. We plan to learn a great deal from the newly launched Assets for Colorado Youth initiative, a five and one-half year social experiment to encourage and support a statewide mobilization around the asset framework. Supported by a major, long-term commitment from The Colorado Trust, this effort devotes significant resources and energy to evaluating the impact of dozens of community asset-building initiatives on youth and adults.

I currently use two images to describe this work. One is "journey." The tasks of naming the elements and molecules of healthy development *and* conceiving how culture and community transform are informed both by emerging scientific inquiry and by the learning that comes from and with communities. This is a journey we are only beginning. We have much to learn.

The second image is of "movement." Healthier development for America's children and adolescents is not about starting another short-term, professional-led program. Rather, it is about some combination of shared vision, passion, and sustained action that touches, encourages, and changes most Americans and most communities. For now, I find *movement* to be the word that best captures this process.

Let the movement begin.

Minneapolis, Minnesota   Peter L. Benson
July 1997

ACKNOWLEDGMENTS

The demands of leading Search Institute in Minneapolis have necessitated that "my" writing be a collaborative activity. Simply put, this book would never have been completed without the enormous skill and generosity of Gene Roehlkepartain (Search Institute's director of publishing and communication) and Marilyn Erickson (my administrative assistant).

In addition, it is a much better work because of other colleagues at Search Institute, who continually contribute new insights about the intersection of human development and healthy community. My gratitude goes to Shelby Andress, Tom Berkas, Dale Blyth, Laura Lee Geraghty, Nancy Leffert, Beki Saito, Peter Scales, and James Vollbracht.

The contributing team, though, is much larger. In addition to Rick Gordon, Rick Trierweiler, and Jean Wachs—each of whom advanced the creation and analysis of the national data on which this work is grounded—my thanks extend to Judy Becker, Ann Betz, Kay Bjorke, Paul Bloomer, Mark Borst, Margaret Chayka, Jean Cunningham, Tessa Davis, Craig DeVille, Tim Duffey, Ed Forbush, Jennifer Griffin-Wiesner, Maureen Heinen, Sheryl Herrick, Jack Jackson, Candyce Kroenke, Ann Machmeier, Jan Mills, Torneya Norwood, Flora Sanchez, Anu Sharma, Adell Smith, Terri Swanson, Serita Tapplin, Kate Tyler, Elaine Varner, Debbie Wynn, and Brian Zdroik. Special thanks to Nancy Leffert for her creative data analysis work, and to Nancy and Peter Scales for the bibliography on developmental assets (Appendix A).

Behind the scenes in all nonprofits is the board. In our case, board members have been significant partners in the evolution and growth of the Healthy Communities • Healthy Youth initiative. I am grateful for the support, wisdom, and experience of Dale Delzer, James Dittes, Kent Eklund, John Forliti, Don Fraser, Judy Galbraith, Gene Gall, Elling Halvorson, Vivian Jenkins Nelsen, Syl Jones, Geraldine Kearse Brookins, Monroe Larson, Mary Olson, Michael Olson, Karen Pittman, Albert Quie, Ruth Randall, Michael Ranum, James Renier, Sharon Sayles Belton, Robert Skare, Harlan Stelmach, and Barbara Varenhorst.

Major support for our work on developmental assets and healthy communities is provided by Lutheran Brotherhood, which offers financial services, community service opportunities, and philanthropic outreach in communities nationwide. Beginning in 1996, Lutheran Brotherhood has expressed its commitment to the social good and the creation of healthy communities for all youth by pledging multiyear corporate support to undergird the development and expansion of Search Institute's Healthy Communities • Healthy Youth initiative. Beginning in 1989, Lutheran Brotherhood has assisted hundreds of communities in both conducting studies on developmental assets and acquiring resources for promoting positive youth development. I am deeply grateful for the organization's leadership, commitment, and support, including the special grant to prepare this manuscript. Its passion for promoting a national asset-building movement is visible in its board, corporate and field staff, and national volunteer system. Special thanks to CEO Robert Gandrud, Executive Vice President Paul Ramseth, Vice President Louise Thoreson, and Ellen Albee, manager of program development, Fraternal Division.

At the same time, I thank a growing number of other partners supporting our work on developmental assets and community change, including the Blandin Foundation, the Cargill Foundation, the DeWitt Wallace–Reader's Digest Fund, the Ford Foundation, the W. K. Kellogg Foundation, the Lilly Endowment, the Norwest Foundation, the Stewardship Foundation, the Vesper Society in Oakland, California, and Robert and Marilyn Skare. A particular debt of gratitude goes to The Colorado Trust for its long-term commitment to launch and grow an asset-building movement in that state.

The initiative is also supported by school districts, city agencies, community collaborations, state agencies, youth organizations, community foundations, and citizens in hundreds of cities across the country.

Many have inspired, supported, and shaped the content of this work. I'm grateful for:

- The scholarship and wisdom of James Comer, William Damon, Joy Dryfoos, Marian Wright Edelman, Joyce Epstein, John Gardner, Fritz Ianni, Joan Lipsitz, Richard Lerner, Ann Masden, John McKnight, Karen Pittman, Merton Strommen, Emmy Werner, and Joan Wynn.

- The splendid counsel and encouragement of Leslie Iura and Christie Hakim, my editors at Jossey-Bass.
- The creative approaches to youth development and community change learned from Karen Atkinson, Bonnie Bernard, Delroy Calhoun, Donald Draayer, Sam Grant, Nan Henderson, Brenda Holben, Carl Holmstrom, Mary Hoopman, Rick Jackson, Vivian Jenkens Nelsen, Mick Johnson, Dick Kinch, Dick Mammen, Colleen Moriarty, Richard Murphy, Jolene Roehlkepartain, Mark and Susan Scharenbroich, Carol Truesdell, Gary Walker in Philadelphia, and Gary Walker in Tempe.
- Robert King and the Trim Tab Foundation.
- The visionaries, change makers, youth advocates, and children and adolescents in the hundreds of cities taking the journey with us.

I particularly want to acknowledge the leaders, adults, and youth of St. Louis Park, Minnesota, for their pioneering and sustained commitment to the developmental asset paradigm, with special thanks to Dr. Carl Holmstrom, who launched the city's Children First movement and who continues to ignite passion for this approach in many communities.

P. L. B.

THE AUTHOR

Peter L. Benson is president of Search Institute, Minneapolis, a national organization that generates knowledge through research and promotes its application to advance the healthy development of children and adolescents, where he serves as author, researcher, consultant, and lecturer on youth development, community development, and the intersection of the two. He also serves as adjunct professor at the University of Minnesota and is the author or coauthor of *The Quicksilver Years, What Kids Need to Succeed, Religion on Capitol Hill: Myths and Realities, Beyond Leaf Raking: Learning to Serve/Serving to Learn,* and *The Troubled Journey: A Portrait of 6th–12th Grade Youth.* He was educated at Augustana College (B.A.), Yale University (M.A.), and the University of Denver (M.A., Ph.D. in social psychology).

About Search Institute

Search Institute is a nonprofit research and educational organization working to advance the healthy development of adolescents and children through research, evaluation, consultation, training, and publications. Founded in 1958, the institute launched its national Healthy Communities • Healthy Youth initiative in 1996. For information, contact Search Institute, 700 S. Third Street, Suite 210, Minneapolis, MN 55415; toll-free: 800–888–7828; web site: http://www.search-institute.org.

CHAPTER ONE

INTRODUCTION

From Peril to Possibility

Imagine a U.S. city that is especially successful in raising caring, responsible, and healthy children and adolescents. What would this community look like? What does it do that makes such a difference?

Some characteristics are fundamental. It has a vibrant economic infrastructure that meets basic needs for adequate income, meaningful work, affordable housing, health care, and safety. Moreover, it provides humane and effective services and interventions for vulnerable families and their children. It aggressively works to reduce the environmental circumstances—poverty, racism, malnutrition, abuse, and violence—that threaten young people's healthy development.

As fundamental as these efforts are, they are not sufficient. A community that truly meets the needs of its youngest generation complements its strong economic infrastructure with a vibrant developmental infrastructure—that is, with community commitments and strategies that accentuate the positive building blocks of human development. In this community, children and adolescents experience:

- Daily support and care provided by one or more involved, loving parents or other caregivers
- Sustained relationships with several nonparent adults in the community
- A neighborhood where everyone knows, protects, listens to, and gets involved with the young

- Opportunities to participate in developmentally responsive and enticing clubs, teams, and organizations led by principled, responsible, and trained adults
- Access to child-friendly public places
- Daily affirmation and encouragement
- Intergenerational relationships, in which children and teenagers bond with adults of many ages and in which teenagers bond with younger children
- A stake in community life made concrete through useful roles and opportunities for involvement
- Boundaries, values, and high expectations consistently articulated, modeled, and reinforced across multiple socializing systems
- Peer groups motivated to achieve and contribute
- Caring schools, congregations, youth-serving organizations, and other institutions
- Opportunities for frequent acts of service to others

This kind of vibrant developmental infrastructure cannot be legislated or enforced by laws. It cannot be created by paid professionals or new programs. It cannot be "purchased" with public or philanthropic funds. And although good families are essential architects for this infrastructure, this foundation cannot be created by families alone.

Forming this foundation is the work of all of the community's residents and institutions. They are the ones who support, encourage, motivate, guide, and empower young people through thousands of individual and group acts of caring and commitment. They are the ones who build relationships day by day that show children and adolescents they are known, valued, listened to, and connected.

In short, this vision of healthy communities focuses on creating a normative culture in which adults, organizations, and community institutions unite to take action guided by a shared vision of positive development. It is this kind of community that nurtures caring and competent youth, ready to become responsible neighbors, citizens, parents, and workers.

The Crumbling Developmental Infrastructure

This image of a healthy community stands in marked contrast to today's realities.

Everywhere we look, U.S. towns and cities are structured—however unintentionally and benignly—to work against young people's healthy development. Instead of the image opening this chapter, we see communities characterized by:

- Age segregation, which separate adults from the lives of children and vice versa
- Silence, inconsistency, and negative messages about boundaries and values

- Mistrust, which undermines relationships between youth and adults, adults and other adults, institutions and residents
- Fragmented, ill-equipped, and isolated socializing systems
- A normative climate that emphasizes privacy and civic disengagement rather than a shared vision and commitment
- The isolation of families

During the first eighteen years of life, it is common for a young person not to know well any adults outside of her own family; to be a stranger in the neighborhood; to be ignored or unwelcome in public places (especially in the company of other youth); to be the object of well-intentioned programs without having any say in their focus or design; to lack safe places to spend time; to be excluded from the community's deliberations; to spend considerable time each day without an adult presence; and rarely, if ever, to join with peers or adults in serving others.

These concerns cannot be dismissed as urban issues alone. Part of the American dilemma is that these issues affect *all* sizes of communities in all parts of the nation. A story from a Midwestern agricultural town of three thousand illustrates the pervasiveness of the problem. I asked what issues concerned local citizens there. The response gave me pause: "We have packs of twelve- and thirteen-year-olds who destroy or vandalize property. And nobody knows their names." What is notable is not just the destruction of property but the perpetrators' anonymity.

Most Americans see the crumbling infrastructure in bits and pieces—something unraveling here, something else going wrong over there. Rarely do we put the pieces together to see their interconnections and the bigger picture of what is happening to the youngest generation.

In 1989, Search Institute introduced a framework of developmental assets, which has begun to put some of the pieces together. Drawing from extensive literature on child and adolescent development, the framework of assets identifies forty experiences, opportunities, and internal capacities essential for health and success in a complex society. (Chapter Two examines the sources and nature of these assets.) They are grouped into eight categories:[1]

External Assets	*Internal Assets*
Support	Commitment to learning
Empowerment	Positive values
Boundaries and expectations	Social competencies
Constructive use of time	Positive identity

This framework provides not only a vision of what young people need from their families and communities but also a vivid picture of what is missing for most young people.

Since 1989, Search Institute has conducted in-depth studies of sixth-to-twelfth-grade students in public school districts across the country. By early 1995, this study had been conducted in more than five hundred public school districts.

For this book, we have aggregated responses from the 460 school districts that assessed all or most students in the sixth to twelfth grades and that conducted either a full census or a random sampling of students. The resulting sample of 254,634 students (most surveyed between 1992 and 1995) is diverse in geography, race and ethnicity, and community size. It represents one of the largest efforts ever undertaken to measure the life experience of America's youth. (Chapter Three provides more information on the survey and sampling process.)

As we survey youth in communities across the country regarding their experiences of developmental assets, we find that the average young person experiences only about half of them. This is true regardless of town size or region. It is true for youth in all ethnic groups. The problem is everywhere: far too few young people are being "gifted" with the positive experiences, opportunities, and relationships that nurture the character and commitment they need to be healthy, productive, and contributing members of society.

Signs of the Crumbling Infrastructure

The relative absence of developmental assets in young people's lives suggests that our culture has lost its way in raising caring and responsible children and adolescents. A report from the American Medical Association captures our nation's dilemma with these words: "For the first time in the history of this country, young people are *less* healthy and *less* prepared to take their places in society than were their parents. And this is happening at a time when our society is more complex, more challenging, and more competitive than ever before."[2]

Everyone who spends time with young people can see the signs. In schools, educators must devote increased attention to managing problems and negotiating social services. Amid public fear about youth violence, precious resources are poured into costly juvenile intervention and justice systems for more violent and younger children and youth.[3] Employers are investing more and more resources in remedial efforts to equip young people who are just entering the workforce with the skills and attitudes that they lack, but that they need in order to be productive workers.

Four streams of evidence document the critical state of affairs for today's young people: the near-universality of high-risk behaviors; historical trends that show deepening concerns; the high levels of problems when comparing the United States to other nations; and evidence of a declining commitment to prosocial commitments among youth.

The Prevalence of High-Risk Behaviors

A majority of American youth engage in health-compromising behavior. In her pioneering *Adolescents at Risk*, Joy Dryfoos concludes that half of all ten-to-seventeen-year-olds are at high or moderate risk of undermining their chances for a healthy life because of substance use; unsafe sex or teenage pregnancy; and school failure and delinquency, crime, or violence.[4]

An important reanalysis of data from the National Survey of Children supports this conclusion. This federally funded project studied children age seven to eleven in 1976 who were then reinterviewed in 1981 and 1987. Researchers found that, before age eighteen, 68 percent of American boys and 55 percent of American girls had taken a serious developmental "misstep," defined as using illegal drugs, running away from home, engaging in voluntary premarital sex, having a child premaritally, or dropping out of high school.[5]

A more recent examination of young people's involvement in risky behaviors is embedded in Search Institute's study of more than 250,000 twelve-to-eighteen-year-olds. This study suggests even higher levels of risk-taking behaviors than were identified in the National Survey of Children. This research measured young people's involvement in one or more of the following high-risk behavior patterns:

- Three or more uses of alcohol in the previous month or drinking to the point of intoxication one or more times in the past two weeks
- Daily cigarette use
- Three or more uses of an illegal drug (for example, marijuana, cocaine, LSD) in the past year
- Sexual intercourse three or more times
- Three or more acts of antisocial behavior (such as vandalism or shoplifting) in the past year
- Three or more acts of violence in the past year
- Reported frequent depression or attempted suicide
- Repeated absenteeism from school

Any involvement in some of these risk behaviors could be considered alarming. A single act of violence, for example, is considered intolerable by most people in our society. However, even when the cutoff points are set at what may be intolerably high levels, 64 percent of all young people are at risk in one or more of these behaviors (Figure 1.1). As we would expect, this percentage is higher in the upper grades: 81 percent of twelfth graders are at risk in one or more of these areas.

Increased Risks Compared to the Past

Not only are high-risk behaviors widespread among U.S. youth, but several national studies document that these behaviors have increased in sheer numbers when compared to previous decades. Generally speaking, in the past decade rates for the following have increased: violent deaths among those fifteen to nineteen; arrests of ten-to-seventeen-year-olds; teenage pregnancy; the percentage of all births that were to single teenagers; number of births for mothers younger than fifteen; the percentage of high school-age students dropping out of school or graduating late; and suicides among fifteen-to-twenty-four-year-olds.[6]

Each of these areas represents a tremendous need and challenge, and society is now faced with costly questions about how to respond to, slow down, and reverse these trends. But taken together, these changes provide striking evidence that this society is profoundly off target—and losing ground—in its capacity or willingness to raise the youngest generation.

FIGURE 1.1. HIGH-RISK BEHAVIOR PATTERNS AMONG PUBLIC HIGH SCHOOL STUDENTS, BY GRADE LEVEL.

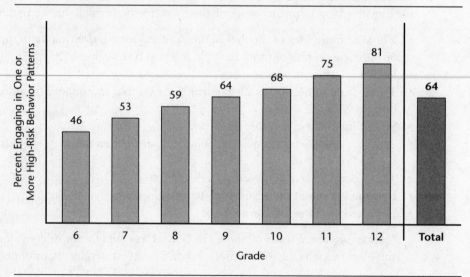

Higher Risks Than in Other Countries

Compared with other technologically advanced nations, the United States has the dubious distinction of being a leader in several problem areas, including teenage pregnancy, adolescent alcohol and other drug use, and school dropouts.[7] This country fairs poorly in rankings on international comparisons of student achievement. For example, thirteen-year-olds in the United States fall behind in both science and mathematics achievement when compared to same-age peers in Canada, France, Hungary, Ireland, Israel, Italy, Korea, Switzerland, and Taiwan.[8]

Additional comparisons are particularly sobering. Compared to other affluent nations, the United States has a high rate of children in poverty (20 percent of all children in 1995).[9] Furthermore, poor children in the United States are worse off economically than poor children in other affluent nations, while, ironically, affluent children in the United States are considerably better off than affluent children in other nations.[10] In part due to these poverty trends, U.S. rates for infant mortality and low birthweight infants are among the highest in comparison with other affluent nations.[11]

Finally, adolescents in the United States are much more likely than young people in other countries to be killed during adolescence by homicide or an accident. Indeed, adolescents in the United States are ten to fifteen times as likely to die from a homicide as in any European country.[12]

Absence of Prosocial Commitments

The prevalence of problems is only one way to ascertain the vitality of a nation's young people. A parallel indicator of vitality focuses on young people's positive commitments and contributions to society. Most obvious of these is a commitment to serving others and the community—a cornerstone of a humane and democratic society.

Given the importance of volunteerism, service, and civic engagement in this democratic society, we take it as another sign of our national disrepair that only 33 percent of public high school students in the United States performed *any* volunteer service within the past two years.[13]

Thus, not only are we failing to protect young people from the problems that can thwart their healthy development, but we are also failing to promote commitments to the common good that are essential to our society's long-term health and vitality. (Part of the problem is that adults do not model such commitments either. Indeed, young people are more likely to volunteer than adults.)

Making matters worse, there is a penchant in public policy, when dollars become tight, to sacrifice positive youth development opportunities and experiences (such as music, art, drama, organized sports, summer employment, work readiness, before-school and after-school care) in favor of preserving or expanding treatment and intervention systems. Too often, it seems easier or more politically expedient to propose building another juvenile detention center than to enhance and expand a community's capacity to nurture and connect all of its young.

Shared Responsibility for Current Realities

It is not completely clear whether growing up now is riskier than it once was, or whether we see differences because we are now better at identifying and measuring long-standing dilemmas. In some ways, it does not really matter. What matters is that there are too many casualties, too many wounded, too many close calls, too much unfulfilled potential among today's youth. What matters is that this society is failing to provide the vibrant developmental infrastructure young people need to survive and thrive.

Why are we in this mess? If blame is to be cast, it implicates a wide range of people and systems. The problem is bigger than scapegoating young people for their problems and society's. It is bigger than families and bigger than schools (though these two groupings are most often blamed for not being up to the task). The problem is deeper than cutbacks in funding and support from the public sector (although such cuts can undermine the efforts that are needed). The problem lies at the core of how our entire society—both individuals and institutions—treats and cares for children and adolescents.

Numerous cultural trends have contributed to the current state of affairs. In what ratio and with what interplay is unclear. In this section, we identify five realities that contribute to the current situation.

Decline in Family Support

The institution of the family is undergoing radical transformation. The combination of comparatively high rates of divorce and separation, the demands of finding and keeping work in an ambiguous economy, and the pursuit of material gain or individual fulfillment interfere with the commitment of families to their number one responsibility.[14]

For many children and adolescents, family life is marked by parental absence—physical and/or emotional. David Elkind captures this absence with his profound insight:

Many of today's parents—offspring of the modern nuclear family but also products of the social upheavals of the 1960s and 70s and the economic pressures of the 1980s and 90s—no longer . . . think of children and youth as requiring a full helping of security, protection, firm limits, and clear values, and many of those who still believe in the goodness of those things no longer have faith in their ability as parents to provide them in today's complex world. As a consequence, postmodern young people are often left without the social envelope of security and protection that shielded earlier generations. Because today's children and teenagers are resourceful, they can cope, to some extent, with these new demands for independence and maturity. But ironically, this demonstration of adaptability often encourages parents, and the larger society, to provide even less security and direction than they might otherwise have done.[15]

The rupture of family support has numerous historical and societal roots, among them changes in workplace demands, changing attitudes of parents regarding their responsibilities, and parents' sense of stress and helplessness to ward off the barrage of messages and influences that undermine family priorities. Although some of the changes are due to choices parents make, others are forces beyond the family that stretch and strain families, making it more difficult for them to fill their essential role in young people's development.

Rupture in Community Support for Young People

A symbol of our difficulty in raising healthy youth is the widespread and growing belief that kids are the responsibility of family. Period. This is a radical departure from the way it has been, when parents were understood to be "representatives of the larger social order," sharing "child-rearing responsibilities with other agents of society."[16]

Part of the problem is that U.S. culture does not, for the most part, treasure its children and adolescents. In fact, as Barbara Kingsolver writes (see "Children: Burden or Blessing?"), the opposite is often true: young people are too often viewed as inconveniences or as problems or burdens to their families and communities.

Children: Burden or Blessing?

The following story by Barbara Kingsolver offers a vivid example of how another culture places a priority on its young in contrast to U.S. attitudes toward children and adolescents.

As I walked out the street entrance to my newly rented apartment, a guy in maroon high-tops and a skateboard haircut approached, making kissing noises and saying, "Hi, gorgeous." Three weeks earlier, I would have assessed the degree of malice and made ready to run or tell him to bug off, depending. But now, instead, I smiled, and so did my four-year-old daughter, because after dozens of similar encounters I understood he didn't mean me but her.

This is not the United States.

For most of the year my daughter was four we lived in Spain, in the warm southern province of the Canary Islands. I struggled with dinner at midnight and the subjunctive tense, but my only genuine culture shock reverberated from this earthquake of a fact: people there like kids. They don't just say so, they do. Widows in black, buttoned-down CEOs, purple-sneakered teenagers, the butcher, the baker, all would stop on the street to have little chats with my daughter. Routinely, taxi drivers leaned out the window and shouted "Hola, guapa!" My daughter, who must have felt my conditioned flinch would look up at me wide-eyed and explain patiently, "I like it that people think I'm pretty." With a mother's keen myopia I would tell you, absolutely, my daughter is beautiful enough to stop traffic. But in the city of Santa Cruz, I have to confess, so was every other person under the height of one meter. Not just those who conceded to be seen and not heard. Whenever Camille grew cranky in a restaurant (and really, what do you expect at midnight?), the waiters flirted and brought her little presents, and nearby diners looked on with that sweet, wistful gleam of eye that I'd thought diners reserved for the dessert tray. What I discovered in Spain was a culture that held children to be its meringues and éclairs. My own culture, it seemed to me in retrospect, tended to regard children as a sort of toxic-waste product: a necessary evil, maybe, but if it's not our own we don't want to see it or hear it or, God help us, smell it.

Source: Excerpted from Barbara Kingsolver, *High Tide in Tucson: Essays from Now or Never* (New York: HarperCollins, 1995).

What is clear is a retreat by most citizens from natural and daily responsibility for nurturing the youth in their midst who are "not my own kids." Not long ago, I visited a small city to share with them results of a study of youth in their community. The finding that most galvanized the community was that fewer than one in five young people reported that their neighbors cared about them. As if to underscore that this statistic was not an anomaly, three young people began the presentation, telling the adults that "people around here really don't seem to care much about us."

It is easy to think of community support programmatically, in terms of clubs, teams, organizations, and places to be. Indeed, such programmatic areas of community life are crucial and need reinforcement. But these programmatic expressions of care should supplement individual commitments to caring, not the other way around. Community support ought to be present from adults who take personal responsibility to "be there" for youth as advocates, affirmers, role models, boundary setters, values transmitters, encouragers, and elders in the routine and daily dynamics of neighborhoods, congregations, workplaces, and public places.

These forms of daily involvement are waning for several reasons. First and foremost is the cancerous spread of age segregation, in which adults and children go their separate ways. The architecture and design of communities and neighborhoods isolates families, and virtually every program and institution is organized to meet age-specific needs at the expense of the richness of intergenerational community. The public perception of danger and the rise of mistrust freezes connectedness and undermines community.

Civic engagement (and the lack thereof) has become a topic of lively debate among academicians and policy makers. There is evidence that people join less, connect less, and engage less in community life.[17] One effect of this trend is disengagement from the lives of children and adolescents.

Exacerbating the problem, our culture overstates the importance of individual gain at the expense of community; "I" is more important than "we." Growing social mistrust fuels the privatization of personal and family life, with citizens disengaging from each other, from civic affairs, and from shared responsibility for the healthy nurture of the youngest generation.

Two other dynamics contribute to this disengagement. One is the current American proclivity to identify, count, and report problems (for example, alcohol abuse, teen pregnancy, youth violence). Any adult who pays attention to the media is barraged with reports of the demise of childhood. This repeated experience overwhelms and inadvertently communicates that the problems are too big, too vast for an average citizen to make any difference.

A second dynamic fueling disengagement from the lives of children is what John McKnight calls the professionalization of care. He writes: "The most significant development transforming America since World War II has been the growth of a powerful service economy and its pervasive serving institutions. Those institutions have [commoditized] the care of community and called that substitution a service. As citizens have seen the professionalized service commodity invade their communities, they have grown doubtful of their common capacity to care, and so it is that we have become a careless society, populated by impotent citizens and ineffectual communities dependent on the counterfeit of care called human services."[18]

These two dynamics lull us into the naïve belief (and hope) that doing better is a matter of introducing more programs and hiring more professionals, usually at public expense. Reclaiming positive community-based socialization hinges on quite the opposite: the resurrection of relational engagement with children and adolescents.

The Loss of Consistency in Socialization

In order to pass on a coherent and constructive worldview to children and adolescents, socializing systems (family, school, youth organizations, religious institutions, agencies, media) need to be on the same page, singing the same song. If we want to nurture the value of environmental responsibility, for example, our success is enhanced when youth are exposed to multiple places that articulate and model this core value.

Consistency used to happen more naturally, without much dialogue or rehearsal. That's because people with similar beliefs lived together in clans, tribes, and small towns. Sometimes, such common beliefs were dysfunctional, as in the case of a shared intolerance for difference. Even in this negative context, though, the principle of consistency could be said to "work": a community of people bound together in this belief was successful in passing intolerance on to the next generation.

Consistency matters for transmitting the best of a culture as well. This includes such key values as responsibility, compassion, integrity, and justice. The growing heterogeneity of our society as well as the mass media expose youth to many ways of thinking and choosing, some of which are inconsistent. And it must be confusing, particularly when family, peers, media, and school are rarely united.

Where now are the consistent voices on things that matter? Such consistency needs to be intentionally reclaimed. I believe that virtually all people in communities—regardless of income, political persuasion, religious ideology, or race—share some common core values about what is good. Subgroups, families, and individuals may have additional perspectives that add richness beyond this common core. But the common core must be named through a process of safe community dialogue. Then it becomes a matter of broad and deep intentionality to articulate, and model, and symbolize these shared commitments in all places of interaction with youth. To do otherwise—via silence or inconsistency—invites confusion and risks soft commitment to the best of this culture.

Take the value of caring. We would expect that if the people of even the most diverse communities were polled, there would be a shared commitment that compassion for others is a personal and social good. Yet, in all probability, communities give mixed signals and, in some cases, may give counterproductive cues (such as: compassion is feminine, not masculine).

If compassion matters as a cherished youth outcome, then compassion must be modeled, articulated, rewarded, encouraged, and expected for youth as well as adults (who are less likely to volunteer than youth). It becomes part of a community's normative structure with informal and programmatic opportunity for caring in family, neighborhood, youth organizations, schools, and religious institutions.

Few experience such consistency in values. Some families pursue it by choosing parochial schools that match family or religious worldviews. Some reduce the amount of inconsistency by proactively monitoring TV viewing to reduce exposure to violence or unbridled consumerism. Home schooling may also be seen as an effort to reduce the inconsistency.

Furthermore, many are wary of seeking to identify shared values out of a (sometimes justified) fear that someone seeks to impose parochial values on them and their community. But communities have the capacity to increase consistency of socialization for all children. It is not without risk, and it takes work. But it's essential if we seek to rebuild a solid foundation for our young.

The Modern Creation of Disconnection

The three dynamics discussed so far require reweaving the tattered web of community life. Another dynamic that interferes with healthy development is dealt with not by rediscovering what has been lost but by seeking a solution to a modern invention. This invention is the period between childhood and adulthood. It includes what we now call adolescence.

Until fairly recent times, societies moved children into the adult roles of work and parenting during the teenage years. Only during the past half-century has a high school or secondary education for all young people become a commonly held standard. This new expectation, a larger peer group, and other changes affecting adolescence (such as the downward trend in the age of onset of menarche) all combine to make adolescence a very different experience than it was only two or three generations ago.[19]

Today's adolescents have to navigate through a long period of ambiguity in which modern society provides few if any rites of passage marking the transition out of childhood and offers few if any roles that give adolescents a stake in community life.[20] Recent Search Institute research suggests that only a third of middle school and high school students think that their community provides useful roles for youth.[21]

In the vernacular of contemporary strategic planning, youth are important stakeholders in community life. But you would not know it by how communities make decisions or conduct their affairs. What we have created is an "in-between" period of development: not child, not adult. Unless communities begin to actively engage their young in the affairs of community—providing places and moments of connection, involvement, partnership, input, and responsibility—we risk reinforcing an antiadult youth culture that overemphasizes self-absorption and the pursuit of immediate gratification. This society hardly needs more of either.

The Proliferation of Developmental Deficits

Developmental deficits are negative influences or realities in young people's lives that make it more difficult for them to develop in healthy, caring, and productive ways. They are liabilities that may not do permanent harm but make harm more possible.

Poverty. Deep and persistent poverty is one of these. As noted earlier, the United States, of all industrialized countries, has an untenably high rate of child poverty. We also seem to be losing our potential will to search for a solution. National economic challenges have led policy makers to dismantle public support for low-income families. All the ramifications of this change in policy are not clear, but it's highly likely that the gap between the haves and have nots will widen.

Other deficits can also interfere with healthy development. Search Institute's study of 460 school districts includes assessments of the ten different deficits in sixth-to-twelfth-grade youth: spending time alone at home, hedonistic values, overexposure to television, attending drinking parties, stress, physical abuse, sexual abuse, parental addiction, social isolation, and negative peer pressure. (For definitions of these deficits and the percentages of youth who experience each, see Appendix B.) The average student in our national study has 2.4 of these ten deficits.

Time Alone. Among these ten deficits, the most common is being alone at home two hours or more per day; three out of five young people report that as the case. This rate reflects that 61 percent of tenth-to-twelfth graders spend this much time alone at home, but a surprising 53 percent of sixth graders also report this deficit. These numbers will only increase if more schools move to shorter school days in response to budget pressures.

Physical and Sexual Abuse. Eighteen percent of all students report physical abuse. Eleven percent report sexual abuse. On both, girls report higher rates than boys (on physical abuse, 21 percent versus 15 percent; on sexual abuse, 19 percent versus 3 percent). Overall, nearly one-third of all girls (32 percent) report having been physically or sexually abused.

Though we do not know if these reports of abuse are about family members or not, it is a reasonable assumption that most are. Accordingly, we find that young people who experience these deficits are less likely to experience many of the positive interactions in the family that contribute to healthy development.

TV Overexposure. Our research finds that watching a lot of television tends to interfere with education (both in terms of school performance and long-term educational aspirations), positive peer influences, development of empathy for others, and involvement in constructive activities (such as music and arts, community organizations, school cocurricular activities). In addition, a litany of previous studies have concluded that increased TV viewing is associated with increased frequency of violent behaviors.[22]

While this book advocates a vision of healthy community that seeks to rebuild the developmental assets young people need, we ought not to be blinded to the fact that there are environmental threats that interfere with healthy development and must be addressed. Any comprehensive effort to raise healthy youth must take these deficits seriously.[23] At the same time, there is growing evidence that focusing on these problems alone is inadequate and short-sighted, in the same way that shipping food to starving people is an inadequate solution for countries that need sustainable development efforts to make starvation less likely. Raising healthy youth requires balancing crisis intervention with efforts that make the crises less likely to occur.

Searching for Solutions

In communities and institutions everywhere, people are looking for solutions to the crisis facing America's youth. The most common approach is to name problems and then develop targeted strategies to reduce or contain them. This approach often involves redesigning or integrating systems, developing prevention programs to prevent specific problem behaviors (such as violence, substance abuse, and teen pregnancy), and, when problems persist, resorting to increasingly expensive treatment, rehabilitation, and incarceration efforts. Despite tremendous resources and energy that have been invested in these deficit-reduction approaches, they are either ineffective in combating the problems they were designed to address or, if they do have a positive impact, they are so expensive to implement that they could never be replicated on a national scale.

Part of the problem has been that the deficit-reduction paradigm and approach tend to be designed to attack problems one at a time. As a result, these efforts depend on sustained interest in the specific problem (such as homelessness, poverty, illiteracy, family violence, child abuse and neglect, unemployment) from people implementing programs and from funding sources. Too often, though, the interest and resources dry up when the initial flurry of concern about the issue is replaced in public consciousness by another, seemingly more pressing issue.

As the interrelatedness and complexity of these issues is recognized, more comprehensive methodologies are now being developed. One focuses on reconfiguring public services to address multiple, interrelated problems. A common expression of this model involves collaborations among the child welfare, social service, and economic development arms of local government, largely to ameliorate poverty-related challenges. In some settings, public schools are brought into the mix to provide a single location for multiple services to children, youth, and families. Another approach is for social service professionals to make home visits and to assist families in finding and using available services to address multiple needs.

Some efforts to develop comprehensive services are particularly innovative, benefiting from foundations' expertise and funding. A good example is the Annie E. Casey Foundation's New Futures initiative, which led five cities through redesigning the delivery of interventions and support systems for high-risk youth. Among its recent conclusions is that, "in some low-income communities, service systems and institutional-change initiatives, by themselves, cannot transform poor educational, social, and health outcomes for vulnerable children and families."[24] Consequently, the initiative has now incorporated economic development into its design.

Other deficit-reduction strategies seek to touch a larger percentage of America's young by reducing developmental risks in the larger population, not just among vulnerable children and families. They include community efforts to reduce access to weapons, reduce teenage pregnancy, and limit youth access to tobacco and alcohol both within and outside the home.[25]

The Limits of Deficit Thinking

Despite the innovations involved and significant investment in these efforts by public, private, and philanthropic sectors, their overall impact has been minimal. Much of the problem is that they are rooted in a deficit-based paradigm that focuses too exclusively on reducing or eliminating individual risks and problems. Though the concerns about the problems are justified, the problem-centered response by itself perpetuates a mind-set of professionalizing services to patch up young people and families, rather than a fundamental rethinking of how this society cares for its young.

Daniel Goleman sums up the weakness of the deficit-centered approach this way: "Over the last decade or so 'wars' have been declared, in turn, on teen pregnancy, dropping out, drugs, and most recently violence. The trouble with such campaigns, though, is that they come too late, after the targeted problem has reached epidemic proportions and taken firm root in the lives of the young. They are crisis intervention, the equivalent of solving a problem by sending an ambulance to the rescue rather than giving an inoculation that would ward off the disease in the first place."[26]

Unfortunately, the deficit-reduction paradigm is deeply entrenched. As the dominant approach to advancing child and adolescent well-being, it is fueled by the predilection of social researchers to name and count the negative. Take, for example, the *Kids Count* report, released annually by the Annie E. Casey Foundation. This highly influential barometer of child well-being focuses exclusively on monitoring state-by-state trends in these ten areas: low birthweight babies, infant deaths, child deaths, teen violent deaths, teens having babies, youth arrested for violent crimes, school dropouts, idle teens, child poverty, and single-parent families.[27] An abundance of other national studies share this bias for naming and counting the negative. They often (and dramatically) repeat trends in alcohol, tobacco, and other drug use.

The paradigm is also reinforced by the print and broadcast media, which in their daily coverage of local, national, and world events tend to emphasize conflict, crime, and violence. A Rocky Mountain Media Watch study documented that 53.8 percent of the news time in a sample of twenty-nine U.S. cities was devoted to crime, war, or disaster stories.[28] This "mayhem index" likely also holds for how news about children and adolescents is repeated.

Language shapes consciousness. The language of deficits dominates nearly all deliberations. Research on youth issues tends to identify and count large and seemingly intractable problems. The media put a human face on these problems. Foundations and government agencies organize funding programs around these issues (violence prevention, drug prevention, teen pregnancy prevention). Social service agencies raise funds and develop programs to respond to these needs.

The deficit language—and the paradigm undergirding it—has a debilitating effect. It makes the public feel powerless in the face of daunting, complex problems. And it fuels the erroneous conclusion that costly programs run by professionals are *the* antidote.

Deficit thinking is akin to the medical model in which the absence of symptoms is (mis)taken for good health. Even if we as a society figured out how to reduce developmental deficits and risks, and even if we found the political and social will to address effectively and compassionately the untenably high rate of family and child poverty, the success of our national effort to raise healthy children and adolescents would be only partial.

In challenging what they call needs-based approaches that focus on a community's problems and needs, John P. Kretzmann and John L. McKnight of the Center for Urban Affairs and Policy Research write: "Because a needs-based strategy can guarantee only survival, and can never lead to serious change or community development, this orientation must be regarded as one of the major causes of the sense of hopelessness that pervades discussions about the future of low income communities. From the street corner to the White House, if maintenance and survival are the best we can provide, what sense can it make to invest in the future?"[29]

The absence of economic, social, family, or personal deficits may make health easier to attain, but such absence is not the same thing as health, just as absence of chest pain does not in and of itself signal cardiovascular health.[30] As Karen J. Pittman, a longtime advocate for positive youth development has said, "Problem free does not mean fully prepared."[31]

A Different Paradigm: The Vision of Asset Building

In his best-selling book, *The Seven Habits of Highly Effective People*, Steven Covey writes: "It becomes obvious that if we want to make relatively minor changes in our lives, we can perhaps appropriately focus on our attitudes and behaviors. But if we want to make significant, quantum change, we need to work on our basic paradigms."[32]

Extending Covey's point, we may be able to improve the situation for our young people and communities by fine-tuning and reshaping programs and services (assuming we can continue to pay for them). But if we want quantum change in the lives of our young people and the health of our communities, we have to revise our basic paradigms.

That work has begun in pockets across the country. People have begun questioning the adequacy of the deficit-centered (problem-centered) paradigm for addressing young people's development. Researchers, activists, and practitioners have begun exploring and experimenting with new approaches. Early signs are that these approaches have tremendous potential for improving the well-being of children and adolescents. Furthermore, they capture people's imagination and renew a sense of hope and commitment.

Search Institute's framework of developmental assets offers communities a new vision that is helping them shift their paradigm. As communities have measured the developmental assets among their own youth, they see the potential of this framework to ignite a positive, communitywide commitment to raising healthy children and adolescents.

The asset-building vision represents the other side of the coin. Instead of focusing on fixing problems, it centers on nurturing the positive building blocks of development that all young people need. This approach contrasts sharply with traditional deficit-reduction approaches, as shown in Table 1.1.

The bottom line is this: assets, as we elaborate on them in the chapters that follow, are developmental necessities. They are important in the lives of all youth, whether African American, Asian American, Hispanic American, Native American, or white. They are important whether rich or poor. And in all rural areas, small towns, suburbs, and large cities across the country, we are failing to provide these necessities.

This gap may be the most pressing social crisis of our time. It requires a shift in language, from naming and counting deficits and problems to naming and

TABLE 1.1. TWO PARADIGMS FOR INCREASING THE WELL-BEING OF CHILDREN AND ADOLESCENTS.

	Deficit Reduction	Asset Promotion
The Problem	Poverty, environmental risks, family dysfunction, high-risk behaviors	Extensive rupture in developmental infrastructure in all towns and cities; deterioration of positive socialization
The Goal	Eliminate or control risks	Promote or enhance developmental assets
The Target	Vulnerable children and adolescents	All children and adolescents
The Strategies	Expansion of social services and treatment systems; early intervention; prevention programs targeted at high-risk behaviors	Mobilization of all citizens and socializing systems to act on a shared vision for positive human development
Who Does the Work?	Professionals take the lead	The people
Who Pays?	Government, foundations	The community
Time Frame	Until funding ends or a new issue grabs public attention	Long-term commitment

counting life-enhancing developmental experiences and resources. The language shift and emphasis puts the power back in the hands of the people and makes possible the kind of broad civic engagement that is crucial for healthy child and adolescent development as well as overall community health.

The asset paradigm does not eliminate the need to address deficits such as poverty, abuse, neglect, and other hardships that are too real and devastating for too many children and adolescents. Nor does it eliminate the need for intentional efforts to confront negative behaviors and choices with problem prevention, intervention, and rehabilitation efforts.

It is not an either-or choice. What communities need is what we might call a paradigm balance, in which deficit-reduction efforts are matched in intensity and power with asset-building efforts. A communitywide commitment to promoting developmental assets may, over time, reduce developmental deficits and risky behaviors, and the extraordinary cost of addressing them.

People who have begun using the framework of developmental assets find that it helps to transform the mood from frustration and despair to hope and possibility. "We find communities with a victim psychology," says Tom English, president of the Oregon Council on Crime and Delinquency in Eugene. He continues: "The difference with asset building is that you look at the assets that a community already has and where they are located. A community then sees that, yes, we do have a lot of things going for us, and through some rearranging we can fill in some gaps. But this is done through a position of strength rather than a position of bleakness. The difference is subtle but absolutely profound in terms of how a community begins to approach taking care of itself and becoming a strong community rather than a victim of circumstance."[33]

Ultimately, the ideal is to create healthy communities for our young: safe and economically vibrant places in which *most* citizens and *all* child-serving organizations and institutions unite around a shared vision of the positive, assume responsibility for asset building, and take concrete, sustained action. Unless we begin to rebuild this developmental infrastructure in our communities and to provide all youth with the assets they need to thrive, we will continue to see disturbing and destructive trends in child and adolescent behavior.

What Is the Village?

Carl Holmstrom may be a retired school superintendent, but his concern for children keeps him working full-time in his community of St. Louis Park, Minnesota.

"People who say our children are in trouble miss the point when they talk about alcohol, drugs, and too much television," he says. "Our children need strong families, institutions, and communities. Those things are everyone's business."

Working through his local Rotary Club, Holmstrom helped raise funds for what has become Children First, the first community in the nation to adopt Search Institute's developmental assets as a foundation for community action. The community adopted the popular African saying, "It takes a whole village to raise a child" as its slogan.

"And what is a village?" Holmstrom asks. "It is the faith communities, city government, school boards, health professionals, institutions, families, and businesses. When everyone shares a vision for a healthy community, our children prosper."

The Vision of Healthy Communities

Given the power of the developmental assets and their relative absence in the lives of most youth, a commitment to asset building should become a top priority in communities across the country. We do not pretend to have the final word on exactly how an asset-building community is organized. This book offers our current thinking as it has been refined and extended by close to two hundred communities (as of early 1997) involved in asset-building efforts.[34] We believe this understanding will grow and blossom as these and other communities move forward with their own innovations.

The term *community* has rich and varied connotations, and a growing number of meanings and usages. In our usage, community is largely a geographic area and refers typically to a town, city, or municipality.[35] We choose this approach because much of the socialization energy that can be mobilized for children and adolescents occurs within geographically overlapping systems of schools, neighborhoods, youth organizations, parks, and religious institutions within a municipality.

In reality, community is more complicated. When systems of socialization overlap (as when school districts draw students from multiple suburbs or when many towns share a school district), community must be thought of as several cities, a county, or other area. In large urban centers, the geography that defines a particular child's community might be a section of the city where most socialization energy is experienced.

Community, then, is a geography of influence and has definable boundaries that can be plotted for most children. We recognize, however, that socialization influence can easily stretch across these boundaries. Television is a prime example of an influence that obliterates community boundaries.

Just as the term community has many different connotations, the phrase *healthy community* is used by many disciplines and can have various emphases. We focus the phrase to refer primarily to geographic communities that effectively organize social life (its residents and its systems) to consistently promote developmental assets among young people, from birth through age eighteen.

Healthy communities for children and adolescents are places with a shared commitment to care for young people. They are distinguished as relational and intergenerational places that emphasize support, empowerment, boundaries, and opportunities. Developmental assets become a language of the common good, and the commitment to engage citizens and systems pursuing this common good is visible, long-term, and inclusive.[36]

Our vision for healthy communities suggests a causal influence. As communities organize their lives to become asset-building places, we expect the health and well-being of youth to improve. The cause-and-effect arrow goes both ways: healthy youth enhance the welfare of the community.

We recognize that ours is a focused definition of healthy community. In the fullest sense, healthy communities are also marked by vibrant economies, affordable housing, and effective treatment and intervention systems. These communities pay attention to the design of space and habitat; they vigorously combat risks and deficits that thwart healthy development, such as exploitation of children, abuse, violence, racism, and economic inequality.

Furthermore, though we focus on the first two decades of life, the vision could be extended to include how a community of people and resources connects with and supports individuals at other stages of the life journey through adulthood.

The focus on children and adolescents, then, is not intended to contradict or interfere with efforts to build other dimensions of a healthy community. Rather, the focus concentrates energy in an area of common concern and builds a foundation for young people that will have long-term payoffs for community life. Indeed, a National League of Cities survey found that six of the top ten issues identified by city officials as deteriorating in the past year deal directly with youth: youth crime, gangs, drugs, school violence, quality of education, and teen pregnancy. (That focus, of course, is again on young people's deficits and problems.)[37] An asset-building approach to taking care of young people can be a positive rallying cry that unites the community, eventually providing a foundation for working together on related concerns for the community's well-being.

A National Movement for Children

This call for a movement for children is excerpted from William Raspberry's Washington Post *column of Feb. 18, 1994.*

We need a crusade to save our children—a crusade as powerful and as broad-based as the 1960s crusade for civil rights. We need a new movement.

In the 1950s and '60s, even before Rosa Parks refused to give up her seat and unwittingly launched the Montgomery bus boycott, there were people across America working at various aspects of civil rights. There were voter registration workers, real estate testers, school desegregators, filers of class-action suits, wade-in-march-in demonstrators. Many of the resisters didn't even know about the work of the others.

Then something happened. Somehow an umbrella was spread over all these independent projects, and they became "the movement."

It was far more than a matter of nomenclature. The birth of "the movement" changed attitudes. We saw change coming, and we wanted to be part of it. We joined a vast alphabet soup of civil rights groups, joined in picket lines, boycotted stores. White people joined us from across America. Sharecroppers joined college students, business executives joined politicians and reverend clergy, and America changed.

There are today people performing all the elements of a children's crusade: helping youngsters with their algebra and their self-esteem, keeping them out of jail, talking to them about life, raising money for their education, helping them to see—and attain—their life possibilities.

I wish I understood by what chemistry these individual and local efforts could be transformed into a movement with the power to reach beyond the particulars of time and place and make our children—and not just black children, either—know that they are valued and loved and counted on.

We'd still have racism, no doubt, but we'd also have a thing that is in woefully short supply, and whose absence, in my view, accounts for most of the problems that afflict our children.

We'd have hope.

Exploring the Vision

This book articulates and explores the intersection of two visions: building developmental assets and creating healthy communities. It begins by examining the shape and impact of developmental assets based on our studies of youth across the nation. Then it moves to presenting a vision and strategies for nurturing healthy communities. Woven throughout are stories of how towns and cities have begun this journey.

The vision of developmental assets and healthy communities for children and adolescents is a work in progress. Because it is a new paradigm, more is yet unknown than known. Communities that have begun this work are, more than anything, our teachers and guides, introducing us to innovative strategies worthy of emulation. Although we expect healthy communities to develop one city or town at a time, we can envision a time when many local transformations constitute the critical mass of energy and insight needed to give birth to a full-fledged social movement for children and adolescents.

PART ONE

BRINGING OUT
THE BEST IN ALL KIDS

CHAPTER TWO

DEVELOPMENTAL ASSETS

Forty Building Blocks of Human Development

In order to rebuild the developmental infrastructure for America's children and adolescents, we need to think boldly and expansively. Positive development in the first two decades of life is not a program or a curriculum. There are no magic potions or quick fixes that steer lives toward success, productivity, and responsibility.

In the past several decades, a deep body of knowledge has emerged on elements of human experience that have long-term, positive consequences for young people. This work explores a wide range of topics, including family dynamics, support from other community adults, school effectiveness, positive peer influence, value development, and the learning of social skills. Too often, however, these areas of inquiry are disconnected from each other in both scholarship and practice, so that each by itself too easily becomes seen as a panacea. What has been missing in national discourse is a broad vision that names all of the core elements of healthy development and all of the community actors (family, neighborhood, school, youth organizations, congregations, and so on) needed to promote these essential building blocks.

The framework of developmental assets embodies this kind of far-reaching vision. In establishing benchmarks for positive child and adolescent development, it weaves together a wide range of essential developmental building blocks requiring broad community engagement to ensure their acquisition. The developmental asset framework enables families, schools, neighborhoods, congregations, employers, and youth organizations to unite around a common language and employ complementary strategies toward a shared goal: healthy children and adolescents.

The importance of a shared language about the terrain of healthy child and adolescent development cannot be overstated. While effective family life is a crucial ingredient in healthy development, it takes more than strong family to raise healthy kids. A major problem in contemporary society is that those outside of the immediate family have forgotten their place in the human development process. A shared language of the elements of positive development is critical for unleashing the significant human development capacity of communities. In this chapter, we describe forty developmental assets, each a molecule of healthy development and each within the influence of residents and social institutions to promote.

Where Developmental Assets Came From

How one names these building blocks of healthy development depends on both where one enters the developmental sequence and one's definition of health. The forty developmental assets are initially framed around the second decade of life, roughly spanning the middle school and high school years. This is a watershed decade, fraught with choices, opportunities, and dangers, significantly predictive of long-term adult outcomes and inextricably linked to developmental experiences in the first decade of life. Although this chapter focuses on the experiences of adolescence, many of the same principles are relevant to both younger children and adults. Thus, Chapter Four looks at the experiences of developmental assets for children, from birth to eleven, as well as some of the implications for adulthood.

The forty developmental assets represent a conceptual model of essential socialization experiences for all young people. The naming of the developmental assets has been guided by a set of lenses, filters, and processes.

Growing out of scientific literature. Each of the assets is rooted in the scientific literature, particularly in the intersection of child and adolescent development and the more applied literatures in prevention, protective factors, and resiliency.

Though the developmental asset framework is new because of its synthesis, integration, and architecture, it builds on the important work of a number of scholars and researchers, in the fields of child and adolescent development, prevention, youth development, and resiliency.[1] Appendix A is a bibliography of selected scientific articles that support each of the forty individual assets.

Connecting to positive outcomes. In synthesizing this expansive and ever-growing terrain of scientific knowledge, my key interest was to locate those developmental factors known to be causative or predictive of healthy outcomes. This brings us to the critical question of defining the elastic concept of health.

This conceptualization of health integrates three dimensions. The first is resistance to health-compromising behavior, or what is often called high-risk behavior. Hence, many of the developmental assets are rooted in the extensive literature on prevention and protective factors, naming those family, school, and community factors that help to inoculate youth against acts of substance use, violence and antisocial behavior, too-early sexual activity or teen pregnancy, driving and drinking, and school dropout.

The avoidance of health-compromising or future-jeopardizing behavior, however, is only part of a fuller conceptualization of healthy development. Equally important in naming assets is locating development experiences that promote forms of thriving. Included here are school success, affirmation of diversity, compassion for others, leadership, and choosing a healthy lifestyle (for example, nutrition and exercise).

And finally, the assets include the dimension of resiliency: the capacity to rebound in the face of adversity. Many of the elements that promote resiliency overlap with those that are known to either prevent high-risk behavior or promote thriving.

Drawing from practitioners' wisdom. The naming of the territory of positive child and adolescent development was not a solitary task. In addition to building on scientific literature, the process of nominating and refining developmental assets tapped the professional expertise of the team of social scientists at Search Institute and the practical wisdom of practitioners.[2]

Through more than a dozen dialogues, workshops, and focus groups conducted in 1995 and 1996, about 150 youth, educators, parents, social service providers, and policy makers were asked to nominate and defend essential developmental assets. These dialogues were designed primarily to understand the developmental journeys of urban youth and youth of color.

Though many learnings emerged through these conversations, one deserves comment. In discussing developmental assets within the category of support, the idea of neighborhood caring and boundaries emerged in many settings across the country. Repeatedly, dialogue participants recalled the power of growing up in neighborhoods where multiple adults took interest in the well-being of children and adolescents, affirming in-bounds behavior and reporting and sometimes censoring out-of-bounds behavior. There was also a deep lament about the loss of this developmental experience in contemporary society. Though there is relatively little empirical literature on this asset, the experiential testimony given to this in many parts of the country, combined with pilot testing of this asset in several cities to ensure it had predictive power for child and adolescent health, compelled us to name it as one of the forty assets. It also, of course, has high face validity as a developmental experience to be both prized and promoted.

Balancing external and internal factors. Several other filters were crucial in designing the asset taxonomy. On theoretical grounds, I sought to give equal weight to *external* (environmental factors) and *internal* (internalized skills, competencies, and commitments) factors known to promote positive developmental outcomes. I then marked the conceptual territory of each category, breaking external assets into assets of support, empowerment, boundaries and expectations, and constructive use of time, and the internal assets into commitment to learning, positive values, social competencies, and positive identity. The task then was to sort into each of the eight subcategories the developmental experiences or processes known to enhance healthy outcomes (for example, prevention of high-risk behaviors, promotion of thriving, resilience).

Applying to all youth. Special attention was given to those elements of development known or hypothesized to have health-promoting utility across gender, race or ethnicity, and income. In this way, my search was an effort to name a common core of developmental assets that matter for all youth regardless of social circumstance.

This filter eliminates some of the positive experiences that are particularly relevant and important for specific cultures and traditions. For example, people sharing a religious tradition often see gaps in the assets in terms of faith expression and experience. Leaders of Native American communities see developmental power in ceremony and ritual.

Not including these experiences in the framework of forty assets is not intended to devalue them. Rather, it is a function of the goal of naming a common core of developmental experiences that are important for all young people in this pluralistic society. This filter allows people from many different walks of life, backgrounds, and perspectives to work together on promoting a common core of healthy development. At the same time, we encourage people and communities to augment the forty common core assets with other historically valued ones.

Building on previous research. The naming of the forty developmental assets and the measurement of each in subsequent community profiles of middle school and high school students has also been guided by a considerable legacy of research at

Search Institute. My initial conceptualization of thirty developmental assets, first articulated in a report titled *The Troubled Journey: A Portrait of 6th–12th Grade Youth*,[3] led to studies of developmental assets in 460 cities between 1990 and 1995. Discussed in more depth in Chapter Three, this research on approximately 250,000 American youth provided a rich database for revising some asset definitions as well as revising how some of the assets are measured. In 1996, pilot studies of the new configuration of forty assets were conducted in all public schools in Albuquerque and Minneapolis.[4] Analysis of data from twenty thousand sixth-to-twelfth-grade students in these two cities encouraged some final adjustments in the naming and measurement of the current configuration of forty assets.

This experience of expanding from thirty to forty assets is a reminder that the forty assets are not intended to be exhaustive. Indeed, the naming of developmental assets should always be considered a work in progress, building on emerging knowledge and wisdom.

Identifying factors communities can readily promote. The developmental assets tilt to covering the kinds of relationships, social experiences, social environments, patterns of interaction, and norms over which a community of people have considerable control. That is, the assets are more about the primary processes of socialization than the equally important arenas of economy, housing, services, and the "bricks and mortar" of a city.

Accenting the human development infrastructure of a community (rather than the economic, social service, or physical infrastructure) implicitly places much of the responsibility and power for promoting positive youth outcomes in the hands of citizens and social institutions. By so doing we seek not to diminish the developmental significance of the economic, service, and physical dimensions of city life but to balance these with deeper attention to crucial processes of socialization.

The Architecture of Developmental Assets

The framework of forty developmental assets is presented in Table 2.1.

Developmental assets fall into two broad categories: external assets and internal assets. Within each of these categories are four types of assets, as follows:

External Assets	*Internal Assets*
1. Support	5. Commitment to learning
2. Empowerment	6. Positive values
3. Boundaries and expectations	7. Social competencies
4. Constructive use of time	8. Positive identity

TABLE 2.1. SEARCH INSTITUTE'S FORTY DEVELOPMENTAL ASSETS.

External Assets

Asset Type	Asset Name and Definition
Support	1. *Family support:* Family life provides high levels of love and support. 2. *Positive family communication:* Young person and parent(s) communicate positively, and young person is willing to seek parental advice and counsel. 3. *Other adult relationships:* Young person receives support from three or more nonparent adults. 4. *Caring neighborhood:* Young person experiences caring neighbors. 5. *Caring school climate:* School provides a caring, encouraging environment. 6. *Parent involvement in schooling:* Parent(s) are actively involved in helping young person succeed in school.
Empowerment	7. *Community values youth:* Young person perceives that adults in the community value youth. 8. *Youth as resources:* Young people are given useful roles in the community. 9. *Service to others:* Young person serves in the community one hour or more per week. 10. *Safety:* Young person feels safe at home, at school, and in the neighborhood.
Boundaries and Expectations	11. *Family boundaries:* Family has clear rules and consequences, and monitors the young person's whereabouts. 12. *School boundaries:* School provides clear rules and consequences. 13. *Neighborhood boundaries:* Neighbors take responsibility for monitoring young people's behavior. 14. *Adult role models:* Parent(s) and other adults model positive, responsible behavior. 15. *Positive peer influence:* Young person's best friends model responsible behavior. 16. *High expectations:* Both parent(s) and teachers encourage the young person to do well.
Constructive Use of Time	17. *Creative activities:* Young person spends three or more hours per week in lessons or practice in music, theater, or other arts. 18. *Youth programs:* Young person spends three or more hours per week in sports, clubs, or organizations at school or in community organizations. 19. *Religious community:* Young person spends one or more hours per week in activities in a religious institution. 20. *Time at home:* Young person is out with friends, with "nothing special to do," two nights or fewer per week.

TABLE 2.1. SEARCH INSTITUTE'S FORTY DEVELOPMENTAL ASSETS, cont'd.

Internal Assets

Asset Type	Asset Name and Definition
Commitment to Learning	21. *Achievement motivation:* Young person is motivated to do well in school.
	22. *School engagement:* Young person is actively engaged in learning.
	23. *Homework:* Young person reports doing at least one hour of homework every school day.
	24. *Bonding to school:* Young person cares about school.
	25. *Reading for pleasure:* Young person reads for pleasure three or more hours per week.
Positive Values	26. *Caring:* Young person places high value on helping other people.
	27. *Equality and social justice:* Young person places high value on promoting equality and reducing hunger and poverty.
	28. *Integrity:* Young person acts on convictions and stands up for beliefs.
	29. *Honesty:* Young person tells the truth even when it is not easy.
	30. *Responsibility:* Young person accepts and takes personal responsibility.
	31. *Restraint:* Young person believes it is important not to be sexually active or to use alcohol or other drugs.
Social Competencies	32. *Planning and decision-making:* Young person knows how to plan ahead and make choices.
	33. *Interpersonal competence:* Young person has empathy, sensitivity, and friendship skills.
	34. *Cultural competence:* Young person has knowledge of and comfort with people of different cultural, racial, and ethnic backgrounds.
	35. *Resistance skills:* Young person can resist negative peer pressure and dangerous situations.
	36. *Peaceful conflict resolution:* Young person seeks to resolve conflict nonviolently.
Positive Identity	37. *Personal power:* Young person feels in control over "things that happen to me."
	38. *Self-esteem:* Young person reports having high self-esteem.
	39. *Sense of purpose:* Young person reports that "my life has a purpose."
	40. *Positive view of personal future:* Young person is optimistic about personal future.

The eight types of assets are further defined by forty individual assets. In this chapter, we describe this structure and define the assets. As noted earlier, Appendix A provides scientific sources that support each of the forty assets.

It is important to note, however, that the most important contribution of this framework lies less in the forty individual assets than in the big picture of healthy development. Thus it is probably more important to understand the larger framework and the eight categories than it is to dwell on the forty individual assets. This macro-level approach serves as a reminder that young people can experience each category of assets through a wide array of relationships and experiences.

A Popularized Understanding of Developmental Assets

Eugene C. Roehlkepartain, director of publishing and communication at Search Institute, provides this useful way of thinking and communicating about developmental assets.

There seem to be at least three kinds of money managers in the world.

First are the ones you read about in the personal finance books. They have a steady income and a well-thought-out budget. They balance their checkbook every month; they only charge what they can pay for at the end of the month; they start saving for college when the baby arrives; and they think of every major purchase as an investment.

Other money managers don't necessarily have less income or greater expenses on average, but their financial picture is quite different. Regardless of how much money they make, they live paycheck-to-paycheck. Bills are paid when their bank balance isn't precariously low, and they put little thought into saving for the future.

The third type of money managers do their best to make ends meet but simply don't have the resources they need. They live paycheck-to-paycheck because they have to; rarely can they pay all their bills on time or save for the future.

While most of us recognize the value of the first approach, the second and third pictures are disturbingly accurate analogies for the way our society has been taking care of our most valuable investment: our children and teenagers. Instead of doing everything we can to guarantee a good "return on our investment," we have spent tremendous amounts of energy just trying to recover from the damage that has already been done because we haven't—or couldn't—invested wisely in our youth. Often times we don't have, or know how to get, the resources to help us understand what we can do to build a solid foundation for our youth.

External Assets

External assets refer to positive developmental experiences that need to be provided to all youth by the socializing systems of a community. These assets emerge from constant exposure to interlocking systems of support, empowerment, boundaries and expectations, and structure.

Young people experience external assets through informal interactions with caring and principled adults and peers. Families, schools, neighborhoods, community organizations, and religious institutions have a role in providing these assets. They must also be supported and reinforced by the larger network of community institutions, including government, health care, law enforcement, civic organizations, community foundations, and others. We place external assets in four types, as follows.

Support Assets

Support refers to a range of ways young people experience love, affirmation, and acceptance. These experiences include both demonstrative forms of verbal and physical approval, symbolic gestures showing that young people matter (for example, calling them by name, listening, including, paying attention to, talking with, showing interest in), and creating environments where young people feel welcome and comfortable.

The support assets appear to be instrumental in a number of developmental outcomes, including internalization of boundaries and values, taking action to help others, and development of empathy and self-esteem. The capacity to learn and accept support may be grounded in the quality of early attachment to one's primary caretakers.

Support for children and adolescents ought to be a daily enterprise. No one knows precisely how many symbols or gestures of support are needed, nor whether some kinds are more important than others. What we do know is that many American young people experience erratic or little support.

Ideally, support should be abundant both inside and outside one's immediate family and include gestures of care in casual, informal daily interaction with adults and peers. In addition, it should be an intentional goal or value in many places where young people spend time, including schools, youth clubs and organizations, congregations, places of employment and recreation, and neighborhood.

Support Assets

1. Family support
2. Positive family communication
3. Other adult relationships
4. Caring neighborhood
5. Caring school climate
6. Parent involvement in schooling

Support Within the Family. Support is obviously a family enterprise. There are hundreds of ways families can provide support. We use two assets to approximate this rich territory in the scientific literature. The first two assets focus on how families provide support through a caring environment in the family and through positive family communication. To measure the asset of family support (#1), we assess the degree to which youth say "There is a lot of love in my family," "My parent(s) (or guardians) give me help and support when I need it," and "My parent(s) (or guardians) often tell me they love me."

The asset of positive family communication focuses on whether youth have frequent, in-depth conversations with their parent(s) and whether they seek their advice or help when dealing with tough issues. In our surveys of youth, fewer than half (47 percent) of students surveyed said they see their parent(s) as a source of social support.

Intergenerational Support. Support is not only a family enterprise. It also belongs to the larger community. Indeed, as children move to day care and school settings, support from other adults (and peers) becomes increasingly important. By the time of adolescence, young people seek and find a considerable amount of support from the larger community.

Asset #3 focuses on nonfamily, intergenerational relationships. Communities ought to provide three kinds of intergenerational support.

The first we might think of as spontaneous gestures of support, or "random acts of support." This refers to a range of experiences, from being called by name in one's neighborhood (see asset #4) to being gently encouraged by a coach or youth organization leader.

A second kind of necessary support is provided by sustained contact with adults other than parents. These are the adults who choose to connect with, know, and spend time with a young person across multiple years. This could be an aunt or uncle, a teacher who pays attention to and takes an interest in a child across more than one school year. It is the adult in a congregation who develops a long-term friendship with a child. It is a neighbor who always acknowledges a child's presence.[5]

How many of these sustained relationships ought a young person to have? Throughout the prevention and resiliency literature, the call is for "at least one."[6] This goal has become a focus of many national reports and calls to action.[7]

We think it important, however, to elevate this benchmark to at least five relationships, and in the ideal, to a dozen or more (a number that has more symbolic utility than empirical grounding). We come to this conclusion by examining in depth the life portraits of our sample of sixth-to-twelfth-grade youth. Young people were asked how many adults they knew who they could go to for help "if you had an important question about your life."

We analyzed how other assets and behavioral choices vary as a function of the number of adult relationships in one's life. We discover that each increase in the number of available adults is associated with positive outcomes. That is, having one adult is better than having none; having two is better than one, and so on. Even the increase from three or four adults to five or more adults generates a higher number of assets and decreases high-risk behaviors such as alcohol use.[8] Some of the asset implications are shown in Table 2.2.

The more adults in one's life, the better. Our research in hundreds of communities shows that only 22 percent of youth benefit from five or more supportive relationships outside one's family.

Number of Adults	Percentage of Youth
None	14 percent
One	15 percent
Two	22 percent
Three or four	27 percent
Five or more	22 percent

Doing better on this asset requires becoming an intergenerational society.

Spontaneous and sustained relationships with nonparent adults are at the heart of a healthy community for youth. Informal and nonprogrammatic, they are premised on adults remembering and acting on their power and responsibility to make a difference in the routines of everyday life.

The third type of nonparent support represents the programmatic expression of intergenerational relationships through mentoring programs. These programs carefully match a caring adult with a young person, most often young people experiencing developmental deficits of one kind or another.[9]

TABLE 2.2. THE VALUE OF RELATIONSHIPS WITH MANY NONPARENT ADULTS.

Number of Adult Resources	Percentage of Youth with Caring Asset	Percentage of Youth with Self-Esteem Asset	Percentage of Youth with Positive-View-of-Future Asset
0	41	33	55
1	49	38	62
2	50	44	68
3 or 4	54	52	73
5 or more	62	60	78

Coordinated by community organizations and sometimes (but too rarely) enhanced by the volunteer arm of employers, these efforts have significant impact. A recent evaluation looked at 959 ten-to-sixteen-year-olds who applied in 1992–93 to Big Brothers/Big Sisters, the nation's most established mentoring program. Using a quasi-experimental design, the research team concluded that, after eighteen months, this mentoring program reduced the onset of alcohol and other drug use, inhibited interpersonal violence, and improved school attendance and performance.[10]

Support in Schooling. The next two support assets connect the issues of care and support with schooling. Starting when children enter preschool or kindergarten, school becomes a major influence in young people's lives, rivaling family and peer groups in potential impact.

The asset of positive school climate (#5) refers to the caring dimension of schools, based on their capacity to mobilize human resources, both adult and students, to provide daily and sustained messages and symbols of personal support. Such support can happen in schools in a number of ways: being noticed, named, included, and encouraged.

Schools tend not to be places of care.[11] Some things increasingly get in the way, such as large and impersonal class sizes,[12] and troubled, overwhelmed, or acting-out students who command a disproportionate amount of adult attention.

But when schools do place priority on being relational and caring places, good things happen to school achievement, self-concept, and learning an ethic of care. Indeed, constructing schools to be places of support may be an essential path to creating academically effective schools. As one research team put it: "We have learned through our research that caring can create possibilities for children—possibilities for learning to read, for recognizing their capabilities and feeling better about themselves, for learning how to work and play with others. Although children may learn in the absence of caring, without the presence of a caring teacher these possibilities are greatly diminished. As a fourth-grader named Candace remarked, 'If a teacher doesn't care about you, it affects your mind. You feel like you're nobody, and it makes you want to drop out of school.'"[13]

Caring is not only an important dimension of elementary schools but of middle and high schools as well.[14] It may be a little more challenging in these settings, requiring among other things training, encouragement, and support for secondary school teachers, counselors, administrators, and support staff.

Parental involvement in schooling (#6) is a much-touted strategy for school improvement. And for good reason. We know that parental involvement enhances school success and motivates students to achieve.[15] We also know that risk-taking behaviors decrease as parental involvement increases. Parental involvement has several dimensions, from actively participating in the life of a child's school, to creating a positive learning environment at home. Ultimately, we ought to think of involvement as something parents (and other citizens) do to ensure effective schools for all children and adolescents within a community, not just advocating for one's own children.

Support in Other Environments. Although the last two support assets focus on support connected with school, the same principles could logically be extended to other environments where young people spend time, including extracurricular activities, youth organizations, religious congregations, places of employment, and many others. In short, the challenge is for all socializing systems to examine their relationships and climate to determine whether, in fact, young people feel cared for, heard, and connected.

Empowerment Assets

A key developmental need is to be valued and valuable. Empowered young people feel good about themselves and their skills. They grow up feeling treated with respect, knowing their strengths, and sensing that they can make a difference in the world. The empowerment assets highlight this need, focusing on community perceptions of youth and opportunities for them to contribute to society in meaningful ways. Those experiences of being valued depend on first feeling safe, the final empowerment asset.

The first two empowerment assets focus on community perceptions of youth, seeing them as positive contributors to community life and then giving them useful roles in the community.

These assets are among the least common for young people to experience. In the first two cities to study their students' experiences of the forty assets, only about one in five youth reported that they believe their community values young people, and only one-third said their community gives them useful roles.

In fact, rather than seeing youth as valuable resources, our society is much more likely to portray youth as problems. A colleague recently attended a neighborhood meeting in which the residents' most animated discussions were over how

---

Empowerment Assets

7. Community values youth
8. Youth as resources
9. Service to others
10. Safety

to keep the kids from causing trouble on their block. Indeed, most popular (and scholarly) literature (not to mention water cooler conversations) about adolescents views them as problems. As Patricia Hersch writes: "Say the magic word 'adolescents' to most adults and you're likely to get a litany of complaints: they spend all of their time in front of the tube or playing video games. They lack ambition and they won't read. They want instant gratification. They have no values, no interests. . . . Most parents feel an uneasiness, at times bordering on panic, about their abilities to help their children through this notoriously rocky time of life."[16]

Asset #9, service to others, has gained a great deal of attention with the national interest in youth service and service learning. A growing body of literature supports the power of youth involvement in service to strengthen both academic and social outcomes.[17] In addition, involvement in service has the potential to contribute to developing many of the other assets as well. For example, serving others can be the catalyst for internalizing values of caring, equality, and social justice. In addition, service activities provide opportunities for constructive use of time. Indeed, if service opportunities are designed carefully, service becomes a strategy for reinforcing all eight categories of assets.

Whereas service to others is valuable both to the community and to the young person who serves, we have a long way to go in engaging youth consistently in serving others (with adults being even less likely to be active volunteers). According to our surveys of youth, most middle school and high school students do not engage in service on a regular basis. When asked how much time they had spent helping others in the past week, 63 percent of youth said they had spent no time. Another 24 percent said they had spent one hour, with 8 percent reporting spending three to five hours.

The final empowerment asset is safety. Young people who feel safe are more likely to feel valued and able to make a difference than youth whose safety is threatened. Growing up in an unsafe or violent environment also shapes the choices young people make. For example, research shows that young people who grow up in violent communities or violent families are more likely to become involved in substance abuse.[18] Thus, creating environments in families, neighborhoods, schools, gathering places, congregations, and other settings where young people are physically and emotionally safe is an important asset-building task.

Boundaries-and-Expectations Assets

Support and empowerment need to be balanced with clear and consistent attention to boundaries and boundary reinforcement. Important here are clear messages about what is in-bounds (for example, respect for people and property) and what is out-of-bounds (violent resolution of conflict, chemical use, etc.).

Boundaries-and-Expectations Assets

11. Family boundaries
12. School boundaries
13. Neighborhood boundaries
14. Adult role models
15. Positive peer influence
16. High expectations

Boundaries have to do with clear signals about what is expected, what is approved and celebrated, and what deserves censure. Ideally, the rules and norms that guide appropriate behavior and the consequences that accrue when boundaries are violated have a kind of symmetry across socializing systems so that a common core of messages are reinforced in settings as diverse as family; neighborhood; school; congregations; and clubs, teams, and other youth organizations.

The methods by which this system of boundaries should work begins with family standards; moves to school, neighborhood, and community policies and norms (for example, underage drinking is inappropriate; conflict is to be resolved peacefully; youth should not stay out late at night); and extends to clear and visible efforts to communicate and model positive expectations.

Many observers of American social life—whether teachers, parents, neighbors, or police—would conclude that the signals are unclear, inconsistent, or unseen. Robert Bly suggests that in this age of self-indulgence, adults refuse to name and articulate their wisdom about what matters, choosing instead to extend their own adolescence indefinitely.[19]

The current American dilemma with boundary-breaking behavior is real and pervasive. Its signs include disrespect for adults, violent resolution of conflict, disregard for personal health, vandalism, disregard for the rights of others, turning away from another's pain, prejudice, and underage chemical use. We could go on. Boundary setting and maintenance require a team of socializing systems giving redundant messages to children and adolescents about both what is in-bounds and out-of-bounds. Such teamwork is rarely visible in communities, partly because there is little public dialogue to establish some semblance of consensus on boundaries.

Psychoanalyst Francis Ianni of Columbia University recommends the establishing of "youth charters," unwritten but widely understood and articulated expectations and standards. When such communitywide expectations exist, good things happen developmentally and behaviorally.[20] Indeed, William Damon asserts that youth charters are "far stronger predictors of wholesome youth behavior than are such widely heralded factors as affluence, ethnicity, geography, family structure, or social status."[21]

There are some clear obstacles, some of which are addressed in assets #14 through #16. Positive adult and peer role models and influence set positive behavior standards that reinforce boundaries and encourage healthy commitments. In addition, high but reasonable expectations keep young people focused on positive goals and can enhance their sense of competence. Although high expectations typically focus on education, the same principle applies to expectations in other areas of life, such as high expectations for how youth live out their social relationships, how they spend their time, and how they live out their values and priorities.

Constructive-Use-of-Time Assets

As the mechanisms of consistent support and boundaries deteriorate for American youth, engaging youth in structured use of time through organizations and programs escalates in importance. Involving children and adolescents in forms of structure is not just a nice thing to do; it is essential. Ideally, these are settings that connect youth to principled and caring adults who nurture skill and capacity through group activities, lessons, relationships, and supervision. The importance of this form of external assets is made more manifest by the high percentage of children and adolescents who lack access to a parent before and after school.

Unfortunately, many youth lack access to developmentally appropriate and enticing programs. However, even for those who do have access, too many young people disconnect from such forms of positive structure, either choosing not to join or dropping out. It is becoming increasingly common for youth to disengage from structured time use just when, in our national history, parental presence is also waning. The combination of parental absence and disengagement shifts socialization away from adults to other influences, to the point where it appears that children are raised less by principled, caring adults and more by their peers and mass media.

Constructive-Use-of-Time Assets

17. Creative activities
18. Youth programs
19. Religious community
20. Time at home

Such connections matter even when a child is blessed with a strong family. More and more youth spend considerable time outside the view of adults. The Task Force on Youth Development and Community Programs of the Carnegie Council on Adolescent Development calculated that 40 percent of young adolescents' waking hours are discretionary (not committed to other activities), and "many young adolescents spend virtually all of this discretionary time without companionship or supervision from responsible adults."[22]

The task force noted that the 1988 National Education Longitudinal Study found that 27 percent of eighth graders spend two or more hours alone after school.[23] However, Search Institute surveys put the percentages even higher. In this research, 47 percent of sixth graders report spending two or more hours per day at home without an adult present. By ninth grade, the percentage has risen to 60 percent, which remains fairly constant throughout high school.[24] Such is the consequence of families in which both parents (or the only parent) work.

But there is also a more positive rationale for involving youth in structured activities: structure provides the kinds of opportunities for personal development and adult connection that augment and extend the effect of family. For those young people with absent, neglectful, overwhelmed, or underskilled families—and there are too many—the power and impact of constructive time use may be a critical factor in whether they become resilient or are trapped by adversity.

In a compelling study of "urban sanctuaries," one finding deserves attention: "What distinguishes the hopefuls from other youth engaged in inner-city survival is their active involvement in some kind of neighborhood youth organization. These young people have 'ducked the bullet' and build hope through their participation in neighborhood-based organizations that offer safety, support, guidance, companionship, opportunities for growth, and engagement."[25]

Creative Activities. We single out creative activities (music, drama, and other art) as one of the assets (#17) for several reasons. The arts provide a daily routine and shape what can become a lifelong skill and interest. Music is a good example. As Bobby McFerrin puts it, "Music teaches the heart." And now the field of developmental neurobiology has contributed a series of studies suggesting that music neurologically triggers improved spatial reasoning and other complex cognitive tasks important in mathematics and related higher-order thinking processes.[26]

Youth Programs. Youth programs (asset #18) cover a rich territory of clubs, teams, and organizations. These include national youth organizations (Campfire, Boys and Girls Clubs, 4–H, Girl Scouts, Boy Scouts, Girls Incorporated, YWCA, YMCA, and Junior Achievement), community-based programs, and school-based after-school cocurricular activities.

This network is an important part of a city's developmental infrastructure, contributing significantly to young people's healthy development through a wide array of activities.[27] All youth ages seven to eighteen should have at least one such connection point. In *A Matter of Time: Risk and Opportunity in the Nonschool Hours*, the Carnegie Council on Adolescent Development presents this challenge: "In a youth-centered America, every community would have a network of affordable, accessible, safe, and challenging opportunities that appeal to the diverse interests of young adolescents."[28]

That said, there are some challenges to providing such contact. These places of constructive time use are least available in communities where young people need them the most. For example, a report by the National Commission on Children found that low-income, urban youth are least likely of all youth to have access to youth clubs and organizations.[29]

Even when programs are available, there are obstacles to participation that must be rectified. These include lack of transportation, disinterest, lack of information about program availability, parental mistrust of leaders or program quality, and a fear for their safety.[30] Some of these obstacles can be addressed by an attentive and intentional community. Others present a greater challenge where safety is a daily concern. There are stories emerging of families who impose a "lockdown" on their kids, keeping them off the streets, out of programs, and within the safety of the home.[31]

It takes a whole community effort to build and maintain this kind of high-quality system of structure. It takes institutional resources, and volunteers. It also takes a community of citizens to guarantee that school-based and cocurricular activities (for example, sports, band, orchestra, drama, clubs) are never sacrificed. When fiscal problems emerge, it is only slight hyperbole to say that it would be wiser to turn off a city's lights before eliminating youth development programs.

Religious Community. Asset #19 calls for involving children and adolescents in activities through religious congregations (churches, mosques, synagogues, or other faith communities). There are several reasons why this involvement promotes positive development. First, religious institutions are one of the few remaining intergenerational communities to which youth have access. It is a place of multiple generations, with people bound together, to a greater or lesser degree, through a shared perspective and shared values. (Congregation-as-intergenerational community, however, represents potential more than reality, since most communities of faith are as age segregated as the rest of society.)

Congregations are also places that are less afraid than other socializing systems to articulate their values. There is a scientific literature that shows that such participation—even after controlling for family background—enhances caring for others and helps reduce multiple forms of risk-taking behavior.[32]

Finally, congregations are places that have the opportunity to provide a range of structured activities for children and adolescents, from weekly religious education to informal youth groups, from service projects to mission trips. Each of these experiences has the potential to build positive relationships and strengthen social competencies. However, many congregations have neglected these opportunities and now struggle to engage youth meaningfully.[33]

Time at Home. The final asset in this category is time at home. We noted earlier that young people spend too much time *alone* at home. But it is also developmentally important that they spend time at home with parents and siblings, reconnecting, resting, relaxing, doing homework, doing chores . . . being family. In too many communities, young people spend virtually every evening away from home at activities or with friends. And while those experiences are also important, they must be balanced with time for families. Thus an asset-building community works to protect time for families to be together.

Is Part-Time Work a Developmental Asset? In our efforts to refine the asset taxonomy, we explored the question of whether part-time employment should be added as a new constructive-use-of-time asset. The case is often made that work provides both asset-building opportunities and deflection from risk-taking pressures and opportunities.

Based on analysis of our national study of assets as well as other research, this does not appear to be the case. Table 2.3 shows the impact of hours of work per week on school problems. (Numbers are the percentage who report skipping school two or more days in the last month or have below a C average, for ninth-to-twelfth-grade students only.)

What we see is that working up to twenty hours a week has no particularly strong effect on school performance. But twenty-one hours or more increases

TABLE 2.3. PERCENTAGE OF YOUTH REPORTING PROBLEMS IN SCHOOL.

		Amount of Work Per Week		
	None	5–10 hours	11–20 hours	21 or more hours
Youth with 0–10 assets	48	47	46	51
Youth with 11–20 assets	19	18	22	31
Youth with 21–25 assets	6	5	8	13
Youth with 26–30 assets	2	1	2	3

school failure for youth having 0–10, 11–20, or 21–25 assets. Those with 26–30 assets are more immune to the deleterious effects of high levels of work.

When we examine rates for repeated experiences with sexual intercourse (three or more times), using the same sample of high school students as above, we are pressed in the direction of even greater caution. As shown below, working 5–10 hours per week may slightly lessen this pattern. But working 11–20 hours increases the rates. They also increase for twenty-one or more hours of work. Similar patterns hold for alcohol use, antisocial behavior, and tobacco use.

Given these findings and those of others in the field,[34] the best policy seems to be to limit working to no more than ten hours per week. At these low levels, work appears at least not to have a negative effect. It is still unclear if it has a positive effect in other areas.

Internal Assets

Promoting external assets is perhaps the easier of the two major tasks of socialization. The other is nurture of the inner life: those commitments, passions, and values that need to be planted deep in the head, heart, and soul of each young person. The nurture of this internal gyroscope, this frame of reference, is particularly crucial in the dominant U.S. culture, which emphasizes—and perhaps overstates—the primacy of the individual.

To a certain extent, the internal assets deserve more attention now than in previous decades. That is because of strong countervailing influences in contemporary society that steer children and adolescents away from responsible, caring, and principled commitments. Without strong community attention to internal assets, the pervasive cultural messages about consumerism, instant gratification, and pursuit of personal interest cannot be adequately tempered.

Internal assets are also grouped into four types: commitment to learning, positive values, social competencies, and positive identity. Strength in these four areas creates a kind of character and centeredness among youth that promotes wise, health-enhancing choices and minimizes risk taking.

Commitment-to-Learning Assets

The first five internal assets are in the domain of commitment to learning. These assets have a dual power. They are crucial in the long run for vocational success and engaged citizenship. They also play a prevention role, inhibiting some forms of health-compromising behavior.

Developing these commitments is far from automatic. One sign of this is the untenably high rate of school dropout in the United States. Several factors may

---

Commitment-to-Learning Assets

21. Achievement motivation
22. School engagement
23. Homework
24. Bonding to school
25. Reading for pleasure

---

erode a commitment to learning. First is the increasingly unclear connection—at least in the perceptual world of contemporary students—between learning and career. Equally important may be educational systems and approaches that fail to take into account young people's developmental needs and styles of learning that are engaging, relevant, and motivating.[35] Third, low or mixed expectations and norms in society regarding the value of education and learning may interfere with young people's making their education a priority. Finally, the widespread cultural message that learning is not fun and that learning and education are synonymous undermines nurturing an internal, lifelong commitment to and interest in learning.

Commitment to learning has a number of sources in the journey through childhood and adolescence. Parental attitudes, encouragement, involvement, and modeling are key. The quality of schooling matters, through both its formal and informal curricula. Norms that encourage high attention to educational tasks, by both peer group and community, are also instrumental. Unfortunately, many youth do not benefit from these kinds of expectations.

The asset of homework (#20) has a dual function. Obviously, the discipline of homework promotes learning and school success. Equally important, however, is its utility in structuring time and creating daily routine.

There is evidence that this is a society of misplaced priorities. Here are the percentages of middle and high school students in our sample who engage in various levels of homework and television watching. The rule seems to be that television rules.

Number of Hours per Day	Doing Homework	Watching Television
None	9 percent	4 percent
One hour or less	68 percent	25 percent
One to two hours	18 percent	33 percent
More than two hours	5 percent	38 percent

Asset #24 reminds us that it is not enough that young people gain knowledge and skills in school. They need to bond to—become invested in—their place of learning. Research has found that bonding to school is a particularly important factor for promoting school success and academic achievement.[36]

Positive-Values Assets

Values have moved to center stage. In the campaign year of 1996, hardly a day went by without a presidential candidate admonishing us that the rediscovery of values is the pivotal issue in national life. Though extreme voices can dominate the airwaves (and there is some contention about whether the issue is values, virtue, or character), there is a growing consensus that personal standards are central to individual and communal decision making.

The debate, of course, is: Whose values? Some values, however, have universal currency, affirmed by nearly all citizens regardless of age, income, or race or ethnicity. Among them are caring for others, honesty, and responsibility.

The values assets naturally fall into two broad categories. First are the two assets related to prosocial values: values of caring and compassion for others and the world. For the well-being of society, young people need to learn how and when to suspend personal gain for the welfare of others.

Within the value of caring we see some disturbing trends, with younger youth being much more likely than older ones to express this value. Overall, 61 percent of those in the sixth to eighth grades express this value, compared to 46 percent for ninth-to-twelfth graders. These numbers suggest that we graduate into adulthood a majority of youth who have lost or never developed the values of caring and compassion.

This decline is particularly true of males, with only about one-third holding these values in grades ten, eleven, and twelve. If not nurtured during the middle school and high school years (and earlier), such values are harder to develop later

---

Positive-Values Assets

26. Caring
27. Equality and social justice
28. Integrity
29. Honesty
30. Responsibility
31. Restraint

in life, with profound, long-term implications for the sustainability of marital relationships, citizen participation, and volunteerism.

Where do caring values come from? There are two primary sources. First, caring, like all values, is passed on by modeling. It is rooted in the experience of being with people who choose to respond to human need with acts of caring and compassion. The more one's sphere of adult and peer influence accents this action, the greater the chances that the seeds of compassion are planted. The second source is practice, the doing of caring (which, of course, relates to the empowerment assets).

How many such caring experiences or what frequency is needed to cement caring values? No one knows for sure. Certainly the answer is many times, not once or a few. Indeed, for caring to become a lasting disposition, the practice of it ought to be in the range of once a week throughout childhood and adolescence.

Communities are organized to deliver neither the modeling nor the practice dimensions of caring. Age segregation—reinforced by institutional structures and cultural norms—thwarts repeated exposure to adult role models. Most youth rarely engage in the practice of caring, ostensibly because such experience is not a lasting priority in community life. Finally, too many adults do not model or value caring behavior themselves.[37]

We must do better. To make caring a more normative experience, service should be a mainstay of developmental experience, being highly valued and promoted in family, congregation, school, clubs, teams, and organizations.

We also propose an even more comprehensive vision for the future. In neighborhoods, four or five families unite and form a compact to engage in service together. Preferably, these "teams" are intergenerational in nature, including small children, teenagers, and adults. Children, youth, and adults select their experiences together, then spend time afterward talking about their experiences. Let's call these service teams, and advocate that all kids and adults participate, making such efforts long-term and normative. Community agencies and congregations that support and use volunteers are equipped to support these teams and match them with "real work" that matches their interests and values.

The next four values assets address areas of *personal character*. These values provide a foundation for wise decision making. Each of these personal character assets is an important predictor of both nonengagement in risk behaviors and of multiple positive outcomes, such as school success.[38] And each is increasingly touted as an essential value for a humane and democratic society.[39]

The final value asset, restraint (#31), focuses on young people's believing it is important not to do some things because they are against their values. One of the areas addressed in this item is a commitment to postponing sexual intercourse. It is based on this item: "It is against my values to have sex while I am a teenager."

How youth respond to this item separates the sexually experienced from the sexually inexperienced. But it seems to do more than this: young people who say it is against their beliefs to have sexual intercourse as teenagers are also more likely to refrain from alcohol and other drug use as well as violent resolution of conflict. Hence, the sexual-restraint value may represent a larger commitment by young people to avoid health-compromising risks.

A Community's Year of Values

"Developing a healthy community has been a long-standing goal in our city," says Scott Richardson, coordinator of the Healthy Community Initiative of Northfield, a college town in Minnesota. Using the survey results of their young people's assets, the community was able "to focus on a specific way to approach our goals for building on our community's strengths."

With the survey results fresh in their imaginations, community leaders gathered to explore ways to implement positive youth development in Northfield. The school district and the Northfield Ministerial Association committed themselves to exploring ways they could develop a "Year of Values" for the city.

"Our task has always been to humanize the information we learned from our Search Institute survey," said Richardson. "Through the Year of Values theme, we were able to get our feet on the ground."

Throughout the school year, parent-teacher organizations all over the city became involved in organizing educational opportunities for families. One focused on the power of the media; another on the importance of positive communication in families. In the fall, every family in the community received a wallet-sized card listing seven values shared by the community.

Social-Competencies Assets

The current genre of alcohol and other drug prevention programs appropriately emphasize the development of social competencies.[40] They inhibit chemical use and are essential ingredients in preventing other high-risk behaviors. And social

---

Social-Competencies Assets

32. Planning and decision making
33. Interpersonal competence
34. Cultural competence
35. Resistance skills
36. Peaceful conflict resolution

competencies are also important for the larger social task of civic engagement and form a foundation of skills for effectiveness in the workplace.

These competencies can be developed in the adult years, but the chances for carrying these assets into adulthood are greatly increased when communities pay attention to their development in childhood and adolescence. Each of these can be informed and shaped by family, school, youth organizations, religious institutions, and informal interactions with peers and adults.

Two of the social-competency assets focus on personal choice making (planning and decision making, and resistance skills). Resistance skills have become an important ingredient in the newest generation of alcohol and other drug prevention programs because of their power in reducing substance use and abuse.[41]

The other three social-competency assets focus more on healthy interpersonal relationships. The competency of peaceful conflict resolution relates not only to prevention of violent behavior but to other risk-taking as well.[42]

Cultural competence—knowing and being comfortable with people of different ethnic or racial backgrounds—is strongly tied to affirmation of diversity.[43] This competence becomes increasingly important for all young people—and adults—at a time when this society is becoming more and more multicultural, to combat issues of intolerance, racism, and prejudice.

Positive-Identity Assets

Identity formation is one of the critical tasks of adolescence, as young people ask: "Who am I? What can I do? Who do I want to become?" This eighth category of assets focuses on young people's views of themselves: their own sense of power, purpose, and promise. Without these assets, young people can become powerless victims without a sense of initiative, direction, and purpose. The positive-identity assets deserve special attention.

Self-Esteem. None of these positive-identity assets has gained as much attention as self-esteem (#38). In recent years, youth professionals and policy makers have

---

Positive-Identity Assets

37. Personal power
38. Self-esteem
39. Sense of purpose
40. Positive view of personal future

acted as though this single asset tips the scale, that building self-esteem is *the* answer. On the contrary, self-esteem is not the most powerful of the assets. It is no more powerful in the construction of healthy development than the others, and, indeed, some research has found that it has little or no impact on many youth outcomes. Thus, elevating self-esteem as the critical variable is greatly overstated; it is one element in the larger formula for healthy development.

In this context, we note that the asset of positive self-esteem is less common among girls than boys, a finding that is consistent with other research.[44] It is an issue that deserves combined community attention and close examination of how opportunity and a sense of being valued are distributed in this culture. But attention to this relative gap in self-esteem ought not to preoccupy communities to the exclusion of other, equally pressing developmental concerns.

Positive View of Personal Future. The positive view of personal future asset (#40) points to the power of hope and optimism to shape life choices. Indeed, a number of researchers—most notably, Martin E. P. Seligman of the University of Pennsylvania—suggest that optimism is a key to healthy development. Seligman persuasively argues that ours is a culture of pessimism and that "pessimism is fast becoming the typical way our children look at the world." Through his research, he has concluded that "pessimism is an entrenched habit of mind that has had sweeping and disastrous consequences: depressed mood, resignation, underachievement, and even unexpectedly poor physical health."[45]

While Seligman's understanding of optimism is more complex than can be captured in a single asset, it suggests the rich potential of this social competency. A similar depth of research and practical tools can be found for many of the other social competencies as well.[46]

Assets as Building Blocks

Two years ago, Dottie Mullikin decided to look in a new direction for the Ozarks Fighting Back initiative. For years, the effort had focused on prevention and education regarding alcohol and other drugs in twenty-one counties in southwestern Missouri.

"We were successful in getting folks together, bringing them to the table to solve problems by implementing solutions," Mullikin said. "But I wanted to move away from always talking about prevention strategies."

Mullikin learned about the framework of developmental assets, and it quickly captured the interest of her planning group and the communities she serves. The initiative shifted its emphasis and is now promoting asset building throughout the counties, using the language of "building blocks."

"We added a new dimension to the Search Institute concept of assets. We decided to call them building blocks and have used the image for our program interpretation and marketing."

Mullikin and her staff constructed blocks, with one asset written on each block. "People can touch and understand the concepts," Mullikin said. "For some reason, stacking blocks to visualize the idea of assets is a real motivation. Instead of constantly planning, we seem to move quickly to implementing ideas."

The initiative is sharing these ideas in other ways:

- Public schools print the assets on report card envelopes.
- More than thirty people have been trained to tell the asset story to various groups in the communities.
- Local department stores teamed with the initiative to sponsor "Building Block Days," during which staff members dressed in building block costumes and mingled with customers, sharing ideas for supporting children and youth.
- Health care providers put brochures in their waiting rooms that asked the question: "How many blocks have you worked on today?"

The framework of developmental assets unleashes these kinds of creative community efforts to mobilize the power of individual citizens, organizations, and social institutions. It does so, we find, because this language of assets unifies communities around elements of positive development that are intuitively and experientially obvious to most residents. In this sense, what is understood to matter scientifically is known, and always has been, by the people in communities.

CHAPTER THREE

THE STATE OF DEVELOPMENTAL ASSETS AMONG YOUTH

Chapter Two presented a vision of forty developmental assets. Each one matters. Each contributes to healthy development. Because of the power of these building blocks, we should do whatever is necessary in our families, neighborhoods, schools, youth organizations, congregations, businesses, and public life to guarantee that every American child and adolescent experiences most of these assets.

But the gap between the ideal and the real is wide in every community and every subgroup of youth. Our initial research on this configuration of forty developmental assets suggests that, on the whole, the average public school student in the twelve-to-eighteen age range has less than twenty of the assets. For most youth, regardless of demographic category, the assets are too fragile, too uncommon, and too undeveloped.

There is, of course, a lot at stake. We cannot be sure what happens in the long run to the high percentage of American youth who do not currently possess asset strength. Some, fortunately, find a way during adulthood to reclaim lost ground. Others carry into adulthood certain gaps in development that spell trouble for themselves and others.

For many, however, the effects of a less-than-optimal experience in the first eighteen years of life are less dramatic or visible. The personal loss could be unrealized potential, or a muting of happiness, productivity, or contribution. Calculated at a personal level, the effects may be somewhat imperceptible. But calculated at a national level, summing across millions of youth, the cumulative effects on society are substantial.

This chapter identifies central themes or patterns in young people's experiences of developmental assets:

- The power of developmental assets
- Developmental assets being too few everywhere
- The poverty of developmental assets for all types of youth
- The absence of specific assets

Chapter Three is based on two research sources. First, most of this chapter presents core themes about developmental assets based on the aggregated results of surveys of more than 254,000 public school students in 460 communities across the United States (which we call the 1990–1995 developmental asset sample). Details on the characteristics of this sample as well as additional findings are presented in Appendix B.

Because this large study was based on the original framework of thirty developmental assets (a precursor to the reconfigured framework presented in Chapter Two), we also draw preliminary findings from the initial wave of dozens of communities that have completed surveys of their youth using the new framework of forty developmental assets, which now undergirds our work. By February 1997, these pioneers in the new taxonomy of assets range from large urban cities such as Seattle and Minneapolis to small towns and suburbs across the country. What we see in these first forty–asset studies mimics precisely the core themes we identified in the hundreds of places where we studied the initial configuration of thirty assets.

The Power of Developmental Assets

Developmental assets are powerful predictors of behavior. They serve as *protective* factors: they inhibit, for example, alcohol and other drug abuse, violence, sexual intercourse, and school failure. They serve as *enhancement* factors: they promote positive developmental outcomes. And they also serve as *resiliency* factors: they help youth weather adversity.

For each important function (protection, enhancement, resiliency), the key dynamic is this: the more assets, the better. That is, the larger the number of assets a young person has, the lower the involvement in high-risk behavior (protection), the greater the positive outcomes (enhancement), and the greater the ability to beat the odds (resiliency). Let's look at each of these areas in turn.

The Protective Power of Assets

The developmental assets inoculate youth against a wide range of risk-taking behaviors, from substance use to violence and school failure. The assets work best in combination. The more of them, the better. Having forty assets is better than having thirty; thirty is better than twenty, and so on. As assets rise in number, all forms of risk taking decrease.

We see strong evidence for the cumulative power of developmental assets in every town, city, or school district we study, whether based on thirty or forty developmental assets. Take, for example, our widely distributed report on public school students in Albuquerque and Minneapolis.[1] As the first cities exploring the forty assets, their data illuminate a pattern seen in towns and cities across the country, from small agricultural communities to suburbs in major metropolitan areas.

Table 3.1 shows the percentage of sixth-to-twelfth-grade students in Albuquerque who engage in patterns of high-risk behavior as a function of how many assets they have.

One of the patterns is alcohol use, defined as three or more uses of alcohol in the past month, or getting drunk once or more in the past two weeks. Among Albuquerque youth who are asset poor (with ten or fewer of the forty assets), 53 percent report this pattern of problem alcohol use. For those with 11–20 assets, the percentage falls to 35. For students with 21–30 assets, the percentage falls again to 16. And for those who are particularly asset rich (31–40), the number reporting an alcohol risk pattern is reduced to 4 percent. This profound drop in alcohol use, as assets rise in number, is similar in Minneapolis.

This inoculating or protective feature of developmental assets applies to tobacco use, sexual activity, and violence, but also to antisocial behavior, illicit drug use, depression and attempted suicide, school failure, driving and alcohol, and gambling. In every case, an increase in the level of assets is tied to a substantial decrease in each form of behavior.

Though the numbers vary a little when one changes the name of the city, the pattern is always the same: as assets rise, multiple types of health-compromising behavior decrease.

When we look at the 1990–1995 developmental asset sample, we see a similar relationship between the thirty original developmental assets and at-risk behavior. As shown in Figure 3.1, youth with few assets (0–10) have the highest rate of risk taking in every one of the risk-taking behaviors. The percentage decreases as youth move up to 11–20 assets. Then it decreases again when youth have 21–25 assets, and again when they are particularly asset-rich (26–30).

Take, for example, the percentage of youth who report sexual intercourse three or more times. When youth have 0–10 assets, 41 percent exhibit this pattern. The rate falls to 27 percent for those with 11–20 assets, to 14 percent if 21–25 assets,

TABLE 3.1. FORTY DEVELOPMENTAL ASSETS AND HIGH-RISK BEHAVIOR PATTERNS: ALBUQUERQUE AND MINNEAPOLIS.

Category	Patterns of High-Risk Behavior — Definition	City	Percentage of Youth Engaged in High-Risk Behavior Patterns			
			If 0–10 Assets	If 11–20 Assets	If 21–30 Assets	If 31–40 Assets
Alcohol	Has used alcohol three or more times in the past month or got drunk one or more times in the past two weeks	Albuquerque	53	35	16	4
		Minneapolis	63	42	24	12
Tobacco	Smokes one or more cigarettes every day or uses chewing tobacco frequently	Albuquerque	36	19	7	2
		Minneapolis	35	18	7	2
Sexual Intercourse	Has had sexual intercourse three or more times in lifetime	Albuquerque	38	28	17	5
		Minneapolis	44	32	17	4
Violence	Has engaged in three or more acts of fighting, hitting, injuring a person, carrying or using a weapon, or threatening physical harm in the past year	Albuquerque	65	41	21	7
		Minneapolis	69	49	31	10

Notes: Albuquerque sample is a census of public-school students, grades six to twelve (*N* = 12,440).

Minneapolis sample is a census of public-school students, grades seven, eight, ten, and eleven (*N* = 5,235).

FIGURE 3.1. THE PROTECTIVE CONSEQUENCES OF DEVELOPMENTAL ASSETS FOR NINE HIGH-RISK PATTERNS OF BEHAVIOR.

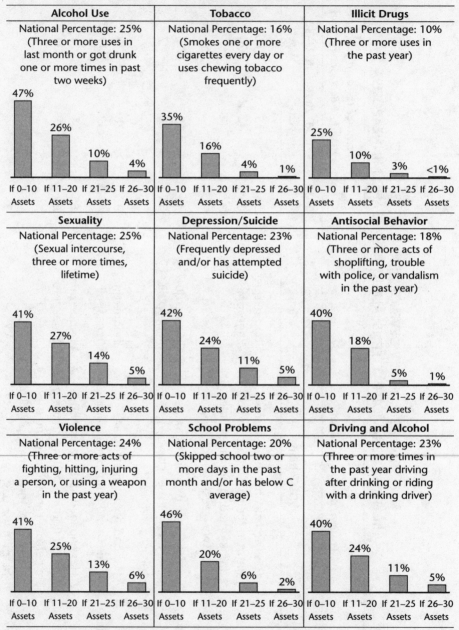

Notes: Based on total national sample of 254,464 students, grades six to twelve.

Percentages indicate how many youth engage in each pattern based on the level of the original thirty assets they experience.

and then down to 5 percent of those with 26–30 assets. That's a difference of eight times when comparing asset-poor youth to asset-rich youth. This kind of relationship to the number of assets holds for all nine patterns of high-risk behaviors.[2]

The strong association between developmental assets and behavioral choices holds not only for the sample taken as a whole but also for demographic subgroups. Assets serve as protective factors in each grade, by gender and by race. (These conclusions and related statistical information on the relationships among assets and various forms of risk-taking behaviors are presented in Appendix B.)

The Enhancing Power of Assets

Healthy development for U.S. youth should not be defined only on the basis of reducing health-compromising behavior. Healthy development also includes the proactive embrace of life-enhancing attitudes and behaviors.

Developmental assets include some of these markers of healthy behavior, particularly in the categories of values and social competencies. They appear to promote positive actions and dispositions. Some might call these "indicators of thriving."

When we switch the outcome to forms of thriving, we also find that positive choices increase dramatically as the number of assets increase. This is true in many different areas of thriving, including school success, affirmation of diversity in one's life and community, choosing to show care and concern to friends or neighbors, gravitating to leadership, and taking care of one's health through good nutrition or exercise.

Figure 3.2 highlights some of the connections between assets and thriving, based on the original framework of thirty assets. For example, in the area of school success, students who report A averages tend to be asset-rich. This finding suggests that the calls to focus on improved academics at the expense of other asset-building opportunities (such as music, cocurricular activities, or climate-enhancing efforts) could, in fact, inhibit academic achievement, not improve it, because young people may be less ready and able to learn without a strong developmental foundation to undergird their academic pursuits.

Similarly, the action of volunteering to help others rises dramatically as a function of asset level. Perhaps young people whose own needs for support, boundaries, structure, and the other assets are met are better equipped to reach out to others in acts of compassion and justice.

Volunteer service is only one way of measuring helping others. Perhaps equally important are more informal and nonprogrammatic forms of helping among peers and within neighborhoods. We also include a measure of informal helping in our studies[3] and find that this kind of prosocial behavior also climbs as assets increase.

FIGURE 3.2. ASSETS AND THRIVING.

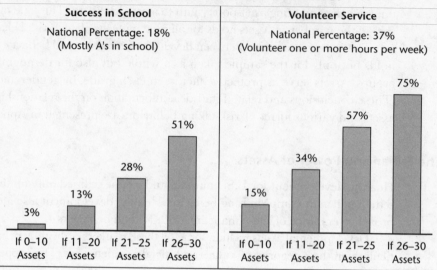

Success in School	Volunteer Service
National Percentage: 18% (Mostly A's in school)	National Percentage: 37% (Volunteer one or more hours per week)

Note: Based on the original framework of thirty assets.

Two forms of optimism—projected future happiness and projected future success—follow the same pattern: as assets increase, so do these indicators of thriving. Personal optimism should not be diminished as a kind of warm-and-fuzzy or soft affect. A number of experts in the child and adolescent fields assert that feelings of hopelessness are among the significant precursors to taking chances with one's health or future.[4]

We are somewhat surprised by the overall rates for optimism (80 percent for future success, 70 percent for future happiness). These percentages suggest a kind of resilience to the vicissitudes of human development. Then again, recall that the sample includes only youth remaining in public schools. Youth who drop out or who are pushed out might alter these findings if they were part of this sample.

The Resiliency Power of Assets

Resiliency is an area of inquiry and practice grounded in the research of scholars such as Norman Garmezy and Ann Masten at the University of Minnesota and Emmy Werner at the University of California, Davis.[5] Resiliency is about beating the odds, or bouncing back from the travails of adversity and trauma. There is plenty of adversity to go around. Developmental challenges include sexual abuse, family violence, alcoholism or other addictions among parents or caretakers, parental psychopathology, divorce, neglect, disabilities, and poverty.

Some young people overcome the odds; others do not. The concept of resiliency refers to those environmental and individual dynamics and characteristics that tilt the scales to beating the odds.

The developmental assets cover some of the same conceptual ground, though there are some differences. The resiliency literature highlights the following areas that are captured in the new framework of forty developmental assets:

- Social competence (for example, empathy, caring, communication skills)
- Caring, attentive family environments
- Surrogate caregivers (extended family members, siblings, nonrelated adults) who provide counsel, safety, and support, particularly when parent or parents are absent or inattentive
- Academic success
- Youth participation in school and community-based programs
- Healthy self-concept and a sense of personal efficacy or control over one's environment
- High expectations
- Assignment of productive roles and responsibility in family or community life[6]

All of these have been documented as distinguishing characteristics of resilient children and the environments that surround them. Particularly illuminating has been Emmy Werner's longitudinal research on an entire cohort of children from Kauai.[7] A similar set of personal and environmental factors have been named in effective social programs that ameliorate some of the negative consequences of high-risk families.[8]

These resiliency factors have a place in the taxonomy of developmental assets. In this way, we might infer that promoting developmental assets functions to buffer youth against adversity. Indeed, our analyses show that the asset profiles of youth who rebound from divorce, sexual or physical abuse, or parental addiction are markedly different from the profiles of those who do not.[9]

We see this profile difference in two ways. First, the assets that reflect the resiliency factors named above are more common among the resilient. Second, the overall number of assets also matters. Resilient youth tend also to have a higher asset average, suggesting that the key is accumulation of developmental assets, in addition to having specific ones.

Perhaps our contribution to the field of resiliency is the consistent finding that all of the assets overlapping the resiliency field are things all young people need, not just those who face challenging odds. They are core and essential developmental experiences that need to be built into the fabric of how communities do business with all their young.

Assets Are Not a Cure-All

Though increasing developmental assets is a necessary and powerful strategy for reducing the kinds of health-related issues youth face, this strategy alone is not enough. Even among youth who experience many of the assets, there is still a small percentage who are not fully inoculated. Some of these young people still engage in negative behaviors.[10]

What this suggests is that behavioral choices are determined by a host of factors. Developmental assets are one factor. Economics, cultural norms, temperament, genetics, and other factors all influence behavior. Hence, we need to tackle healthy development from many angles. There is a place for prevention programs that directly target behaviors such as violence and alcohol and too-early sexual activity. It is also crucial that this society begin to recognize the danger of glamorizing such actions as violent resolution of conflict and alcohol use. Building assets can take us a long way, but not the whole way.

Gaps in Experiences of Developmental Assets

As we show in the previous section, the developmental assets are powerful influences in young people's lives. Children and adolescents are best able to navigate through the challenges of growing up when they are armed with these assets. Yet too few young people experience these assets, suggesting a major factor in the challenges the nation faces in caring for its young.

Overall Levels of Assets

Our surveys of public school students find that the average sixth-to-twelfth grader experiences slightly more than half of the original thirty developmental assets (16.5).[11] Our initial findings from schools surveying youth on the forty assets suggest that the average for the new framework is slightly under half of the forty. Unfortunately, these averages would look even worse if the samples included youth who drop out before completing high school.[12]

Reaching more than twenty-five of the original thirty assets (or thirty-one of the newly configured forty) is a worthy, though challenging, benchmark. But few young people attain these standards, as shown in Figure 3.3. In fact, three-quarters of the youth surveyed have twenty or fewer of the original thirty assets. Only 4 percent reach what ought to be a standard for all: twenty-six or more of the thirty. Furthermore, meeting this goal is uncommon regardless of gender, grade, race or ethnicity, or town size. Though there is some variability (see Appendix B), there is no subgroup for which we can say we are now organizing community life in an optimally asset-promoting manner.

FIGURE 3.3. PERCENTAGES OF YOUTH EXPERIENCING DIFFERENT LEVELS OF ASSETS.

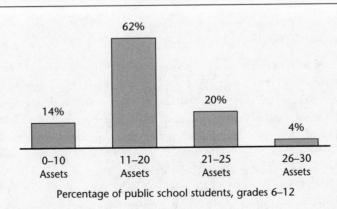

Percentage of public school students, grades 6–12

Note: Based on the original framework of thirty assets.

The Universality of Asset Depletion

A particularly striking finding is the universality of asset depletion. In each of the communities that have conducted this study of developmental assets, the average student has too few of them. We are not talking about just those young people labeled "at risk." We are talking about the way young people in general grow up in this society—whether Caucasian or of color, female or male, rural or urban.

Across the hundreds of communities we have studied using the thirty–asset survey, the average number of assets for each community occurs in a fairly narrow range, from fourteen to eighteen. Eighty-three percent of school districts have an average between 15.0 and 16.99; 3 percent have an average of fourteen; 15 percent average seventeen; and less than one percent average eighteen.[13]

Contrary to what many might expect, the average number of assets stays quite constant across town-size categories. The range is from 16.8 in small cities with 10,000–50,000 population to 16.2 in metropolitan areas, larger than 250,000. In small and mostly rural towns under twenty-five hundred, the average is 16.3. This violates the romantic notion that the quality of socialization is stronger in small towns than in large cities. Maybe this was once true. But it is not the case now.

In the first wave of studies on the forty developmental assets, we continue to see that the average number of developmental assets among public school sixth-to-twelfth-grade students is far below what citizens and experts alike might consider ideal. In each of the first twenty-four communities viewed through the lens of forty developmental assets, the average number of assets is in the range of sixteen to twenty. If we adopt having thirty-one or more assets as a benchmark, we note across the first twenty-four cities that fewer than 10 percent of public school students have reached this level.

The Downward Trend

As disturbing as the overall level of assets is the downward trend in assets, from an average of 17.8 in grade six to 16.1 in grade twelve (based on the original thirty assets). Granted, this is not a study that tracks the same young people across their adolescent journeys, so we do not know the extent of the change in assets in individuals across time. But it is a reasonable hunch that what we see in these grade-by-grade differences reflects this culture's propensity to release adolescents too early, to give little guidance and support (or none at all) after age fourteen or fifteen. What many of us forget is that although specific ways of expressing them change as young people mature, adolescents need as much daily support, structure, boundary-clarification, and value socialization as do five-year-olds.

Missing Assets

We focus attention on the cumulative issues in asset development, but it is noteworthy that some of the developmental assets are in particularly short supply. These findings suggest that the lack of some essential developmental ingredients is becoming normative in this society.

Typically, for every town or city in which we've documented developmental assets, whether with thirty or forty assets, we find that only a minority of youth benefit from:

- Relationships with nonparent adults
- A caring school climate
- Parental involvement in schooling
- The value of caring about others
- Homework
- Clear and consistent boundaries
- Engagement with music or other creative activities

If the first communities conducting the profile of forty assets are indicative, we forecast that the assets of neighborhood caring, neighborhood boundaries, community valuing youth, youth as resources, service to others, reading for pleasure, resistance skills, adult role models, and high expectations will be fragile in all communities as well.

TABLE 3.2. FOUR COMBINATIONS OF DEVELOPMENTAL ASSETS: NATIONAL PERCENTAGES.

	Low Internal	High Internal
Low External	81	11
High External	4	4

Four Asset Profiles

One final way of looking at the depletion of assets among American youth is to place each student in one of the four categories depending on how many of the original sixteen external assets he or she has and, likewise, how many of the original fourteen internal assets. Each young person was scored as high or low on each type of asset category. High on external assets means eight or more of the sixteen; low is fewer than eight. For internal assets, seven or more is high; fewer than seven is low.

Ideally, we would raise a generation that is high on both external and internal assets. But as shown in Table 3.2, only 4 percent of the national sample reaches this standard.[14]

This finding puts our national dilemma in clear relief. It is now normative for our youth to be insufficiently grounded in both external and internal assets. This happens because in all communities studied (and we suspect this is literally *all* cities in the United States), youth experience too few of the assets in any of the eight categories. As long as this asset profile continues, we will see legions of youth who are uncentered or unfocused, susceptible to risk taking and negative peer pressure, and ill-equipped to become the next generation of parents, workers, and leaders.

Differences in Developmental Assets

To this point, we have highlighted the similarities among all youth in their experiences of developmental assets. This emphasis is intentional, for it underscores that the problem is universal and cannot be isolated to one group of youth or another.

At the same time, there are important questions regarding differences among various populations of youth. Our data on the thirty assets allow us to explore how the developmental assets play out by gender, race or ethnicity, and family composition. We come to these conclusions:

- Boys lag behind girls in asset development.
- Differences among categories of race and ethnicity appear to be small.
- On the average, assets are stronger in two-parent families, but some single-parent families are asset-rich.
- Family income appears to have some impact, but not a dramatic one, on asset levels.

Gender

In recent decades, significant strides have been made to advance opportunity for girls. Appropriate attention has focused on promoting equity in schooling and access to higher education and professional occupations.[15] In terms of traditional measures of success and status, ours has been and continues to be a society organized to benefit males. At the same time, however, many forms of social pathology—crime, violence, and substance abuse, for example—disproportionately touch the lives of boys and men.

If the developmental assets represent a way of assessing healthy development, then society needs to pay particular attention to how it raises its boys. As shown in Figure 3.4, boys develop fewer assets than girls. A difference of about two assets can be seen in each grade between six and twelve (in both the original research on thirty assets and the preliminary research on forty assets). The gap is widest in grade twelve: 17.3 versus 15.9. (For detailed differences, see Appendix B.)

The Self-Esteem Difference. When comparing girls and boys on each of the thirty assets, there is only one in which boys excel beyond girls: self-esteem (53 percent for boys, 43 percent for girls). This difference is not hard to understand, given our social proclivity to base personal worth on power, professional status, and Madison Avenue and Hollywood images that set particularly unhealthy standards for females.

The gap between boys and girls in self-esteem widens a bit between middle school and high school, a phenomenon that has been seen in a number of studies.[16] A decrease in self-esteem between middle school and high school, however, is particularly visible among white girls, and to some extent, among Asian American girls. African American, American Indian, and Hispanic American girls appear more resilient to this loss of self regard.

However, boys in all five racial groups report higher self-esteem than girls. A number of explanations for this are possible. Decades ago, for example, Simone de Beauvoir offered the influential idea that, during adolescence, girls in Western culture discover that power unevenly accrues to males.[17]

Strengths for Girls. Self-esteem aside, all other asset differences favor girls. Such differences are particularly pronounced in the categories of boundaries and expectations, constructive use of time, commitment to learning, and positive values.

FIGURE 3.4. AVERAGE NUMBER OF THIRTY DEVELOPMENTAL ASSETS, BY GRADE AND GENDER.

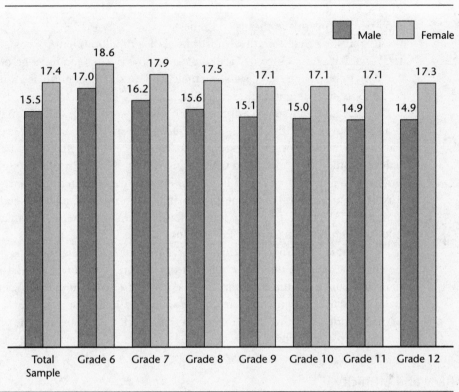

The boundaries-and-expectations and constructive-use-of-time differences may reflect, in part, the greater caution with which families raise daughters. Cross-culturally and across time, societies tend to be more protective of girls. Girls often perceive this inequality in boundaries as unfair or repressive, and families often pay a price for this: conflict between child and parent is more pronounced for adolescent girls than boys.[18]

Gender differences in assets reflect a kind of cultural tradition to "let boys be boys." That is, give boys more leeway to explore, experiment, and be on their own. This may be the way it's always been done, and it may be easier. But it is not wise. In terms of the long-term social good, we must pay attention to the development of both girls and boys, but we may have more work to do to raise asset-rich boys.

A case in point is the caring asset. This asset is about giving and compassion, knowing how and when to sacrifice personal gain for the good of others. Nurturing this disposition is essential for a healthy society. Although this asset is lacking for many youth, our success with boys is particularly pathetic. Only about one-third of boys graduate from high school carrying with them the value of helping others. The rates are 33 percent for eleventh-and-twelfth-grade boys (compared to 54 percent of girls in these two grades).

It is striking that about two-thirds of sixth-grade boys have the asset of caring. What happens? One view is that we give boys permission to let go of caring. We seem to be saying that caring is female stuff, and male identity is grounded in things more instrumental and self-enhancing.

The decline in female caring is also notable (from 79 percent in sixth grade to 54 percent in twelfth grade) and reflective of a society that overstates the primacy of individualism and personal gain. We can celebrate that about half of females transition into adulthood with caring values, but the lopsided commitment reinforces a gender stereotype in which females are expected to offer a disproportionate amount of their energies to shared commitments and needs in the community. We need the girls' commitments, but we need them to be matched by renewed commitments among boys in our society.

The value of caring for others is the glue that holds relationships together, the energy source that fuels everything from attentive parenting to civic engagement and pursuit of the common good. We are at a moment in this society when such prosocial values are also needed to weather the demise of publicly funded services. Addressing this fundamental issue is crucial, and boys are the ones who need the most attention.

Race and Ethnicity

The average number of the original thirty assets varies little when comparing by race or ethnicity. As shown in Figure 3.5, the five groups vary by less than 1.5 of the assets—a smaller difference than the one we found for gender.

It is important to note that the sample on which these findings are based is public school students. School dropouts (who are disproportionately youth of color) are excluded from this analysis. If the study included dropouts—some of whom also live in deep poverty—the racial differences might be more pronounced.

With some caution, then, we include in Appendix B percentages by race on each of the thirty assets (as well as risky behaviors and deficits). Two factors drive this caution. The first is concern that what appear to be racial differences may indeed be confounded with other factors such as family income (a variable that is difficult to measure well in youth self-report surveys such as the one used to gather these data). Second, we are not sure how productive it is to continually hold up race as a defining variable. Over time, such efforts may inadvertently fuel we-versus-they thinking.

FIGURE 3.5. AVERAGE NUMBER OF
THIRTY ASSETS, BY RACE OR ETHNICITY.

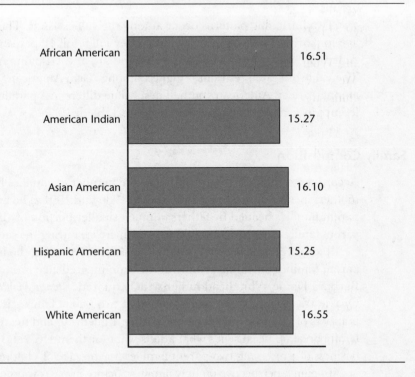

The value of comparing levels of assets among racial or ethnic groups is not in showing the differences but in showing that, on most of the thirty assets, differences are rather small. On many of them, the difference between the largest and smallest percentages is less than 10 percentage points. If anything, this is a reminder that the lack of developmental assets is a widespread phenomenon touching the lives of most American youth, regardless of demography.

When sizable differences occur, they tend to be in the internal assets, most noticeably in the categories of educational commitment and social competencies. On the educational commitment assets, Asian American youth are relatively high, and American Indian and Hispanic American youth are relatively low. In the area of social competencies, African American youth excel, particularly on the assets of self-esteem and a positive view of one's personal future.

Returning to the theme of self-esteem explored earlier, we note that this asset is most common among African American youth.[19] Furthermore, both African American girls and boys report self-esteem at rates considerably higher than their counterparts in all other racial-ethnic categories. The gender difference in self-esteem is less pronounced among African American youth than is true in the other groups.

Two intriguing patterns occur among the values assets. The lowest percentage for caring is among white youth. They fall a full 10 percent below African American, Asian American, American Indian, and Hispanic American youth. The value of sexual restraint is highest among Asian American youth and lowest among African American youth. These value differences parallel a reported difference in sexual activity (see Appendix B, Table B.10).

Family Composition

According to the U. S. Census Bureau, the number of families headed by single mothers increased by 25 percent between 1980 and 1991. The number of single-parent families headed by fathers (a much smaller portion of the overall single-parent family structure) saw a 92 percent increase during the same years.[20]

Recent years have seen considerable debate regarding the impact of single-parent families on children and youth. Gaining credence is the belief, stated by Barbara Dafoe Whitehead in her widely quoted *Atlantic Monthly* article "Dan Quayle Was Right," that "the dissolution of two-parent families is harmful to large numbers of children." It's time, the author argued, "to end the quiet tolerance of family breakup because it's what adults want for themselves and get down to the business of preserving two-parent families for the sake of children."[21]

To gain a perspective on how family structure impacts young people, we compared those young people who live in a single-parent family because of divorce or separation with those in intact two-parent families. (The sample of single-parent youth did not distinguish those whose mother had never married.)

Youth in single-parent families are, on the average, clearly more at risk than those in two-parent families. On many ways of defining risk, single-parent youth tend to show more health-compromising behavior than do youth in two-parent families, even when we statistically control the factors of race and levels of maternal education (a reasonable proxy for family income).[22]

But we err if we generalize to all single-parent families. Almost half of younger youth in single-parent families are at low risk (none or one at-risk behavior out of twenty), as are one-fourth of older youth. Youth in some two-parent families are at high risk. Table 3.3 gives the percentages of youth who are at low (0–1 at-risk behaviors), moderate (2–4), and high (five or more) risk in single-parent and two-parent families.

Thus, although youth in single-parent families are more likely to be at risk, it is not inevitably so. Fate is not sealed based solely on family composition. The

TABLE 3.3. PERCENTAGE OF YOUTH AT RISK, BY GRADE AND FAMILY CONFIGURATION.

		Low Risk	Moderate Risk	High Risk
Grades 6–8	One parent	46	33	21
	Two parents	65	26	9
Grades 9–12	One parent	26	31	43
	Two parents	41	31	28

challenge, then, is to discover what is happening in single-parent families where youth thrive. Part of the answer lies in the developmental assets. Overall, two-parent youth tend to have more of these assets in their lives (16.9 on average out of thirty) than one-parent youth (15.2 on average).

Examining the specific assets shows interesting patterns. On many assets, differences between single-parent and two-parent youth are relatively small. Others, however, show greater differences. For example, single-parent youth are much less likely than two-parent youth to report having a family life that provides love and support. Whether the lack of caring is a result of family conflict, or of a parent's preoccupation with personal concerns, or some other family dynamic is an important question worthy of further research.

Another important area of difference deals with involvement in various structured activities. Young people in single-parent families are much less likely than two-parent youth to report involvement in all types of structured activities. Since these activities often demand financial and time commitments from parents, they may be less accessible to single-parent families. Or it may be that single-parent youth feel out of place in some of these settings (because of an enduring stigma on single-parent families or because the sponsoring organizations presume two-parent families in their planning). Whatever the reason, the result is that many single-parent youth miss important opportunities for positive structure.

Beneath the overall differences between single-and two-parent families, however, lies important news: some single-parent families find ways to provide many of these assets. In a previous report,[23] we presented twenty of the original thirty assets that most discriminate between single-parent youth who thrive (no or one at-risk behavior) and those who have problems with growing up (five or more at-risk behaviors). In all cases, single-parent youth who thrive are more likely to experience these assets in their lives. Many of the differences in assets between single-parent youth who thrive and those who do not point toward the support systems around families:

- Supportive, quality schools
- Friends who are a positive influence
- Involvement in extracurricular activities
- Involvement in religious institutions

It may be that this external network of support is the key to success in single-parenting. And it certainly suggests that communities and institutions that serve families and youth can have a positive impact on the health of these families.

These analyses remind us that categorical statements about two-parent families being good and single-parent families being bad overstate the case. True, two-parent families have an edge. Yet, being in a two-parent family is no guarantee that a young person has the nurture, boundaries, opportunities, and guidance needed to grow up healthy. Many two-parent families do not live up to their potential.

At the same time, being a single parent is tough work, and living in such a family structure is not, generally speaking, optimal for children. But with special effort—and with the support of individuals, communities, and institutions around them—single-parent families can also be supportive, healthy families in which young people thrive.

Family Income

Many questions are raised about the impact of family income on asset development. Unfortunately, it is difficult if not impossible to gain accurate information on family income from youth self-report surveys. But we do have some information suggesting that family income makes some difference. However, by itself, it is insufficient to explain a young person's experiences of the developmental assets.

In Minneapolis, we looked at how much the developmental assets vary among the city's eleven planning districts, which vary graphically in average family income, property values, and resources.[24] Across these eleven geographical areas of the city, the average number of forty assets ranges from 16.7 to 20.1. Not surprisingly, as average wealth rises, assets also rise. But the differences between less affluent and more affluent neighborhoods are relatively small: only about three out of the forty developmental assets.

Once again, these findings reinforce the message that nearly all American youth face a sizable gap in the formation of developmental assets. It's time to get beyond competitive blaming and handwringing to determine what needs to be done in all communities to rebuild the developmental infrastructure for young people. Certainly some of the strategies and challenges are different among different communities and populations of youth. But the goal is the same.

Which Assets Are Most Important?

When we share the research on developmental assets with various audiences across the nation, one of the most common questions we hear is, which assets are the most important?

The question is an obvious one in our society. We have come to expect or wish for a single panacea or quick fix for each challenge we face. We hope and wish that there are programmatic interventions that will turn the tide for whatever worries us at the moment. An example might be the fondness for self-esteem enhancement programs, with the hope that increasing self-esteem solves all our problems.

Finding a single program that alters the course of development would be efficient and convenient, freeing most of us from having to make fundamental changes in our lives and community. Altering our individual commitments and the nature of community is messier and more complicated and interferes with personal agendas. But it's the way we need to go. Positive human development is not a big bang, not one grand program. Rather, it is more like the accumulation of thousands of positive socialization moments that shape both external and internal assets.

A variant on the quick-fix question is whether some of the assets matter more than others. Rather than worrying about all of them, couldn't we focus on the two or three that are most powerful?

A somewhat flippant answer is, "If I knew that several mattered most, I wouldn't say." This uncooperative response is fueled by the fear that communities would then program one or two things and eschew the deep mobilization needed to alter the overall asset profiles of young people. The question is similar to asking which single nutrient or food group the body needs, rather than working to ensure a balanced diet.

In actuality, there is no concise answer to the question, for it depends on which behavior we are trying to explain. Some assets matter more for alcohol-use prevention, while others matter for restraining sexual behavior. Still others are relatively important for enhancing school success or compassionate actions. The judicious approach, then, is to act on the fact that the assets are cumulative and that, as each of them builds in strength, we reap broad and significant influence on protection, enhancement, and resiliency.

This said, there are some interesting themes in how the assets relate to specific behavioral choices. For example:

• The asset of self-esteem is strongly related to prevention of depression and suicide. However, it is much less related to all the other patterns of high-risk behavior.[25]

• The asset of behavioral restraint ("it is against my values to have sex while I am a teenager") has surprising power. It is strongly related to sexual behavior, but it is also one of the strongest predictors of tobacco use, violence, and alcohol use. That is, those with the asset of sexual restraint have lower rates on all these patterns of risk behavior.[26] Apparently, a commitment to sexual restraint is part of a larger commitment to caring for oneself, or a reflection of the strength of moral conviction.

• The asset of parental standards (a boundary asset) tends to be more important than family support (a support asset) for preventing alcohol, tobacco, and other drug use. However, for preventing depression and suicide, the roles are reversed, with family support being more powerful than parental standards.[27]

• Grades in school are most strongly correlated with a number of internal assets, including achievement motivation and many of the social competencies (planning skills, decision-making skills, self-esteem, and a positive view of one's future), as well as with each of the structured time-use and positive-peer-influence assets.

• Spending time helping other people is most strongly correlated with the value assets and the structured-time-use assets.

The power of a communitywide approach to raising healthy children can be seen in the ten assets that most inoculate youth against antisocial behavior. These ten, in the language of the original thirty assets, are:

External Assets	*Internal Assets*
Parental standards	Behavioral restraint
Youth programs	Achievement motivation
Religious community	Educational aspirations
Family support	
Positive peer influence	
Positive school climate	
Time at home	

Search Institute colleagues Dale A. Blyth and Nancy Leffert deepened this understanding of community impact by comparing healthier communities (relatively low risky-behavior rates by its ninth-to-twelfth graders) with less healthy communities (relatively high risky-behavior rates).[28] The healthier communities were marked by a number of assets, including higher rates for family support, positive school climate, achievement motivation, and youth engagement in structured activities. Hence, many of the same assets seem to define both high community health and individual health.

Too much attention to this maze of idiosyncratic connections between assets and youth outcomes makes it difficult to see the forest through the trees. The big picture is that every asset plays an important role, but its role is shaped by the outcomes in question. If our commitment is to broad, positive outcomes for all of our youth, the best policy is to organize community life in a way that maximizes the full range of developmental strengths for all children and adolescents.

Putting the Challenge in Perspective

In hundreds of audiences of professionals and community residents who hear us discuss this research, there are two frequently asked questions: Are assets weaker now than in previous decades? And how do we compare to other nations?

These are difficult questions. Most of the cross-time studies of American youth have been designed to measure risk-taking behaviors, not the quality of the developmental infrastructure. And we know of no available comparative cross-cultural data. Some inferences can be made, however.

We know that since World War II, there have been major social trends in the direction of family disruption, single-parenting, and women in the workplace, a triumvirate of factors that have likely increased parental absence. The advent of television as a daily influence is a second social factor that likely interferes with asset development. As many parents and other adults have become consumed by work or anxious about the loss of it, it is likely that community attentiveness to children and adolescents has decreased, replaced by more programmatic efforts to support our young (day care, after-school programming) and a concomitant increase in sustained intergenerational relationships.

We infer that a higher percentage of adolescents today work more than fifteen hours a week than at any time since World War II. As mentioned in Chapter Two, too much work interferes with asset development. We also note that many of the institutions that serve children and teenagers (schools, youth organizations, religious institutions) are constantly seeking reform, a sign perhaps that there is now a major disconnect between institutions and the needs, interests, and wants of children and adolescents. Neighborhoods are more likely now to have closed and locked doors than open ones.

One way of summarizing these trends is this: the four major sources of influence on child and adolescent development are adult interactions (including parent interactions and intergenerational relationships), social institutions, mass media, and peer groups. Since the 1960s, the first two have decreased in their constructive influence and the latter two have filled the void. If this hypothesis is true, it would seem axiomatic that developmental assets are in greater disrepair now than at any time since the middle of the century. The relatively high rates of children in poverty now compared to twenty or thirty years ago does not help.

On an international scale, it is likely that other developed societies have also seen a rupture in their capacity to sustain positive development of their youth. We can use some reverse logic to suggest that the United States, though, has a comparatively deeper problem with developmental assets. On many indications of "problem behavior," such as teenage pregnancy, adolescent alcohol and other drug use, and school dropouts, we are a leader among the world's developed nations.[29] To the extent that developmental assets shape behavioral choices and reduce risky behaviors, assets are in relative trouble in U.S. society.

In some ways, though, these are not the most pressing issues. Comparisons to the past or to other places, though important, can also deflect attention to the real crisis and challenge: in all of our communities, we are losing young people because we have failed to provide them with the basic building blocks of development. This is partly because we have been unable to protect them from the deficits that interfere with healthy development. But it is also largely due to the fact that we have, in general, let the developmental infrastructure crumble for far too many of our young.

CHAPTER FOUR

EXTENDING ASSETS FROM BIRTH TO ADULTHOOD

As my colleagues from Search Institute and I share our understanding of developmental assets with communities and other groups across the country, we often hear reactions such as, "Aren't these assets things everyone needs, not just adolescents?"

Indeed, the need for a strong developmental infrastructure doesn't suddenly surface at puberty and disappear at high school graduation. The assets that adolescents need have deep roots in childhood, and they provide a foundation for lifelong health and well-being. So while Search Institute's research has focused primarily on sixth-to-twelfth-grade youth, we have begun developing a deeper understanding of the developmental path of young people from birth through age eighteen. We also believe that this same path continues into and through adulthood.

This understanding is consistent with the developmentalists' perspective that child and adolescent development is not a set of unrelated stages or steps but rather a continuous process, with early experiences and opportunities helping to shape later ones. This does not mean, of course, that everything a child does predetermines what happens later in life. Events, both positive and negative, occur that can alter the course of development.[1] But this perspective calls for continuous attention to the foundations of healthy development—developmental assets—throughout the life span. This chapter summarizes Search Institute's conceptualization of assets for children from birth through fifth grade—based on a report titled *Starting Out*

Right: Developmental Assets for Children[2]—and offers some initial thoughts about what assets might look like for adults.

Developmental Assets for Children

Recent years have seen a plethora of information emerge on the healthy development of children. This information has been applied in a wide variety of contexts, including highly visible national programs such as Head Start, Success by Six, and other early childhood and family education programs.

These efforts have focused considerable energy on addressing children's needs at critical times in their development (usually from birth to age three or six). What has been missing, however, is a broad picture of how these pieces fit together, that is, a multifaceted vision of healthy child development in which everyone in a community sees her or his role in contributing to the well-being of young people.

Like the assets for youth, the asset framework for children embodies such a wide vision. When combined with Search Institute's previous work on assets for twelve-to-eighteen-year-olds, the assets identified for children offer a comprehensive vision of what young people need in the first two decades of life to become healthy, caring, responsible, and contributing members of society.

Although this framework grows out of extensive research, we expect that like the framework for middle and high school youth it will evolve through a process of inquiry and dialogue. But for now, these proposed assets for children represent a consistent, developmentally based road map for understanding and addressing the needs of all children.

The assets for all ages of children are arranged into the same eight categories used for the assets for youth (see Chapter Two). Although the children's assets do not have the same kind of empirical data to support their cumulative impact that we have on adolescents, they are deeply rooted in existing literature on child development.

It is important to note that the distinction between external and internal assets offers a useful lens for clearly understanding the asset categories, but the distinction is not directly applicable to infants and young children. During infancy and early childhood all of the assets essentially externally surround the child through important relationships. Infants, toddlers, and preschoolers are more dependent on adults than are older children. For this reason, the responsibility for building both external and internal assets for infants and young children is in the hands of parents and other caregivers.

With this context in mind, we turn now to a brief overview of the children's assets.

External Assets

Positive development requires constant exposure to interlocking systems of support, empowerment, boundaries and expectations, and constructive use of time. The first twenty assets for children provide this web of safety and support that is so important for stimulating and nurturing healthy development.

Support. Support refers to the many ways adults love, encourage, comfort, and affirm children. From birth, infants need parents and caregivers who take the time to be with them, meet their needs, and be emotionally available. Through mutually gratifying interactions that occur between the child and parents and caregivers, relationships develop over time. These relationships are essential to a child's positive development.

In infancy, the groundwork for the beginnings of attachment is laid as caregivers and infants consistently connect. As children grow, support provides the security children need to try new tasks, master new skills, and gain confidence. Children without support are more apt to feel afraid, insecure, and isolated.

Empowerment. Children who are empowered feel good about themselves and their skills. They grow up in homes where they are treated as separate individuals with unique strengths and needs and who are encouraged to act independently in age-appropriate situations. Empowered children feel their actions can make a difference.

Yet we live in a society that tends to either ignore children because they get in the way, or, conversely, we expect them to act like miniature adults. Often children take on the role of parent, or at the other extreme we tend to err by not giving them meaningful, developmentally appropriate roles. Too often we assume that they want to focus only on themselves, thus neglecting their sense of concern and ability to contribute. In addition, we do so many things for them that they are left with few useful opportunities or roles in their families and communities.

Boundaries and Expectations. Children need to know how to act and how not to act, and they need to hear clear instructions, not conflicting messages, from parents and other caregivers. Boundaries are part of what makes our society civilized and safe.

One of the first boundaries an infant is given, once he is physically capable, is to sleep through the night. Toilet training, looking both ways before crossing the street, giving things back that you borrow are only a few of the many boundaries and expectations that young children learn between the ages of two and ten. Through the thousands of interactions between the child and the adults surrounding her, the child learns what is acceptable and what is not, in terms of safety, socialization, and values.

Constructive Use of Time. All children need a balance of structured and unstructured time that allows them to grow and develop. All children need quality time, as well as a sufficient quantity of time, with their families to ensure healthy development. And as they grow, children also need access to high-quality, affordable activities that build their competencies and expose them to caring adults beyond the family.

One of the characteristics of a healthy community for children is a rich array of constructive opportunities for children as young as seven or eight and for families with younger children. This has become particularly important as large numbers of parents of young children work outside the home, leaving some school-age children with little or no supervision in the after-school hours. Whether through schools, community organizations, religious institutions, or for-profit centers, these structured activities stimulate positive growth and also contribute to the development of a number of other assets.

Internal Assets

Responsibility for children does not end with providing external assets. There needs to be a similar commitment to nurturing the kinds of internalized commitments, values, competencies, and identity needed to guide choices and create a sense of centeredness and purpose. Adults who model these assets when children are young lay the foundation for children to observe, learn, and gradually internalize these assets.

Children typically do not begin to have the cognitive or emotional abilities to internalize certain behaviors, values, and competencies—the internal assets—until ages six to nine. They develop these values and competencies through a slow process of observation, social learning, and internalization, a process that continues through early and middle adolescence. Early childhood experiences provide a foundation for children to internalize these assets as they develop cognitive, moral, and social capacities.

Commitment to Learning. Children are naturally curious. They love to explore, learn, and try new things. Yet many children's curiosity wanes and their desire to learn fades somewhere along their journey through childhood. Many adults do not have or take the time to teach and encourage children, or model the joy of learning. Often, parents and teachers are seen as the only ones who can influence a child's commitment to learning, thus reducing children's access to other positive role models and educational advocates in the community. Furthermore, societal influences often cast learning in a negative light or focus on extrinsic rewards and punishments (such as grades and prizes) that may inhibit the development of intrinsic motivation.

Within the category of commitment to learning are five assets. From birth to age five, they focus more on what adults provide in an environment that encourages learning. As children enter school, the assets emphasize development of the internal commitment to and motivation for learning.

Positive Values. Values encompass our attitudes, the standards for our actions, and our beliefs. Values are the important internal compasses that guide people in developing priorities and making choices.

The foundation for value development begins during infancy and slowly evolves through childhood and adolescence, all the while becoming more sophisticated and complex. People do not suddenly become honest and responsible when they become teenagers or adults. The development of these values is a long process that entails many interactions between children and adults.

Social Competencies. During infancy, children learn skills through observation, taking in information by observing the people around them. Toddlers begin to experiment by talking and doing. As children progress through the preschool and elementary-school years, they expand their skills through more in-depth discussions and practicing more complex tasks. How people behave around a young child affects his growth and the development of social competence. Children's development of social competence is affected by interactions with their environment.

Positive Identity. Forging an individual identity is a lifelong process, but the process starts in infancy. To form a positive identity, children need love and support, they need to know and understand their limits and boundaries, and they need to feel empowered. Children also are more likely to feel good about themselves when they enjoy learning, find their activities stimulating and enriching, acquire positive values, and develop social competencies.

Thus, many of the other assets play a part in building a positive identity. The ways others respond to the child also greatly impact her identity. Children who are given clear, logical boundaries that are enforced consistently and with sensitivity are more likely to feel good about themselves, which in turn affects how they interact with other people. Children who feel loved and supported unconditionally are more apt to feel secure enough to take appropriate risks, learn more, and grow into competent, healthy, and productive adults.

How Do Assets Develop in Children?

We believe that the process of asset development is a continuous one, and that development is a complex interaction of nature and nurture. External assets (such as support and empowerment) are absolutely essential in the early months and years, and they are helpful in building the internal assets (such as positive values and positive identity formation). Even though an infant does not have the "ability" to be honest or responsible, the infant does begin to learn about these values by observing the behaviors of her parents and by the caring, honest, and responsible way parents and caregivers care for the infant and young child. The young child can also begin to sense the parents' views about themselves and the world. These feelings and attitudes gradually become internalized by the child as part of his worldview.

Infants take in their world by what they see, hear, and feel. When infants are surrounded by assets and are exposed to many situations that build assets, the foundation is laid for internalization as they grow and develop. Developing the capacity to communicate verbally, young children begin to talk with adults about feelings and beliefs, although these conversations are simple and concrete in the early childhood and elementary school years. Children also observe adults talking and acting in consistent ways, which adds to this slow process. During the elementary school years, verbal skills and reasoning ability increase, opening the door for more explanatory and in-depth conversations between adults and children.

The relationships available to the child are a key component of asset development during childhood. During infancy, most of the infant's time is spent with his immediate family and with one or two primary caregivers if the infant goes to child care. Gradually the child's world expands. When a child goes to preschool and then to elementary school, she begins spending more and more time away from the parent's direct supervision. If children get consistent messages from all socializing systems, parents are helped with the job of child rearing, and asset development is strengthened.

The Shape of Children's Assets

The framework of children's assets was developed to advance the dialogue about how our society can better care for its children. In bringing together the collected wisdom of many people and fields, it presents a new lens for examining the place of children in the United States and examining where the nation needs to invest time, creativity, and resources to ensure that all children have a positive foundation for life.

We do not have the empirical data to evaluate how well families and communities are doing, as a whole, in providing these assets for children. Nevertheless, our extensive research on adolescents, information from other research sources, and the views of experts and others all suggest that these assets may be in short supply for many American children, just as they are for adolescents.

Developmental Assets Among Adults

Conventional and professional wisdom would dictate that asset development during the first eighteen years of life is predictive, if not determinative, of adulthood. If so, how can these assets be claimed, or reclaimed, during adulthood? How do adults continue to nurture the resources and experiences that undergird their continuing psychological health and well-being?

We are thinking here not so much about each of the specific assets identified for children and adolescents, but about the eight major categories of assets. It seems these categories help to script the nature of adult competency. We submit two hypotheses.

First, adults who are asset-rich (for example, who feel supported and empowered, are clear about their own boundaries and values, spend their time constructively, are committed to lifelong learning, hold positive values, have social competencies, and have a positive sense of self) are best able to develop assets in children. In particular, asset-rich parents have a leg up on others in raising asset-rich children. Researcher John Bowlby found, for example, that young children have trouble with attachment when their parents have "a diminished capacity for empathy, low tolerance for frustration, low self-esteem, and heightened dependency."[3] (Chapter Eight suggests the qualities needed to be an asset-building adult; many of these qualities could be considered adult assets.)

Second, a large percentage of adults in their twenties, thirties, and forties are not now rich in assets. In part, this is due to a diminished community capacity for asset building when they were growing up. We don't know exactly when this dilemma began, but there are indications that assets tend to be fragile for many baby boomers.

One sign is the high American rate of divorce and separation. Another is the burgeoning interest in self-help, spirituality, and related personal growth efforts. Then there is the provocative thesis by Robert Bly: American adults have become a massive hoard of self-centered adolescents, unable and unwilling to take on adult responsibility.[4]

If these hypotheses have merit, then part of the community renewal needed to grow the assets of children and adolescents is a community focus on helping adults, including parents, develop their own assets. A key strategy for raising healthier youth, then, could be to develop parent-focused initiatives that pay attention not only to education about effective parenting but also to building the personal strength of parents themselves.

Furthermore, there is a growing understanding of adult resiliency and health that suggests the value of many of these same kinds of assets for adults.

One example of the literature in this area is Daniel Goleman's best-selling book, *Emotional Intelligence,* in which he contends that being able to manage emotions is critical to success in life. For example, he suggests that what he calls "emotional competencies" are essential to resolving marital disputes and having harmonious marriages. Among the competencies he finds to be important are empathy and listening skills, which fit nicely in the category of social competencies.[5]

Goleman also suggests that emotional intelligence is critical to workplace success. He writes: "The single most important factor in maximizing the excellence of a group's product was the degree to which the members were able to create a state of internal harmony, which lets them take advantage of the full talent of their members. . . . What makes the difference between the stars and the others is not their academic IQ, but their emotional IQ. They are better able to motivate themselves, and better able to work their informal networks into ad hoc teams."[6]

Finally, Goleman links physical health to emotional intelligence. Pointing to emerging fields of medicine such as psychoneuroimmunology, he argues that one's emotions play an important role in health and healing, actually affecting the autonomic nervous system. He notes that fear and anxiety can slow healing after surgery, and pent-up anger can do serious harm to the heart. "Being prone to anger," he reports about a Duke University study, "was a stronger predictor of dying young than were other risk factors such as smoking, high blood pressure, and high cholesterol."[7]

Another growing body of literature regarding adults is the whole area of social support. In the book *Creating Community Anywhere,* Carolyn R. Shaffer and Kristin Anundsen survey a variety of studies on social support and conclude: "Contemporary medical, psychological, and sociological literature overflows with studies that point to the life-prolonging, even life-saving qualities of interpersonal support."[8]

Finally, a fascinating perspective on adult strengths is found in *Common Fire: Lives of Commitment in a Complex World.* The researchers interviewed more than one hundred adults "who had sustained long-term commitments to work on behalf of the common good, even in the face of global complexity, diversity and ambiguity." In reflecting on these lives, the researchers found important patterns undergirding these people's strengths—patterns that are highly consistent with the framework of assets.[9]

These examples are not exhaustive or systematic, but they do suggest the potential of creating a framework of assets for adults that would show the continuing nature of development, from birth through all stages of adulthood.

Continuing the Vision

One of the things that seems self-apparent as we work with the developmental assets is that they truly represent a new paradigm. Their language and perspective begin to reshape the way we look at ourselves, our young people, our communities, and our world.

As these concepts are integrated into the fabric of communities, we look forward to discovering the many ways that this work can strengthen community life not only for adolescents (the original focus of our work) but for everyone in our communities. Clearly, this journey has only begun.

CHAPTER FIVE

A CALL TO ACTION

Twelve Critical Culture Shifts

Chapters Two through Four offer a vision of healthy development for children and youth based on the framework of developmental assets. We've seen that although these assets have tremendous power for shaping behavior in positive ways, far too few young people experience or develop these assets. This gap represents a crisis of caring for our children and youth that puts an entire generation—and the future of the nation—in jeopardy.

How do we respond to these findings and the crisis they represent? We believe there are twelve fundamental culture shifts (summarized in Table 5.1) that are essential for building the developmental infrastructure for children and adolescents. Some of these shifts happen at an individual level, as people from all walks of life take personal responsibility for caring for the young people whose lives they touch. These shifts also call upon youth-serving systems—schools, youth organizations, congregations, etc.—to examine and reshape programs to focus energy on asset building. Most importantly, these shifts ultimately call upon communities to rally together around a shared vision and commitment to rebuild the developmental foundation for all children and youth.

Culture Shift #1: From Deficit Language to Asset Language

When communities form task forces or coalitions on youth, the focus is almost always on addressing a particular problem: teen violence, teen pregnancy, teen suicide,

TABLE 5.1. ESSENTIAL SHIFTS NEEDED TO BUILD THE ASSET FOUNDATION FOR CHILDREN AND ADOLESCENTS.

From . . .	To . . .
• Deficit language predominant	• Asset language common
• Focus on troubled and troubling youth	• Focus on all children and adolescents
• Focus on ages 0 to 5	• Focus on ages 0 to 18
• Age segregation	• Intergenerational community
• Self-interest	• Shared responsibility
• Approach: buy and implement new programs	• Approach: expand asset-building actions by residents and systems
• Fragmented agenda	• Unifying vision around developmental assets
• Disconnected socializing systems and conflicting messages	• Connected socializing systems and consistent messages
• Efficiency	• Redundancy
• Youth as objects of programs	• Youth as actors in the process of change
• Constant switching of priorities	• Long-term commitment
• Civic disengagement	• Engaged public

teen drug abuse. The list could go on, depending on the current issue in the news. One reason for this is that many community organizers believe that the only way to get residents involved is to name a problem or an enemy that needs to be fought.

Compounding the problem, public and private funding sources require those seeking funding to combat a particular problem. This pattern results in a series of "wars" that are declared but never really won. In a report on young adolescents, my colleague Peter C. Scales relates the following incident: "In preparing this report the author talked with an official of an important children's advisory body. The official explained that since they had had little luck receiving funding for a generic and comprehensive prevention model, they had been forced to retreat to a single-problem focus on preventing adolescent pregnancy, alcohol and other drug abuse, dropout, and whatever issue was dominating the prevention headlines."[1]

The collective focus in our culture on young people's problems also results in feelings of hopelessness and powerlessness among adults. Few individuals believe they have the capacity to intervene in the problems that have defined adolescence. The result is that they often avoid young people rather than getting involved in their lives in a positive way.

For example, focus groups by Public Agenda found that a major reason people do not take action for children is that they have little to offer. "The public's definition of the problem—which focuses on broad moral and economic problems—makes them feel that there is very little that can be done to help children," researchers summarized. "Their tolerance for the problems of children stems, in other words, not from indifference but from a feeling of helplessness."[2]

In many ways, we have adopted a conventional medical model in caring for young people. Unless they are "sick," we don't treat them. The result is that too many are showing up needing urgent or emergency care—at a high cost to society and the young people themselves.

Like the medical community, which is beginning to emphasize the need for promoting wellness and health, we need to shift energy to building the positive foundation for development that young people need to thrive. What's needed is a major shift in thinking that unites communities around a shared, positive vision and commitment to young people.

Such a shift will not be easy. In our culture, adolescence has come to be defined (falsely) as a time of storm, stress, and conflict. We expect young people to rebel and have problems. Thus, major work needs to be done in reshaping public attitudes toward youth while at the same time reexamining policies and programs that reinforce negative public perceptions.

Culture Shift #2: From Some Youth to All Youth

Our culture's focus on problems has led us to put all or most of our collective energy into young people who are most "at risk." Young people rarely get attention from society until they are causing problems that we're no longer willing to tolerate.

The reality is that nearly all children and adolescents need more developmental assets than they now have. Systems of support, boundaries and expectations, constructive time use, value socialization, and competency building tend to be too fragile for most youth. It is crucial to pay special attention to those children who have the least economically or emotionally, but the central challenge is to reclaim the kind of communitywide attention to positive development that benefits all young people.

Furthermore, an emphasis on strengthening community for all youth helps to destigmatize young people who are currently labeled and targeted because they are at risk. As Karen Pittman and Michele Cahill suggest in arguing for an emphasis on youth development, "Rather than stratify and segregate at-risk and 'problem-free' young people, [youth development] connects intervention, treatment and prevention with development."[3]

Culture Shift #3: From Early Childhood Only to the First Two Decades of Life

A corollary to the societal focus on "problem youth" is the in-vogue focus only on young people in the first five years of life. To be sure, these years are crucial years in development, setting the stage for many life patterns. But the demand for attention to developmental needs does not end at age five, or ten or fifteen. Although the specific needs may change—as suggested by Search Institute's presentation of assets from birth through age eighteen—the foundation for healthy development must be continually reinforced throughout childhood and adolescence.

Asset development in the life of a child begins on day one (or before, with education and care for expecting parents). Attention to assets, though, should be sustained throughout childhood and adolescence. Each stage of development requires persistent attention to support, empowerment, boundaries, structure, competency, and values. Though doing so is crucial in the first five years of life, the demands for these are equally significant at ages 6–10, 11–14, and 15–18. Each phase of life builds on the previous experiences, either positive or negative. Asset-building efforts are most effective when they recognize and build on this developmental perspective.

This emphasis on the first two decades of life reinforces the need for involvement of the whole community, not just families. In the first five years of life, family and other caregivers dominate in influence. Community, though, is still an important influence, as expressed through neighborhood, child care, social services, parent education, and other resources.

As young people grow up, however, schooling, the growing influence of peer groups, mobility within neighborhoods, and access to structured activities elevate community influence. By the time young people enter middle school, we hypothesize that a young person's development is heavily, if not largely, shaped by influences beyond the family.

The point is that it takes more than good family to nurture healthy youth. All along the spectrum from birth to age eighteen, nonfamily influences (aka community) matter profoundly. Without healthy community, healthy development is seriously compromised.

Culture Shift #4: From Age Segregation to Intergenerational Community

At the heart of the American dilemma with its young is the evaporation of intergenerational connections. Indeed, our entire society has been segmented into narrower and narrower age groups, often pitting one generation against another.

A typical young person has little meaningful contact with people from another generation. She spends most of her time with her peers, watching TV shows aimed at her demographic subgroup, or shopping in specialty stores for her age. In school, she may have little contact with teachers or other adults because of large class sizes. If she is involved in other activities through clubs, teams, religious institutions, or other organizations, her time is spent largely with her peers in activities designed specifically for her and her peers.

Once again, there is an important place for age-specific opportunities. But society has become so age-segregated that these experiences define the world for young people, isolating them from the rich experiences of intergenerational relationships. Furthermore, the exclusive emphasis on age-specific opportunities has increased fragmentation and isolation within communities.

Most communities are not now highly relational places. Youth tend to lack sustained relationships with adults and feel alienated from adults in neighborhoods, schools, and religious institutions. Most youth feel ignored and insignificant in their neighborhoods and cities, and, in some settings, rejected or despised. Several lines of evidence tell us where we are and the distance we have to travel:

- Of the 254,000 middle school and high school students we have studied since 1990, only 22 percent have five or more adults they know whom they "would feel comfortable going to for help." The majority (51 percent) have two or fewer.
- Almost half of middle school and high school students in studies of two cities report that they know no one in their community who is older than sixty-five.[4]
- St. Louis Park, Minnesota, began an intentional asset-building initiative in 1994. One of the members of the thirty–person vision team that guides the effort is an eighth-grade student. He decided to count the number of adults who diverted their gaze away from him when he passed on the street. His conclusion: 80 percent.

If there were only one thing we could do to alter the course of socialization for American youth, it would be to reconstruct our towns and cities as intergenerational communities. The cross-generational contacts would be frequent and natural, and they would come in two forms: kids bonding with multiple adults, and adolescents bonding with younger children. Imagine the developmental power (for both the teenager and the child) if every six-year-old had at least one sixteen-year-old who thought he or she was the most special human being in the universe.

Every young person should have several sustained relationships with dozens of adults in neighborhoods, religious institutions, teams, organizations, and schools. These relationships should include adults of all ages, from young adults to senior citizens, who can be "elders" and "grandparents" to young people. Equally important is connecting adolescents to children in bonds of sustained caring. It is a dramatically important relationship for both, yet such intergenerational forms of support are rare.

Culture Shift #5: From Self-Interest to Shared Responsibility

An important challenge is to shift cultural norms regarding young people so that all residents in the community understand and act on their responsibility to the young. The goal is for every young person to experience many points of formal and informal relational support on a daily basis. Even seemingly small gestures— calling children by name, acknowledging their presence, exchanging greetings, smiling when passing a young person on the street or in a hall—are important molecules of support that, when accumulated over time, create a critical mass of positive nurture.

In a society built around self-interest, paying attention to "other people's" children can be a low priority. Martha Minow and Richard Weissbourd take note of "the difficulty [of] mobilizing adult constituencies to care about children who are not their own or who do not seem like their own."[5] While Minow and Weissbourd's focus is political action on behalf of children, the same barrier is present in trying to mobilize many community members to become personally involved in the lives of youth.

An extreme example illustrates an often-hidden attitude. A California-based group called ChildFree Network is organizing to do away with any special considerations for families, including elimination of tax benefits for people with dependent children and dealing with what they see as workplace inequities, such as giving parents time off to be with their sick children. They want to capitalize on the growing number of married couples without children in the United States (predicted to rise from 24.1 million in 1995 to 30.2 million in 2010). Founder Leslie Lafayette puts her perspective this way: "Let's be truthful about it. We do not need children, except for the continuation of the human race, which we do not have to worry about."[6]

There are, however, signs of hope. A poll of voters taken after the 1996 national elections found that, for the first time in history, children's issues played a major role in the presidential election. The poll found that children's issues (such as children's education and health care, child abuse and neglect, drugs, violence) ranked first among a list of key concerns that influenced voters' support for presidential and congressional candidates, with more than four in five voters identifying children's issues as important to them in driving their voting behavior.[7] The challenge now is to shift the focus from children's problems to their healthy development, and to match this political energy with an equally strong commitment to personal involvement in the lives of young people.

Culture Shift #6: From a Program Focus to a Relational Focus

One of the effects of age segregation, the problem focus, and the abdication of responsibility for the young by most nonparent adults is that we have turned over much of the responsibility for caring for our children and adolescents to professionals. From child care for infants to youth programs in community centers and congregations, responsibility for young people is given to people who are paid to be with them. While there are many good reasons for advocating professionalism in these many settings, a side effect is an increased sense that one has to be professionally trained in order to be effective in caring for youth—or, for that matter, to contribute to community life.

John McKnight suggests that a key reason people do not feel empowered to take personal action is that society is organized around services, not community. We no longer have any expectation that citizens (other than parents and those who are paid to do it) take any personal responsibility for the well-being of children and adolescents. He writes: "Many of us have come to recognize that as we exiled our fallible neighbors to the control of managers, therapists, and technicians, we lost much of our power to be the vital center of society. We forgot about the capacity of every single one of us to do good work and, instead, made some of us the objects of good works—services of those who serve. . . . As institutions have grown in power, we have become too impotent to be called real citizens and too disconnected to be effective members of community."[8]

Furthermore, when individuals are called upon for involvement, they are asked to lobby government or institutions to release resources or to take action to address a particular problem. Rarely are individuals equipped to take direct action themselves with the hope that their action will contribute to young people or the community. The point here is not that political action is inappropriate; rather, political action is rarely balanced with motivation and opportunities for personal engagement in the lives of children and adolescents.

Our overdependence on programs and policies rather than relationships can be illustrated in addressing an issue that is taking center stage in national life: transmission of values and boundaries. As consciousness about these issues grows, we fall prey to a common American solution: let's teach the good stuff programmatically, which often means expecting schools to add another obligation to their curricula.

Teaching values through programs is useful, but it is secondary in impact to the way cultures have always passed on the best of human wisdom: through wisdom modeled, articulated, practiced, and discussed by adults with children around them. It is learning through engagement with responsible adults that nurtures value development and requires intergenerational community. Whereas programs are an important reinforcement, they are not the primary process.

Asset building has less to do with hiring more professionals and starting new programs than it does activating and enhancing the capacity of community members to build sustained, informal, positive relationships with children and teenagers. Through such relationships, care is given, expectations and boundaries are communicated, desirable social behavior is both modeled and affirmed, educational commitment and school success are nurtured, and values are "caught."

Unfortunately, far too few adults (other than professionals) are involved in helping young people thrive. As the National Commission on Children wrote, "Too few adults invest the personal time and effort to encourage, guide, and befriend young people who are struggling to develop the skills and confidence [we would say assets] necessary for a successful and satisfying adult life."[9] In its recommendations, the commission concluded: "Voluntarism and generosity are hallmarks of American life. In this tradition, we call on all Americans to reach out to an unfamiliar child as instinctively as they reach out to the ones they hold dear. This is a responsibility that cannot be laid at government's doorstep. Government programs never loved a child or helped with homework or counseled a troubled teenager. These are the tasks of caring adults."[10]

There are, of course, programs that can enhance asset-building and relationship-building efforts, such as mentoring and volunteer programs (designed to connect generations) and peer helping programs (designed to generate youth-to-youth support). Programs and professionals are still needed as a supporting cast within a community. But it's critically important that programs revert to being a *supporting* cast, not the lead actors in caring for our children and youth.

Culture Shift #7: From a Fragmented Agenda to a Unifying Vision

Implicit in many of the changes already suggested is the need to shift from fragmented, competitive agendas to a unifying vision for children and adolescents. If all socializing systems in a community share a commitment to a vision of healthy development, each can see its own niche in the larger vision. Everyone doesn't have to do everything, but all recognize that they are on the same team, working for the good of young people, rather than vying for attention for their particular agenda.

What does it look like when a community shifts from a fragmented agenda to a unifying vision? The story of Nampa, Idaho, is instructive.[11] For five years, this fast-growing town seventeen miles from Boise has been involved in a effort "to make Nampa the healthiest place to live in the Northwest." To that end, many different individuals and institutions in the community have rallied together with a focus on raising healthy youth.

Initially, the community brought together people representing critical "spheres of influence": the local college, the city, the school district, the business sector, congregations, and the area's largest health care provider, Mercy Medical Center. The resulting group focused on common ground and began with a bold plan to unify the community with a recreational and cultural center.

Soon the entire community was rallying together around the community center. Nearly half of the residents hold passes to the center, in part because of efforts to ensure that the center is accessible and welcoming to all residents, in part because of community fundraisers to buy passes for young people who can't afford them.

The community center is just the beginning of the vision for creating a healthy, unified community. "We're taking a hard look at what building a healthy community really means," says Lynn Borud of Mercy Medical Center. "We've come to understand the basic premise, which is that we need all parts of the community involved. Schools can't do it alone. Parents can't do it alone. Police, community agencies, service clubs, congregations, the business sector—all are parts of the bigger picture."

There are, of course, other ways communities can unite around a shared vision. While Nampa chose a visible project to unite the community, it's equally important for communities to work toward a shared commitment in less visible ways. This includes the intentional ways in which all socializing systems—including families, neighborhoods, religious institutions, youth organizations, social service organizations, health care providers, employers, and others—organize, set priorities, and implement strategies and programs that contribute to asset development. As examples, the capacity of neighbors to be asset builders is enhanced when they gather to plan how to communicate the names and interests of area children to all residents, or establish mechanisms to build social trust among households. The asset-building capacity of schools is enhanced when schools are designed to permit students to have the same teachers for multiple years; when asset building informs how teachers are hired, evaluated, and promoted; and when high school students become tutors for young children.

Thus the uniting vision of asset building calls for shared action on a communitywide basis, but it also challenges individuals and institutions within the community to examine their own priorities and programs to determine how they build assets and what they can do to be more effective in contributing to this larger community vision.

Culture Shift #8: From Conflicting Signals to Consistent Messages

For asset development to be most effective, children and teenagers need to be exposed to similar messages about what is important and valued in many moments and many settings during their journey through the first two decades of life.[12] Unless socializing systems share a script about what is in-bounds and out-of-bounds, about values and expectations (integrity, honesty, fairness, respect, justice, caring, academic motivation), then youth experience only inconsistent, conflicted messages.

This sense of consistency has eroded. Francis Ianni wrote: "The difficulty that the American people are experiencing in the accomplishment of group purpose is traceable in part to a disintegration of shared values; and unfortunately, the soil in which such values are rooted and nurtured—family and community—is being blown away in the dust storm of contemporary life."[13]

Consistency in socialization, particularly around the asset categories of boundaries and values, has immense power. The eminent sociologist James Coleman provides evidence of this power in his analysis of school success, demonstrating that academic achievement is advanced when students are surrounded with multiple organizations and institutions (family, school, congregation) articulating a shared core of values.[14]

The challenge is to learn from and adapt these historical forms of consistent socialization to contemporary life. The glue that promotes and sustains this consistency is less and less likely to be a shared religious or cultural worldview. If we look hard enough, however, we see that such consistency still exists. In the current climate of contentious political and social life, we hear much more about the places of disagreement than the places of agreement.

There are universal truths—rooted in millennia of community life and perhaps encoded genetically—that favor compassion, generosity, justice, and belonging. These transcend place, income, creed, and race. Our problem is that we too easily assume that such shared convictions do not exist.

There are legitimate reasons for caution about identifying shared values in a pluralistic, multicultural "nation of nations." However, focusing on identifying shared values and boundaries is not the same as insisting on uniformity. Rather, it is a recognition that true community is only possible when people share some kinds of commitments. As John Gardner writes: "To require a community to agree on everything would be unrealistic and would violate our concern for diversity. But it has to agree on something. There has to be a core of shared values. Of all the ingredients of community this is probably the most important."[15]

The widespread pessimism about the common good may be due to a fear or misunderstanding of diversity. We submit two hypotheses. First, in all localities, there is a common core of values that all people hold; and second, this common core is discernible through the lost art of public dialogue and consensus building.

We do not mean to imply or advocate that all people in a geographical place can or should affirm the same worldview. However, people of all political, religious, philosophical, and social perspectives share some instincts, impulses, and commitments, particularly regarding the primacy, centrality, and urgency of caring for children.

Naming a common commitment is essential for reclaiming consistency. Around the fringes of this common core, healthy communities also debate and disagree on other goals and values of community life.[16] It should be that way.

Culture Shift #9: From Efficiency to Redundancy in Asset Building

In recent years, the word *redundancy* has developed a bad reputation. It is oft-maligned as a source of economic waste in government agencies and service delivery systems. The call today is to eliminate redundancy for the cause of streamlined efficiency.

In raising healthy young people, however, a certain type of redundancy is essential. What we mean here is that communities should provide multiple exposures to the developmental assets. There really is no efficient way to do this. Building and living relationships—the core of asset building—is not, and cannot be, efficient.

Support, for example, should be a feature not just of family but also of neighborhood, school, religious institutions, and the informal settings in which adults and youth interact. Ideally, such redundancy enhances, replicates, and expands on solid, intentional, and daily asset building in families.

The importance of redundancy escalates when we focus on the too-high number of American youth with neglectful, preoccupied, or absent family. In these cases, writes A. G. Blackwell, "We need a system of redundancy that is fail-safe, so that if children are not getting what they need at home they will surely get it in the community."[17]

Culture Shift #10: From Youth as Objects to Youth as Actors

Young people themselves have tremendous influence and potential for asset building in themselves and their peers. They can form relationships; model appropriate behaviors, values, and commitments; reinforce boundaries with each other; and contribute in other ways to community life. Tapping this resource not only strengthens young people's own asset base but deepens the resources available for rebuilding community.

Yet, as we noted in Chapter Two, most young people do not feel as though they are valued in their community. In fact, the opposite is often true: they are often dismissed as too young or too irresponsible, or they are feared as menacing or dangerous. The only time they receive much attention is when they get into trouble or accomplish amazing feats, particularly in athletics.

The asset-building perspective calls on communities (including organizations, families, and other systems) to begin seeing youth as valuable resources and active players in rebuilding communities. In an essay with the provocative title "It Takes a Child to Raise a Whole Village," John P. Kretzmann and Paul H. Schmitz write:

> In the cliché, people (adults) in villages act to "raise" young people. Young folks are the objects of the action, never the subjects. They are defined as deficient— of knowledge, of skills, of any useful capacities—and relegated with their cohorts to the filling stations we call schools. The assumption is that, magically, at age 18 or 21, young people will emerge from their years of being filled, and re-enter the community as full and useful contributors.
>
> This formula is a disaster. Not only has it produced a generation of young people who think of themselves as useless, but it has isolated that generation from productive interaction with older generations. It has relegated more than a third of our citizens to inaction or worse and has deprived our youth of the experience necessary for fulfilling their roles as citizens and contributors to the community.[18]

Involving youth as actors in their communities can take many forms at all levels of community life. It begins with families that involve young people in decisions; it embraces neighbors who take kids' concerns and ideas seriously, schools and other organizations where youth have a role in decision making, and communitywide efforts in which youth take the lead. Each of these strategies and others give young people practice in being active community members while also contributing to community life in meaningful ways.

Culture Shift #11: From Shifting Priorities to Long-Term Commitment

The problem-centered focus perpetuates a cultural tendency to shift attention and priorities from one issue to the next, depending on whatever is foremost in public consciousness. We design programs with goals to "reduce [insert problem X] by [insert Y percent] before [insert year Z]"—which is when the funding runs out.

The developmental assets provide a framework for long-term action that recognizes the importance of ongoing, positive opportunities and relationships across at least the first two decades of life. Within this larger vision, there are opportunities for focused, time-limited activities, but they are seen as contributing to the larger vision, not as self-contained quick fixes and easy answers.

Such a shift is not easy. Policy makers want to be sure that a vote for funding has an impact before the next election season. Foundations and corporate givers expect to see measurable results by the end of the grant. And the public is easily swayed to shift its attention to a new issue or problem. The challenge, then, is to find creative ways to sustain an asset-building emphasis while also meeting the short-term needs of policy makers and other funders, and while continuously renewing public commitment and involvement through focused efforts that build toward the larger vision.

Culture Shift #12: From Civic Disengagement to Engagement

Underlying many of the culture shifts advocated in this chapter is the larger issue of civic engagement: individuals getting involved in the public life of their community. This shift challenges the widespread (if rarely articulated) assumption that people are primarily—if not only—responsible for their own lives and those of their family members.

The tradition of commitment to democracy and the "common good" has eroded and been left in the hands of a few. Frances Moore Lappé and Paul Martin DuBois write: "What's missing has been the core insight that democracy—whether it works or not—depends on how each of us lives our public life, our lives outside our families. Also missing has been an understanding that without meaningful public lives we can't protect and further the well-being of those we care about most in our private lives."[19]

Many social commentators are calling for the renewal of civic engagement. Too often, however, this engagement is equated with political involvement. There is certainly a need to address the disengagement of far too many people from the political system that undergirds our democracy, but such an emphasis should not overshadow the need for people to reconnect with their fellow citizens in relationships of mutual support, care, and shared responsibility. The asset-building approach provides a foundation upon which these relationships can begin to form, recreating the sense of community that is needed to undergird public life.

This brief articulation of the need to activate all citizens and sectors for sustained and unified commitment to the next generation is a good place to note several other shifts that must occur. One is to move from an overdependence on schools as being a place for addressing human development issues to seeing schools as one of many players, that is, working in concert with asset-building neighborhoods, families, congregations, youth organizations, and employers. A second is to move from the isolation of family to the integration of family within community.

Theoretically, the family has high potential to promote developmental assets. But even the best of families cannot, without the active assistance of other sectors, optimize asset building. This is profoundly demonstrated by Dale Blyth in an important analysis of Search Institute's studies of youth. Comparing communities with high rates of healthy youth to communities with lower rates, he discovered that the factors differentiating the two kinds of communities are associated less with what families did and more with how well other socializing systems acted on their asset-building capacity.[20] This encourages and demands a necessary shift from the naïve view that family is solely responsible for kids to the conviction that all members of a community are responsible.

Uniting Communities for Asset Building

When added together, the culture shifts identified herein as essential for rebuilding the developmental infrastructure for children and adolescents call for fundamental changes in the way community life is currently organized. Although some of the shifts can and should begin in individual families and programs, the ultimate vision of asset building is for entire communities to unite around a vision for healthy development.

We see the seeds of these changes being planted in communities across the country. At the time of this writing, almost two hundred municipalities (as well as a statewide initiative in Colorado) have begun communitywide asset-building efforts that seek to address the shifts outlined here.[21] In many other places, organizations, school systems, and individuals have begun efforts within their own spheres of influence. Over time, they may be the catalysts for a wider movement in their communities.

Thus we have come to the intersection of healthy development and healthy community that is the crux of this book. For healthy development to occur for all young people, it is essential that we begin rebuilding communities where people and institutions feel engaged, connected, responsible, and committed to young people. The chapters that follow focus in more detail on the practical issues involved in reshaping community life within the asset-building framework.

PART TWO

WHAT WE ALL CAN DO

CHAPTER SIX

UNITING COMMUNITIES AROUND YOUTH

Seven Essential Goals

In the 1996 presidential campaign, the African wisdom that "it takes a whole village to raise a child" was coopted by campaign spinmeisters into pithy sound bites designed to polarize the electorate. Lost in the political posturing was much constructive dialogue about what kind of village it *really* takes to raise a child.

In many ways, the politicization of "it takes a village . . ." is a parable for the inadequate responses to the challenges facing children and youth that dominate public life. One side too easily equates the "village" with the public sector's commitment to young people. The other side too quickly dismisses the responsibility of anyone beyond the family to care for the young. Each extreme misses the point of the phrase and, more importantly, the real challenge we face in caring for the young.

Perhaps the most urgent task facing American society is rebuilding a sense of community, of village, in which everyone reclaims or accepts their shared responsibility to—and stake in—nurturing the youngest generation. The framework of developmental assets offers a vision to guide communities in setting priorities and taking action. We turn now to examining the principles and processes that undergird a community change process that supports the asset-building vision.

This vision is more expansive than many other visions for youth development. Often, youth development initiatives focus primarily on programs, seeking to equip community-based organizations, schools, and other institutions to be effective in their work with youth. This emphasis is clearly an important part of the vision.

But our vision for healthy communities reaches beyond programs and schools to focus energy on mobilizing and equipping individual residents and all community sectors to reclaim their responsibility to "be a village" for young people.

In this chapter, we survey some of the foundational issues in growing healthy communities, including a discussion of recent community change efforts, underlying principles for effective community change, and key goals of community change related specifically to asset building. The chapters that follow explore the practical issues of mobilizing a community and engaging multiple parts of the community—individuals, families, youth-serving systems, other institutions—in a shared vision for asset building.

Recent Community Change Efforts

In the past several decades, a flurry of projects have sought to tackle difficult and perplexing social problems at the local level. These experiments in social change typically seek to alter some combination of the economic, physical, and institutional infrastructure of communities as a means of enhancing the quality of life for residents.[1]

Notable among these are multifaceted efforts to breathe new life into distressed neighborhoods. These classic community development initiatives include the Ford Foundation's pioneering Neighborhood and Family Initiative in Detroit, Hartford, Memphis, and Milwaukee;[2] the Dudley Street Neighborhood Initiative in Boston; and the Marshall Heights Community Development project in Washington, D.C.[3] Each emphasizes building the capacity of local residents and systems to enhance the economic and social vitality of neighborhoods.

A second type of community-building work is designed to provide more efficient, humane, and effective delivery of health, educational, and support services to vulnerable children and families. A prime example is the Annie E. Casey Foundation's New Futures project, intended to restructure social institutions in Dayton, Bridgeport, Little Rock, Pittsburgh, and Savannah to be "more responsive to the needs of at-risk youth and their families."[4] New structures were built to coordinate the work of previously fragmented service systems, and a case management system was developed to support students' academic success and help them avoid early pregnancy and parenthood.

Testing a different service redesign model, the Chicago Community Trust has launched the nine-year, $30 million Children, Youth, and Family Initiative. It seeks to integrate two approaches: revitalize "primary" services (libraries, recreational programs, youth organizations) to build the capacity of youth, and build the capacity of "specialized" services focusing on addressing family deficits. Both the

Chicago Trust and the New Futures initiatives seek to alter institutional infrastructures to build human and social capital. A statewide effort aimed at similar ends is exemplified by California's Healthy Start initiative, designed to place comprehensive support services for children and families in schools. Such collocation of service models has precedent in many cities.

These two incarnations of community-building—economic development and service redesign—tend to target the most vulnerable and seek to address the causes and consequences of poverty. They also tend to be extraordinarily expensive.

Another genre of community-building efforts addresses broader issues of community wellness, seeking to enhance the quality of life for residents. Grounded in mounting worries about the fragmentation of cities, the disengagement of residents from civic life, the decay of infrastructure, public health challenges, and economic vulnerability, a number of cities have launched intentional efforts to plan and implement needed policy, programmatic, and collaborative changes. A premium is usually placed on engaging citizens in the visioning process.

The National Civic League has triggered dozens of these healthy community initiatives.[5] Similarly, the Western Consortium for Public Health in Berkeley has launched the California Healthy Cities Project. Through this effort, community stakeholders identify successes and needs in a wide range of areas, including employment, the economy, housing, education, the environment, health, transportation, and youth issues. An ongoing civic forum has created Sustainable Seattle, a citywide effort to name indicators reflective of sustained community and develop citizen capacity and interest in renewing civic wellness.[6]

In addition to initiatives designed to strengthen all levels of community life, a number of recent initiatives are focusing specifically on positive youth development. For example:

- The Kellogg Foundation of Battle Creek, Michigan, has partnered with three communities in Michigan in a twenty–year investment to develop new models for improving the lives of youth. (The framework of developmental assets has become an important tool for some of these efforts.)[7]
- In 1995, Public/Private Ventures of Philadelphia began the Community Change for Youth Development demonstration project, which provides six neighborhoods in six cities with a structure to work together to provide youth with the supports and opportunities needed for positive development. Central to this initiative is a rigorous evaluation design to examine basic questions about the community change process.[8]
- The Center for Youth Development and Policy Research in Washington, D.C., is designing a major mobilization initiative to build and sustain partnerships for youth development at the local, state, and national levels. The center hopes

to form partnership agreements with local communities to build a youth development infrastructure in those sites.[9]

- In 1995, the Indiana Youth Institute began partnering with other organizations to create "caring communities" that provide supports for children and families in the state.[10]

These examples illustrate some of the many efforts under way in communities across the United States. Some efforts are coordinated nationally, while others are independent local efforts. Each initiative has a slightly different emphasis and brings different groups together around different needs. But as these efforts continue, the opportunity is ripe for deepening knowledge about what works and what does not.

These numerous efforts suggest significant energy and possibility for improving community life for children and adolescents. However, the efforts have not yet developed a clear set of guidelines and priorities to shape the efforts. A report from the Chapin Hall Center for Children laments that the community-building field is "evolving with little strength of consensus on the primary focus of CCI's [comprehensive community-building initiatives], the nature of the change process initiatives attempt to engender, or who will be responsible (and to whom) for the process and the products. . . . Without a robust and ongoing discussion of the theories and assumptions underlying these initiatives, . . . the practice of comprehensive community building will inevitably become a series of independent demonstrations rather than the progressive, cumulative learning process it should be."[11]

Underlying Principles for Effective Community Change

At the same time, a consistent set of recommended strategies for community change is beginning to emerge, and it appears to be valid regardless of the civic issues under examination (economy, physical infrastructure, service delivery, public health, children and families). Community change must be comprehensive, collaborative, long-term, and marked by significant levels of resident engagement. We now explore the implications of these qualities for community-based, asset-building efforts.

Comprehensiveness

Comprehensiveness usually refers to the understanding that social issues are interconnected. Hence, change is facilitated when the effort seeks to alter all the interconnected parts. For example, economic revitalization requires mounting strategies to simultaneously tackle housing, employment, wages, job training, and education.

In the case of child and adolescent welfare, comprehensiveness means in part that threats to health such as teen pregnancy, alcohol and other drug use, school failure, and antisocial behavior cannot be solved one by one, but rather must be seen as interlocking symptoms with pervasive underlying causes, which we describe primarily as the decay of the developmental infrastructure.

Comprehensiveness also has two additional meanings in asset-building efforts. First, an asset-building initiative must seek to promote all of the recommended assets and not one, or two, or even a subset. This meaning of comprehensiveness reflects the cumulative nature of the developmental assets. Second, asset-building efforts necessitate comprehensive strategies, in which policy, programs, and human relationships are united to create a daily web of asset building for all children and teenagers.

Collaboration

All socializing systems in a town or city must be active players in an asset-building community. These systems include families, schools, youth organizations, religious institutions, and neighborhoods. These all have high potential for directly promoting developmental assets, and the success of an initiative depends on how well each system is activated, trained, and supported in its efforts.

At the same time, there are actors whose influence is more indirect but whose participation in a communitywide spirit of responsibility is necessary. One such system in local government, which, through policy, resource allocation, and advocacy, can advance the power of socializing systems. Others include community education, libraries, health care, universities, and the media, each of which have an important teaching and mobilization role.

The business sector has both direct and indirect influence. The former can be exercised through its support for and mentoring of adolescent employees. The latter is exercised through policies that enhance asset building, including family-friendly policies and paid release time for employees to serve as mentors, volunteers, or coaches. In addition, the business and corporate sector can play an important role (along with other philanthropic entities) in providing resources, financial and in-kind, to support the community mobilization process.

Citizen Engagement

For a community-building effort to be successful, the people it seeks to benefit must participate meaningfully. This principle has become so axiomatic that it's surprising how many social change efforts still fail to follow through on it. Perhaps the gap grows out of the difficulties that sometimes emerge when trying to engage diverse groups in a process. Or perhaps it grows out of a bias that the "clients" most in need of help (for example, the poor, or residents of urban neighborhoods) are thought to lack the skills and capacities necessary for deep involvement. Or perhaps it results from structures that reinforce political, social, and economic power systems within the community that keep some residents locked out. Whatever the reasons, unless concerted efforts ensure that all the key stakeholders are meaningfully involved, the chances of cultural transformation are slim.

In building healthy communities for youth, the critical actors are all the people who live or work within the boundaries of community. It is they who have the power and capacity to build assets in the young. The role of traditional leadership (policy makers, public officials, and other civic leaders) is to support a movement of the people, not to control or dictate the shape and direction of the movement.

There are many stakeholders who must be actively engaged. Since a major part of the vision is to change the way adults and systems care for and guide young people, a broad spectrum of people must be engaged in shaping the community's vision, including parents, senior citizens, and low-income residents, as well as business and organization representatives. Many of the implications of asset building affect these groups, and they should be involved in shaping the agenda and priorities.

Furthermore, the ultimate clients or stakeholders are children and adolescents. This creates a conundrum. What is their place in creating, planning, and implementing an asset-building movement? It is easy at this point to slide into old ways of thinking and assume that social change is something we do *to* the client rather than *with* the client—to treat children as objects of our good intentions rather than as partners in change. ("Opportunities or Alcohol? Youth Find Out" gives an example of how communities are engaging youth in the community-building process.)

Opportunities or Alcohol? Youth Find Out

When YouthNet was started in 1988 in Kansas City, Missouri, it was formed because of the fear of gangs coming to the community. But today, the focus of YouthNet has shifted dramatically, and assets are part of that shift.

In fact, the board adopted a new mission for YouthNet in December 1995, saying it is to increase access for every young person in Kansas City so he or she has a safe place within walking distance of his or her home. At that safe place, the young person will have access to caring adults and positive activities.

To begin accomplishing its mission, YouthNet set up an eight-week summer program to have eleven-to-fourteen-year-olds find out what's available for youth in Kansas City. Seventy young people were hired to work on the questionnaires, go out in teams to survey 110 square miles, do all the data entry, and make phone calls for more information. YouthNet had kids from the west side surveying the east side, and kids from the east side going to the west and south side. "That was an immediate asset in itself," says Deborah Craig, director of development, "getting kids together and having them see parts of the city that they would have no occasion to ever explore or get to know."

The young people filed over six hundred locations in the database and immediately noticed something. Why were there more liquor stores in Kansas City than places for kids?

At the end of the program, the staff of YouthNet noticed many positive benefits from the program. The eleven-to-fourteen-year-olds (who were too young to be employed) enjoyed working for a stipend. The kids became invested and interested in their community by being exposed to new neighborhoods and cultures. A couple of the kids asked staff members for autographs. "They got to interrelate with positive, caring, employed adults," Craig says.

YouthNet now plans to analyze the data and learn more about the community. In the future, it hopes to set up a telephone youth line where kids can call and find out what's available to them near their address.[12]

We contend that the long-term success of asset-building initiatives leaps forward to the degree that youth are partners with adults. On some things, youth know more than adults. Included here are defining the nature and dynamics of effective support, transforming a city's structured activities to become more engaging and enticing, and transforming social institutions into places of care, consistency, and empowerment.

The Long Run

Social change takes time. The status quo has become deeply entrenched and is reinforced by decades of attitudes, values, and behaviors regarding who is responsible for meeting the needs of children (only parents and professionals) and who is responsible for solving community problems (government). These norms will not evaporate easily or quickly.

Becoming an asset-building community—just like becoming a socially just or economically vibrant community—requires a commitment to stay with the change process over the long haul. Many obstacles get in the way of long-term change. Among these is the whimsical nature of government and foundation interests. Communities are called to action one year to prevent alcohol and other drug use. The next year, the interest shifts to teen pregnancy. Then to school reform. Then to violence.

Another major obstacle is grounding the commitment to change in elected or appointed officials. Their interests are also mercurial and too often merely expedient. Such leaders come and go with shifts of commitment in civic priorities.

Engagement

A final obstacle is the difficult nature of change itself, particularly when it cuts to core issues and norms in society. It requires dedicated, painstaking, and ongoing attention to examining and challenging often unspoken cultural norms and expectations, and how they are expressed concretely in attitudes and behavior. For example, it takes years of vigilance to counter the mistaken notion that all adolescents rebel and that adolescence is *by definition* a turbulent period.

Long-term change has its best chance when a profound passion for becoming an asset-building community becomes deeply grounded in the passions and self-definitions of the people. It is the people (neighbor, parent, parishioner, shop owner, coach, teacher) who can sustain a movement across many incarnations of leadership. It is also they who can begin to embody the shifting norms and encourage their peers to do the same. Thus, our vision for healthy communities emphasizes the importance of individual transformation and action alongside organizational commitments and actions.

Seven Essential Goals for Community-Based Asset Building

Comprehensiveness, collaboration, long-term perspective, and deep engagement and ownership by the people are the current mantras of community building. Though essential, they are not enough. The vision of transforming geographies of place into asset-building communities requires attention to additional goals to guide the community change process. In this section, we identify seven of these goals. We acknowledge that they represent a work in progress. Much of what is described here has evolved from the dialogue between Search Institute and close to two hundred towns and cities that have begun intentional asset-building initiatives.

Before reviewing the goals, however, it is important to note that asset building is not a substitute for a thriving economic and service infrastructure. Table 6.1 seeks to show that asset-building emphases are different from but compatible with efforts to strengthen the economic and service infrastructure, with emphasis on transforming communities into asset-building places. The chart serves as a reminder that a healthy community for youth is simultaneously asset building, risk reducing, service providing, and economically thriving. In our view, communities make a serious mistake when they vest energy in risk reduction, service delivery, and economic vitality while ignoring developmental assets (the prevailing pattern across the nation). It is equally off target, though, to seek the latter and ignore the former.

We now turn to the seven goals for asset building.

TABLE 6.1. SEVEN ESSENTIAL GOALS FOR COMMUNITY-BASED ASSET BUILDING.

Economic and Service Infrastructure	The Human Development Infrastructure (Developmental Assets)		Planned Acts of Asset Building	

Economic and Service Infrastructure

- Economic vitality
- Affordable housing
- Access to quality day care
- Access to quality health care
- Access to quality human services and interventions
- Neighborhood preservation
- Environmental protection
- Public safety
- Citywide efforts to minimize threats to human development (e.g., poverty, racism, family violence, abuse, neglect)

The Human Development Infrastructure (Developmental Assets)

1. A Shared Vision of Positive Development

2. Shared Norms and Beliefs
- Children and adolescents belong to all of us
- All residents have asset-building capacity and responsibility
- All residents and organizations expected to take action
- Commitment to inclusivity
- Commitment to intergenerational community
- Commitment to youth engagement and empowerment

3. Connections Across Socializing Systems
- Consistency
- Redundancy
- Cooperation

4. Everyday Acts of Asset Building
- Informal support (hundreds of experiences per year for each child)
- Inclusion of youth in decision making and leadership
- Adult articulation and modeling of boundaries and values
- Nonfamily relationships (all youth experience three or more)
- Intergenerational gatherings, dialogue, and activities
- Youth-to-youth asset building
- Teenagers bonding with children
- Informal, nonprogrammatic, intergenerational service
- Discovery and affirmation of residents who already engage in asset building

Planned Acts of Asset Building

5. Engagement of Organizations and Systems
- Families
- Schools
- Religious institutions
- Neighborhoods
- Youth organizations
- Employers
- Health care providers
- Police
- Media
- Agencies
- Civic organizations
- Parks and recreation
- Coaches
- Libraries
- Local government

6. Identifying, Affirming, and Expanding Current Asset-Building Activities
- Peer helping
- Mentoring
- Intergenerational connections
- Community service, service learning
- Clubs, teams, organizations
- Leadership development
- Family education
- Cultural heritage
- School readiness initiatives
- School-to-work initiatives

7. Introduction of New Initiatives
- Safe places for youth to go
- Gender-appropriate programs
- Family celebrations
- Celebrations of asset-building people
- Family support centers

1. A Shared Vision

We are currently a culture that easily falls victim to divisiveness. It gets in the way of community building. In a recent examination of and polemic against our culture wars, Todd Gitlin suggests that "for too long, too many Americans have busied themselves digging trenches to fortify their cultural borders, lining their trenches with insulation. Enough borders! Enough of the perfection of differences! We ought to be building bridges."[13]

The developmental assets are bridge building. The framework and language make possible broad public acceptance of the concept and importance of promoting the positive. In our work with rural, small-town, suburban, and urban communities, we have found that the asset framework stands above the political and religious foray, unifying citizens who usually doubt the possibility of consensus. It appears that the concept of developmental assets provides a language for the common good.

This is not to say we seek to minimize real and significant differences. Indeed, subgroups across this land—whether defined by religion, culture, race, economics, or ethnicity—have worldview and value accents that are not included in the conceptualization of developmental assets. That is appropriate. The assets serve as a common core of developmental necessities that cut across these worldviews. They are not intended to be exhaustive. The list of assets can and should be augmented in those places where unique accents are worthy of preservation.

There are many ways a community can articulate its asset-building vision. Crafting this vision can occur in public dialogues or town meetings. We have never seen the crafting of a vision to be contentious or labored. Once worded, the vision becomes not simply a beacon to guide but a benchmark against which to assess current realities and progress in the community transformation process.

In our experience, a shared vision, combined with a local study of developmental assets among youth, becomes a powerful tool for communicating the gap between the real and the ideal among "our" youth and for motivating all citizens and systems to redirect their energy toward fulfilling the vision.

The importance of stating and constantly restating the vision cannot be overestimated. As Merton P. Strommen and I. Shelby Andress have noted, "If people have a clear mental picture of the future they desire, they will have more energy to achieve that future."[14]

2. Widely Shared Norms and Beliefs

Activating a community's asset-building power requires broad acceptance of two beliefs: (1) all residents have the capacity to promote assets, and (2) all residents have the responsibility to do so.

These beliefs need to become self-perceptions internalized by all residents and normative expectations that residents have for each other.

Neither of these beliefs is widely held in our culture. Indeed, many cultural norms run counter to these beliefs. Thus, challenging and shifting current cultural norms becomes a difficult, long-term task for asset-building efforts. It involves challenging assumptions regarding individualism and responsibility. It involves assisting people in rediscovering their own capacities for caring. It involves reshaping systems, regulations, policies, and norms that interfere with asset building.

3. Building Connections Across Socializing Systems

Currently, socializing systems in cities work in isolation. Building partnership across neighborhood, family, schools, religious institutions, youth organizations, and businesses requires creating mechanisms of dialogue and consensus building. The goal of connection building is to increase consistency in asset building across socializing systems and through redundancy (that is, repeated exposure to asset building in many places and moments).

Peter Scales captures the importance of these connections when he writes: "Family, school and community resources must work together to promote positive youth development. Young people are more likely to say they feel cared for in their communities when they see all these institutions collaborating. . . . Moreover, there is evidence that when young people see all these sectors of their lives delivering the same messages about expected behavior and providing the supports to act on those expectations, their behavior in fact becomes healthier and their risks decrease."[15]

One mechanism for building connections across socializing systems is to create vision teams representing all socializing systems and community sectors, organized at the level of the neighborhood or across an entire community. ("Involving Many Sectors in the Asset-Building Vision" shows how one community has organized its efforts to build connections across sectors.) Another mechanism is a citywide dialogue to build consensus on values and boundaries. Somewhat to their surprise, some of the cities involved in asset-building initiatives have discovered that residents share a common core of values and expectations. The discovery unleashes actions of modeling, articulation, and intention that previously were frozen by the fear of offending someone.

Involving Many Sectors in the Asset-Building Vision

The city of Albuquerque, New Mexico, has made asset building a major focus for work across many sectors of the community. Under the auspices of a nonprofit organization, Albuquerque Assets, public school students have been surveyed regarding their assets, and efforts have begun to mobilize various sectors in the community to become engaged in asset building. Here are some of the ways sectors have become involved:

- The Albuquerque public schools have integrated asset building into plans for training, to address low test scores and high dropout rates among students.
- A homeless shelter for youth is about to begin training AmeriCorps volunteers to build assets with individual youth who seek services.
- Congregations formed an interfaith network for training and support that focuses on building assets.
- A local radio station is airing public service messages on asset building in both English and Spanish for a year.

Supporting this work are community committees, each of which focuses on mobilizing individual sectors: schools, congregations, neighborhoods, government, and media and business. "It is just incredible how our communities resonate with the message of the importance of building assets for youth," says Flora Sanchez, a prevention expert deeply involved in Albuquerque Assets.

4. Unleashing Spontaneous Acts of Asset Building

Perhaps more than half of a community's asset-building potential resides in daily relationships—some fleeting, some sustained—between young people and adults, and children and adolescents. These asset-building interactions are the small molecules of support, affirmation, acknowledgment, recognition, boundary setting, rewarding, including, listening to, modeling, skill building, leading, helping, and empowering that accumulate over time and shape how a child belongs to and has a stake in the community. Some of these acts are simple gestures, some are conversations, some are moments of recognition and value.

To get empirical about it, imagine a city of one hundred thousand adults and twenty-five thousand children. The goal is to unleash two hundred thousand acts of asset building per day (two per adult). That translates into eight asset-building experiences per day per child. Multiplied by 365 days, that yields 2,920 moments of asset building annually for each child, all done for free in the daily routine.

This kind of revolution in community life is triggered by a shared vision and a normative climate of capacity and responsibility, augmented by supporting messages built into the citywide communications system. The worldview to be created among residents has these underlying elements:

- Positive development for children and teenagers requires daily community attention to asset building.
- It takes more than good family to build assets; it also requires broad and persistent community involvement.

- All residents have the potential to build assets.
- By virtue of being members of their community, all residents have responsibility to promote assets.
- No one can do the work of asset building alone. It takes everyone.

These ideas are currently countercultural. They violate the too-easy belief that (1) positive development is primarily, if not solely, the work of family, and (2) there is a cure-all program that can repair lives when family is not working at full capacity.

Because communitywide asset building is countercultural, unleashing resident action on behalf of youth requires a massive, intentional, long-term "social marketing" strategy to transform people's perceptions, attitudes, and behaviors. This requires using the tools of research to analyze and identify target messages to multiple audiences, so as to communicate redundant, compelling, and empowering messages to the public; provide systems for competency building, support, and affirmation that ensure that individuals are successful as asset builders; and develop institutional commitments that reinforce the individual action.

Chapter Eight looks in more detail at the processes and tools for individual transformation. Chapter Nine extends individual action to the family level, looking at ways the asset-building framework can be a useful tool in family life and its implications for family-serving systems in a community.

At the heart of community transformation is storytelling about the actions people take. Stories become both tools to motivate and vehicles for rearticulating the vision. The search for stories often leads to people who already embodied asset building long before the language of assets was developed or a communitywide initiative was launched. Here are some of the stories we have heard about individual action as people are inspired to build assets:

- Police officers spend lunch hours serving food to children in school cafeterias as a way of developing positive relationships.
- Ten senior citizens acquire several vacant city lots and with thirty neighborhood children turn the eyesores into flower and vegetable gardens.
- A mayor of a large city devotes Saturday mornings to neighborhood children, inviting them into her home for cookie making, conversation, and the transmission of wisdom.
- A varsity basketball team, despite the hectic pace of the season, volunteers in a public library to read to children.
- A family decides to alter its frantic pace and chooses three meals a week at which parents and children are together.
- A retired man with a private backyard tennis court starts to give lessons to neighborhood children.

- A couple sends birthday cards to all the children in their neighborhood.
- A baby-boomer father, preoccupied with life and work, begins intentionally dialoguing with his children's friends.
- Dozens of adults commit each morning to stand at bus stops with children, offering umbrellas, safety, and words of care.
- A fifty-year-old father of three adult children volunteers to lead ten weekend retreats a year through his local Boy Scout troop.

Take a Letter: Every Adult Counts

Educator and parent Lynn Stambaugh believes passionately that "a healthy community starts with responsible and caring adults." As board chair for the Cherry Creek Community Prevention Project, Stambaugh works to help kids stay drug- and alcohol-free in a large suburban area southeast of Denver. The project blends a risk-focused approach with an asset-building strategy that emphasizes the community's responsibility to give young people positive opportunities and developmental support.

Not long ago, she drew up a list of all the adults who interact regularly with her kids: not just teachers, but coaches, janitors, bus drivers, music teachers, and others. Then she wrote each of them a letter, saying in part, "As an adult working with young people, you play a very important role in the lives of our youth in these 'very hard to grow up' years." She described Search Institute's research into developmental assets, highlighting those assets she thought were most pertinent to each adult's role.

"You make a difference," she concluded. "Thank you for all your hard work and for your dedication."

Her letters drew what Stambaugh calls "an amazing response." Many recipients wrote or phoned to thank her, and others responded with special warmth to Stambaugh's four kids, who range in age from nine to almost fifteen.

What's more, asset-building letters have caught on as Stambaugh has shared her experience in parenting classes she leads.

"The letters are great because they open communication between families and other adults involved in kids' lives," Stambaugh comments. "And they build awareness—they help make assets a common language."

Source: Excerpted with permission from *Assets: The Magazine of Ideas for Healthy Communities & Healthy Youth* (Autumn 1996). Copyright © 1996 Search Institute.

5. Unleashing the Power of Organizations and Systems

In the same way that individuals must be moved to build assets, a parallel goal is to stimulate and empower organizations and institutions to become intentional about asset building. Included here are the primary socializing systems (families, schools, religious institutions, neighborhoods, youth organizations) that have regular, ongoing, and direct contact with young people. In addition, secondary systems (such as businesses, health care providers, foundations, justice systems, the media, and government) play an important role, as their actions and policies undergird—or interfere—with creating a caring community for young people.

Intentionality necessitates planning. It can be directed to many dimensions of organizational life. In schools, for example, the asset-building framework has implications for climate, curriculum, school design, cocurricular activities, infusion of values deep into school life, utilization of parent contact as a means for enhancing the asset-building power of family, and service learning.

The same careful planning is important in a secondary support system such as in local government. What role can government leaders, both appointed and elected, play in bringing stakeholders together, creating a climate of mutual trust, directing resources and emotional energy, and otherwise undergirding asset-building efforts in the community? Here are some glimpses of ways organizations in various communities have begun acting upon a commitment to asset building:

- A school district redesigns its staffing arrangements so that teachers have the same students for a minimum of two years.
- A hospital gives all new parents a kit of materials about asset building.
- A foundation shifts its giving guidelines from deficit reduction to asset building.
- A congregation's leadership council decides it will use the developmental assets as a filter through which all decisions pass.
- A network of family service providers develops a training system to aid social workers in using the asset model in interactions with parents.
- A high school incorporates assets into its homeroom advisories.
- A grocery store prints asset-building messages on its grocery bags.
- A restaurant lists the assets on its placemats.
- A radio station airs asset-building messages throughout the day.
- An urban district has named asset-building as one of its primary objectives for school improvement. This, in turn, compels each school to be intentional about creating and implementing a plan.
- A mental health agency hires a full-time staff person to build assets in the community.
- A network of volunteer athletic coaches ask for and receive training in how to promote assets.
- A probation officer uses the asset framework to design programs for troubled youth.
- Four congregations begin after-school programs for children.
- A large business specializing in the manufacture of building materials pays full wages while employees mentor students or attend parent-teacher conferences on company time.

- A team of pediatricians uses the assets with parents, children, and teenagers as a model of health promotion.
- A shelter for homeless and runaway teenagers designs an intensive, yearlong asset-building initiative for the youth.
- A school board changes the position description for the school superintendent, freeing her to devote half of her time to being a community ambassador for asset building.

Later we look at the role of primary (Chapter Ten) and supportive (Chapter Eleven) institutions in creating a healthy community for children and adolescents.

6. Identifying and Expanding the Reach of Formal Asset-Building Activities

Though asset building is largely a relational process, it also needs a programmatic face. Programs not only offer structured opportunities for intentional and focused asset building; they give opportunities to enhance asset-building skills and strengthen relationships.

Asset-building programs already exist in all communities. They are called by such names as mentoring; peer helping; family education and support; cocurricular activities in schools, clubs, youth organizations, and congregations; school readiness initiatives; and school-to-work initiatives. Each of these is about support, competency, and structure, and some seek explicitly to transmit boundaries and values. An asset-building initiative elevates the importance of these opportunities for young people and reminds citizens why these programs are important. The call for communities is to identify these programs, make them known and available, equip them, and celebrate the people who lead them. Then do everything possible to double or triple or quadruple their reach.

At the same time, the asset framework becomes an important tool to use in evaluating and strengthening youth-serving activities, ensuring that they address the range of developmental needs of the young people they serve. For example, a youth club can begin asking how it provides a supportive environment for youth, how to emphasize youth empowerment through leadership opportunities, how it emphasizes values, and so forth.

Expanding the Reach of Asset-Building Activities

The City of Minneapolis established the Youth Coordinating Board (YCB) in the 1980s. A partnership linking public-sector entities in the city and county, YCB has now promoted youth development policies and programs for more than a decade. One of these was Success by Six, a multisector initiative designed to stimulate school readiness.

Now YCB is focusing on seven-to-fourteen-year-olds with an effort to increase participation in youth development clubs, teams, and organizations. In 1995, YCB commissioned Search Institute to conduct a thorough study of the youth organization terrain and the degree of access to and utilization of these resources by seven-to-fourteen-year-olds.[16]

Discovering that many of the programs were underutilized—in part because of lack of knowledge by families and young people of available resources—in June 1996 YCB launched What's Up. Started and run by youth, What's Up is a telephone hotline that links the caller to clubs, teams, and organizations by interest and location. The hotline is one mechanism meant to boost participation from the 50 percent rate of 1995 to 90 percent by 2000. A second mechanism in development is to redesign public school transcripts to include a record of a student's participation in organizations and community service.

7. Introducing New Initiatives

What else transpires in an asset-building community? New initiatives should be planned and implemented, guided by an audit of what is and is not available. The audit could cover these issues:

- Do we have safe places for teenagers to gather?
- Do we have organized activities that develop girls' self-confidence?
- Do we have organized activities that help boys maintain and grow caring and compassion?
- Do all children and adolescents have access to creative activities (music, art, drama)?
- Do congregations have quality programs for adolescents?
- Does our community celebrate families?
- Do we provide opportunities for youth to be resources and activists in the community?
- Does our community celebrate the people who devote their professional lives to nurturing children and adolescents?
- Is there adequate funding and training for day care?
- Do parents of young children have adequate support?

In examining the asset-building gaps, four issues should be given priority:

1. *Think intergenerationally.* In all communities, people have become too comfortable with disconnected generations. People, places, and programs that connect old and young, adults and youth, teenagers and children should be named and held up for others to celebrate and emulate.

2. *Expand the reach of family support and education.* Families are a powerful source of developmental assets. All parents and guardians—regardless of income or life circumstances—need multiple opportunities to learn, remember, build skills for, and act on developmental assets. Agencies, schools, community education, religious institutions, the media, public health, and other community-based organizations should work together in delivering this effort, with particular emphasis on promoting responsible fathering.

3. *Elevate the importance of service.* It ought to become the norm for children and youth to engage in acts of caring and compassion for others and for the common good through youth organizations, families, neighborhoods, schools, and religious institutions. Service to others both solidifies caring values and provides opportunities for building the assets of social competencies, empowerment, and positive identity. When combined with intentional reflection, it becomes a powerful tool for shaping learning, positive values, and competencies. A goal is to ensure that all youth engage in acts of service many times a year from ages five to twenty.

4. *Deepen exposure to cultural strengths and traditions.* For many youth, there is considerable strength in the traditions, symbols, and values of their cultural heritage. Particularly for youth of color, this heritage includes the concept of elders, the primacy of intergenerational relationships, respect for figures of authority, the value of caring for others, and wisdom about what matters. Being in touch with and affirming these strengths represents an important dimension of cultural competence, in addition to knowledge and contact with cultures beyond one's own.

An asset in its own right, the embrace of heritage can enhance self-concept, positive values, and a sense of belonging. Programs and people that help to deepen these roots should be supported and expanded.[17] It is also crucial that communities provide ways for the large percentage of youth who view themselves as biracial or multiracial to claim cultural strengths.

Asset Building Isn't Everything: Maintaining an Economic and Service Infrastructure

With these seven goals for asset-building communities in mind, we reiterate that focusing on asset building is not the only thing communities must do. Well-being is also fostered by other community dimensions, including economic vitality, affordable housing, and access to quality day care and health care. These arenas have direct consequences and indirectly shape the amount of attention families and others can devote to asset building.

A healthy community also provides a range of city and agency services to help children and families weather adversity and cope with change, as well as providing interventions that give youth a second chance. Examples of essential services include special care for low-birthweight babies, pediatric care for low-income families, and comprehensive, school-based health programs. Joy Dryfoos's portrait of *Full-Service Schools: A Revolution in Health and Social Services for Children, Youth, and Families* needs to be given a careful look by all city leaders, particularly in urban areas.[18]

Quality space is a resource of significant import. Neighborhoods uncluttered by danger and debris and uninterrupted by highways are important allies in healthy development. So, too, is the preservation of natural habitat. Richard Louv, in *Childhood's Future,* bids us to remember the value of nature: "the natural world is the ultimate web, and essential to the emotional health of children."[19] City planning departments must be cognizant of this fact and honor this value in the face of ever-aggressive developers.

By its design decisions, government has considerable power in promoting or destroying neighborhood, space, and habitat. In partnership with the business community, cities can be proactive in creating child-hospitable places. A prime example is Seattle's Kids Place, an intentional effort—through architecture, planning and advocacy—to create child-centered urban landscape.

A healthy community also takes responsibility for naming and reducing threats to development. Included here are systemic issues such as poverty, racism, and gender stereotyping, as well as the presence of family and environmental risks such as exposure to exploitative adults; abuse; family violence; access to tobacco, alcohol, and other drugs; and neglect.[20]

It is also important to note that the positive focus of developmental assets is highly compatible with views of economic development, risk reduction, and services that emphasize community empowerment and capitalizing on local resources or, in the terminology of John McKnight, *community assets* (which we tend to refer to as *community resources*).[21] McKnight and Kretzmann's work on asset mapping and community empowerment dovetails nicely with our emphasis on strengthening the developmental infrastructure for youth. Thus, although it is not the focus of this book, we believe that communities must also reexamine the approaches they take to economic development and service provision to ensure that they, too, focus on building capacity and strengths, rather than on deficits and the view of clients as helpless victims.

Putting the Pieces Together: An Overview of the Change Process

Figure 6.1 weaves together strands from many earlier chapters, providing an overview of the process for strengthening the developmental infrastructure. As it is laid out, the change process appears linear, with vision and strategy combining to change prevailing norms and that in turn leading to individual and organizational-level changes.

FIGURE 6.1. OVERVIEW OF THE CHANGE PROCESS FOR STRENGTHENING THE DEVELOPMENTAL INFRASTRUCTURE.

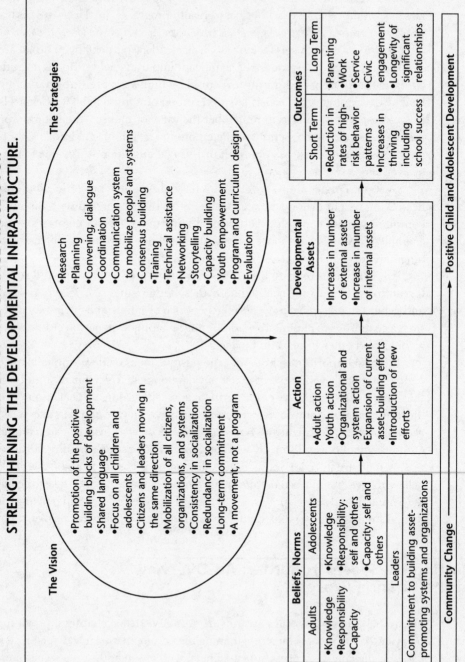

The Vision

- Promotion of the positive building blocks of development
- Shared language
- Focus on all children and adolescents
- Citizens and leaders moving in the same direction
- Mobilization of all citizens, organizations, and systems
- Consistency in socialization
- Redundancy in socialization
- Long-term commitment
- A movement, not a program

The Strategies

- Research
- Planning
- Convening, dialogue
- Coordination
- Communication system to mobilize people and systems
- Consensus building
- Training
- Technical assistance
- Networking
- Storytelling
- Capacity building
- Youth empowerment
- Program and curriculum design
- Evaluation

Beliefs, Norms		
Adults	Adolescents	
• Knowledge • Responsibility • Capacity	• Knowledge • Responsibility: self and others • Capacity: self and others	
Leaders		
Commitment to building asset-promoting systems and organizations		

Action
• Adult action • Youth action • Organizational and system action • Expansion of current asset-building efforts • Introduction of new efforts

Developmental Assets
• Increase in number of external assets • Increase in number of internal assets

Outcomes	
Short Term	Long Term
• Reduction in rates of high-risk behavior patterns • Increases in thriving including school success	• Parenting • Work • Service • Civic engagement • Longevity of significant relationships

Community Change ──────→ Positive Child and Adolescent Development

As the actions spread and become normative themselves, assets increase, with short-term and long-term consequences. In reality, the process of change is likely to be multidirectional, with, for example, action feeding back to further the process of norm changes, and progress in building assets feeding back to refresh and reenergize the vision.

Evaluation efforts are being launched to track the progress of ongoing and emerging healthy-community initiatives. At this point, we can document how the initiatives are being implemented and the kinds of innovative individual and system action that are being unleashed. Measurable changes in assets, we predict, will not occur until initiatives enter their fourth or fifth year. As our evaluation plans are fully implemented—including longitudinal studies of youth and across-time studies of adult norms and beliefs—we will be able to begin building a knowledge base on how and under what conditions communities move the asset needle, and the impact that asset change has on choices made and paths taken.

CHAPTER SEVEN

FROM PLANTING TO HARVEST

Strategies for Growing a Healthy Community

Many different verbs are used these days to talk about community change. People including this author often talk about "building" community and "creating" community. In some ways, those terms suggest a more precise and controllable process than reality indicates. After all, builders have specific blueprints and materials that are made to specifications. Creating community implies that the whole process depends on a mastermind creator.

The process of community change is more organic and unpredictable than these words connote. It is more like gardening or farming. No metaphor is perfect (gardening, for example, may seem a less relevant metaphor to some in urban areas), but the image of *growing* healthy communities suggests several important characteristics.

First, much of the garden's success depends on the garden itself: its soil and nutrients, the sunlight, its location. Similarly, most of the essential elements needed for growing a healthy community are within the community itself.

Second, gardening is as much about art and intuition as it is about precision and science. Sure, there is much to be learned from soil analysis and carefully following the directions on the seed package. But plants grow in sometimes surprising ways! And gardeners find all kinds of novel ways to make their vegetables grow. Similarly, a healthy community initiative depends as much on the creativity and intuition of its leaders as it does on carefully following particular instructions.

Third, there are many different ways to grow a garden—even on a given plot of land. No two gardens need to be exactly the same to produce bountiful harvests (though gardeners are notorious for borrowing ideas from each other). Similarly, each initiative discovers its own approaches . . . often with the counsel of friends and peers.

This chapter highlights a set of generic strategies for planning and implementing communitywide asset-building movements. Yet communities are not generic. Each community's efforts must be shaped by local needs, resources, and opportunities. In the state of Alaska, for example, asset-building resources are being redesigned to integrate the potential socializing power of native ceremony and ritual. In our emerging statewide initiative, Assets for Colorado Youth, a premium is placed on translating resources into other languages.

Fourth, though it is certainly easier to grow a garden in some places than others, almost any plot of land can be cultivated to produce a garden. There are spacious gardens in back yards, community gardens in neighborhoods, patio gardens on balconies and rooftops, and herb gardens in kitchen windows. It may take years of careful attention and creative planning, but a garden can grow anywhere. In the same way, some communities are already cultivated and ready for asset-building work; they may have a history of "growing" similar things in the past. Others require significant investments to make them ready.

Finally, although each garden is different and each gardener has her own knack for how to do things, some underlying principles and techniques give gardeners a place to start and a way to plan. Growing healthy communities involves some basic steps and basic tasks (which, of course, each community adapts to fit its own growing conditions). This chapter outlines our initial thinking about five phases, or "seasons," of community initiatives and the key tasks in each phase.[1]

Another reason the gardening metaphor is appropriate for describing healthy community initiatives is that the process takes time. It is not a quick fix, and it cannot be rushed. Rather, like the gardener who tills the soil in the spring in order to have a harvest months later or years later in the case of perennials, so must community leaders commit to action in hopes of a harvest in the future.

Major Tasks in All Seasons of an Initiative

The gardener must do certain things throughout a growing season. Similarly, there are central tasks that must be maintained throughout a community's asset-building initiative. Each task takes on different levels of importance in different seasons and changes in focus, but all remain important throughout the process.

We have identified six broad task areas that fit into three types: planning, action, and reflection.

Planning

The first two major task areas fall into the broad area of planning: the area of visioning and leadership for one, and planning and coordination.

Visioning and Leadership. Asset building is a process that depends on visionary leadership. To borrow from Stephen Covey, the major task here is to be sure that the ladders being climbed in the community efforts are leaning against the right walls. "If the ladder is not leaning against the right wall, every step we take just gets us to the wrong place faster. We may be very busy, we may be very *efficient*, but we will also be truly *effective* only when we begin with the end in mind."[2]

Planning and Coordination. Planning is different from leadership. Indeed, people who plan well are often not those who are effective at holding up a vision. Perhaps the biggest task in planning and coordination grows out of the fact that an asset-building initiative is not a centralized program, but an attempt to create a web of asset-building activity in the lives of every individual and every organization in the community. Thus the central task is not to plan lots of activities but to prompt and coordinate others in the community to integrate asset building into their efforts.

Action

In addition to the vision-bearing and coordination roles, an asset-building initiative must work to mobilize and equip individuals and institutions to build assets within their own spheres of influence. This is the focus of action for the initiative.

Engaging Residents. As we have repeated often throughout this book, an asset-building initiative puts great emphasis on getting individuals to commit to asset building in their own lives and families. Chapter Eight examines in more detail how to prompt asset-building action by individuals and families.

Engaging Institutions. Similarly, each institution in a community is a potential resource for asset building. Bringing these organizations onto the team and providing the coaching needed expands the vision for asset building into many systems that already exist within the community. Chapters Ten and Eleven focus on the roles of specific institutions in an asset-building effort.

Reflection

The opportunities for sustaining and improving action depend on intentional reflection on the change process. This reflection has at least two major components.

Evaluation. Evaluation is sometimes thought of as a necessary evil to satisfy funders or appease critics. But it serves much more important purposes. First, if it occurs throughout the change process, it provides opportunities for course correction. It also gives insights into improving activities the next time around. In the larger view, careful evaluation of many individual community initiatives lends insights across communities for what is working and what is not in different situations. Finally, evaluation opens doors for the next task area: celebration.

Celebration. Because changing developmental assets is a long-term task, it is essential to have marking milestones along the way for maintaining visibility, commitment, and momentum. Celebrations can range from individual recognition to annual community events.

Sometimes we think of these tasks as linear, beginning with visioning and planning, then moving to action, and, finally, reflecting on what was done. In reality, these tasks are continuous and cyclical. The vision must be shaped and reshaped, shared and reshared, affirmed and reaffirmed throughout the community-growing process. Similarly, evaluation and celebration begin along with the process, even if in small ways, to allow for course corrections as well as celebrations that renew energy and broaden involvement. Thus, these themes are woven throughout the outline that follows.

The Seasons of Community Initiatives

As we examine literature on community change and collaboration and watch communities begin the asset-building process, we see at least five seasons or phases. This section describes the characteristics of each and major issues that surface as priorities in each stage or season. They are summarized in Table 7.1.

Season 1: Envisioning the Garden

This first season of a healthy community effort typically begins when one person or a handful of people in a community learn about the framework of developmental assets and see its benefit to their own community. Many questions emerge during this phase:

TABLE 7.1. SEASONS AND TASKS IN GROWING A HEALTHY COMMUNITY.

Season	Key Tasks
1. Envisioning the Garden	•Work with a small group of initiators •Gather information about readiness
2. Preparing the Soil	•Identify and cultivate leadership •Gather information on youth and the community •Engage in dialogue about the vision with many people •Create a positive, shared vision •Develop initial action plans
3. Planting the Seeds	•Cultivate initiative leadership for vision bearing, management, and coordination •Develop an organizational structure •Broaden involvement and ownership •Plan for early, visible successes •Keep activities to manageable levels •Raise awareness and increase knowledge •Monitor, coordinate, and celebrate action •Draw in existing institutions •Embrace innovations from the community •Establish mechanisms for evaluation
4. Tending the Growing Garden	•Keep the end in mind •Do not neglect maintenance tasks •Network with other communities •Renew the energy
5. Harvest	•Evaluate •Celebrate •Renew

- How would this approach enhance or focus our efforts on behalf of youth in our community?
- How does this framework fit with existing efforts in our community, such as those focused on intervention, problem prevention, or health care?
- Is our community ready for this type of effort? Would it compete with other efforts and foci? Are resources (people and financial) available to make it work?
- What do we need to do to get started in our community?

The primary task at this early stage is to gather adequate information to give a group of initiators confidence in advocating for an asset-building approach. The key task is to nurture in these early adopters a commitment and willingness to put energy into launching an effort. This occurs in some communities where an individual promotes asset building through workshops and other communications methods, which motivates a group to join together and move into action. For example, one organization in the community (perhaps a school) begins a public education campaign that generates interest and enthusiasm for more systematic and collaborative efforts.

In some communities, an informal initiator group, usually four to six people, adequately represents the community. More often, though, it is an existing group (a civic club, a group of educators or clergy, etc.) that then reaches out to include others as their commitment grows. This group is most effective when it includes or has the support of influential people in the community—people who can successfully convene other stakeholders in the community.

Season 2: Preparing the Soil

Taking time to plan the garden before planting seeds is not always essential in a backyard patch, but it is essential in growing a community initiative. Once the initiator group has decided to advocate for a communitywide initiative, several key tasks need to be addressed in order to "prepare the soil" for an effective initiative.

Identify and Cultivate Leadership. Because the asset-building vision calls for communitywide responsibility for youth, involving many different stakeholders is important from the outset. A mixture of motivated residents and their leaders provides a nice balance.

Many communities have developed a "vision team" with representatives from many sectors (schools, government, law enforcement, congregations, local foundations or philanthropic organizations, service agencies, business, health care, civic organizations), grassroots organizations, and individuals such as young people, parents, and other residents (including senior citizens and people from various racial or ethnic and socioeconomic groups).

The quality and makeup of this vision team is vital to the success of the effort. First, the team needs a commitment to asset building and a bias toward identifying local capacity and resources. Kretzmann and McKnight describe the issue this way:

> Building a team of community leaders who are clearly oriented toward finding
> and mobilizing the already existing gifts and capacities of residents and their
> associations is crucial to the success of the community building enterprise. . . .
> Fortunately, every community is blessed with residents who are fundamentally
> committed to what might be called a capacity-oriented view of the world.
> These are the folks who understand well the fact that the proverbial glass is
> both half empty and half full, but who insist always on focusing first on the
> fullness, on the gifts and capacities of their families, friends, and neighbors.[3]

Second, the team must be balanced among organizational leaders and other residents. Vision teams that lack the organizational power of positional leaders have difficulty moving the vision into the structures and systems of the community. Teams that lack participation by many types of residents risk alienating a particular constituency.

In all urban settings reside networks and leaders who represent important segments of the population, each of which belongs at the center of any successful social change movement. Among these important networks are those representing historically disenfranchised peoples. Any successful urban initiative nurtures their advocacy and involvement prior to the official launch of the effort. So doing dramatically shapes how the movement is planned, organized, and implemented.

One key, but often overlooked, constituency is young people themselves. However, even though they have much to offer as partners in the community-building process, strong social realities and norms interfere with involving them as equals.

Perhaps the greatest challenge in engaging youth in the process is the uneven power between adults and youth in our culture. Ruthanne Kurth-Schai writes, "Though attitudes are changing, we still live in a society that places the concerns and interests of adults over those of children and youth. . . . Good intentions—though essential and now more widely shared—are not enough to ensure that young people are valued and supported for the unique gifts they offer."[4]

Kurth-Schai suggests that the central need in building adult-youth partnerships is not "age-blindedness" but "age sensitivity." She goes on to suggest that "adults must also be encouraged to approach adult/youth relationships with *humility*—always assuming they lack complete understanding of the context and experiences of a young person's life—and with caution—always taking care not to dismiss the validity of a young person's point of view."[5] The text "Principles for Engaging Youth in Community Building" suggests some important principles for involving youth in community-building efforts.

Principles for Engaging Youth in Community Building

John P. Kretzmann suggests the following principles for involving young people in community-building efforts:

1. Always start with the gifts, talents, knowledge, and skills of young people—never with their needs and problems.
2. Always lift up the unique individual, never the category to which the young person belongs. . . .
3. Share the conviction that (1) every community is filled with useful opportunities for young people to contribute to the community, and (2) there is no community institution or association that can't find a useful role for young people.

4. Try to distinguish between real community building work, and games or fakes—because young people know the difference.
5. Fight—in every way you can—age segregation. Work to overcome the isolation of young people.
6. Start to get away from the principle of aggregation of people by their emptiness. Don't put everyone who can't read together in a room. It makes no sense.
7. Move as quickly as possible beyond youth "advisory boards" or councils, especially those boards with only one young person on them.
8. Cultivate many opportunities for young people to teach and lead.
9. Reward and celebrate every creative effort, every contribution made by young people. Young people can help take the lead here.
10. In every way possible, amplify this message to young people: *we need you!* Our community cannot be strong without you.[6]

There are several important tasks in forming an effective vision team:[7]

- *Bring people together.* When inviting them, highlight the benefits of their involvement for both the organization or individual as well as the larger community. Once people are together, give them time to get to know each other, and to learn about each others' perspectives and hopes.
- *Build trust.* The time spent building trust is more than recuperated later when efforts face less jockeying for position and power, less suspicion of other participants, and more eagerness to contribute and support each other. A key to trust is having clear expectations and roles, and having meetings that are carefully designed to meaningfully involve all members. Also important is to take time for all participants to honestly disclose their self-interests and how the effort could affect their own organization or constituency.
- *Educate about asset building.* Do not assume that everyone on the vision team automatically understands the asset framework and its implications. Unless people internalize the many dimensions of the asset framework, asset building risks becoming a shallow campaign to "be nice to kids." Repeating key messages about assets lays a foundation for a more thoughtful, well-rounded response.
- *Take time to do it right.* It may take several meetings to get the "right people" into the room together. Each individual and group has its own agenda and needs, and many may not have a solid grasp of the asset-building focus. Working through—rather than rushing through—these challenges helps create a shared commitment that will pay off in the long run.

Gather Information. "Testing the soil" is an important part of the planning process. In gardening, whether it is done more scientifically (using a soil test kit from a nursery) or more informally (feeling the soil for its consistency and humus content), this assessment stage helps to assure that the seeds planted are likely to flourish.

Quality information gives people a shared reference point for reflecting on the needs, realities, and resources in the community as they shape their vision for the future. Otherwise, you risk shaping an initiative that does not adequately connect with the people and organizations in the community. Information should be gathered in several areas:

- *Young people's assets and needs.* Many communities find that a survey of young people can be an important catalyst for creative and sustained action. Unfortunately, most available local research on youth focuses on problem behaviors, not strengths. More than six hundred communities have used a Search Institute survey service to measure the assets in their own youth.[8] In addition, focus groups and other in-person techniques can give a deeper understanding of young people's connections to and attitudes toward their community. Young people can be exceptional partners in gathering this information.
- *Adults' attitudes and capacities.* Given that much of the energy in an asset-building initiative focuses on changing the way adults interact with youth, it is valuable to gather information on adults' attitudes, values, commitments to youth, and capacity to contribute. This information is fundamental in setting priorities for developing public awareness messages, designing systems to ensure success, knowing the obstacles to involvement, and setting priorities for training. Several communities with asset-building initiatives have used a model of convening neighbors in their homes to talk about the community, its youth, and their own vision. Not only do you gather useful information but you begin the process of community building in neighborhoods. More formal focus groups, surveys, or telephone polls can also yield valuable information.
- *Community resources.* What resources lie within the community that can provide the backbone for asset building? These may include:

  Gifts of individuals
  Cultural strengths and traditions
  Commitments of informal groups such as block clubs
  The organizational capacity of the schools, businesses, and other institutions
  The physical assets of the community's buildings, parks, and landmarks

  This information can be gathered through interviews with residents and leaders, surveys of program providers, walking through neighborhoods, or other methods.
- *Community readiness.* Not every community is appropriate for an asset-building initiative. Several factors should be examined in determining whether or how a community should begin an initiative:

A tradition of and commitment to cooperation across sectors is an important ingredient for early success in asset building. If it is not in place, much more energy must be put into building trust and cooperation before significant cooperative work is possible.

Existing efforts can either enhance or detract from a new asset-building initiative. In some communities, existing efforts around health care, prevention, civic engagement, character building, and other community needs have become the primary allies and advocates for asset building. At the same time, care must be taken to ensure that new initiatives do not compete with existing, worthwhile efforts.

A key to the success of asset building is having a champion. Unless someone (preferably several people) is available to dedicate time and energy to getting started, the effort drags on too long, losing its energy and focus.

A highly politicized climate characterized by power struggles and infighting is not conducive to any type of communitywide efforts, including asset building. One of the greatest dangers in this situation is for asset building to become a tool of one group to use against another, which undermines both the spirit and the potential of the approach.

Finally, an initiative based on asset building does not have to be expensive, but it needs a base of financial resources (some of which may be in-kind contributions) upon which to draw.

In gathering information on the community, care should be taken to assess both strengths and resources as well as needs and gaps. Then the process of building a vision allows the community to find innovative ways to use its own resources and strengths to address community needs. Focusing exclusively on the problems results in paralysis when faced by overwhelming needs; focusing exclusively on the resources does not provide adequate information for knowing how best to use the resources.

Engage in Ongoing Dialogue. One of the challenges in our culture is the lack of opportunities for true public dialogue around issues of the day. Rather, public concerns are addressed in win-lose, politicized debates. What is needed, suggests Michael K. Briand, "is the ability and willingness to deliberate, and to make sound judgments as a public."[9]

As a community begins to plan its asset-building efforts, care must be taken to shape the process as deliberative dialogue, not partisan politics. To do this well, Briand suggests four principles for a legitimate and deliberative decision-making process:

1. Ordinary folks as well as politically active elites must have the opportunity to participate.
2. Discussion must be face-to-face.
3. Discussions must take place in a safe, respected setting where all citizens will feel inclined to deliberate together.
4. The process must enable a large number of people to carry on a sustained discussion.[10]

Create a Positive, Shared Vision. A critical task in the first season is to create a shared vision of the community for youth that builds on the leadership that has been formed and the information gathered regarding the community's values, strengths, and needs.

Research on community building suggests that a shared vision is a critical component of the process, even though it can be difficult and time-consuming to develop. The temptation may be simply to start implementing the ideas gathered. Yet the vision is needed to give direction, focus, and consistency to each effort.

A positive vision helps groups lay aside political and ideological agendas to work together because of their shared commitment to the well-being of children and adolescents. Peter Senge describes a vision this way: "Vision is a picture of the future that you really care about. It is an expression of your core values, your sense of purpose. . . . What makes a vision different from mission statements and strategic objectives is that vision brings something from within and says, 'I really want to put my life energy into creating this.' "[11]

In studying the role of vision in organizations, Richard R. Broholm has found that a vision-centered planning process addresses four concerns:

1. It shifts the focus from reaction to creative action.
2. It changes the mood from fatalism to hope.
3. It encourages collaboration rather than competition.
4. It encourages a systems approach to change rather than a problem-solving approach to change.[12]

These characteristics have certainly been true for the communities that adopt an asset-based vision for their efforts. Furthermore, the initial energy of the vision sees early results as people catch the vision and act on their own. In contrast, a mission statement can take months to refine, which drains the early energy and focus of the initiative.

There are dozens of effective visioning processes that can be adapted to create a vision for an asset-building community. The most effective ones build on quality information about the past and present (surveys and the like), involve a wide range of community members in shaping the vision (instead of an individual or group trying to "sell" the vision to others), and free people to dream about their future desires for their community.[13]

Develop Initial Action Plans. Now that you know where you want to go (your vision), you can begin developing the plans and strategies that help move you in that direction. Once again, there are many specific approaches to developing action plans. In our experience, the planning should address the following areas:

- Visioning and leading
- Planning and administering
- Engaging residents
- Engaging institutions
- Evaluating
- Celebrating

Each of these areas is an ongoing task area for a healthy community initiative. Each is explained in more detail later in this chapter.

In addition, three questions should be considered in developing the specific plans:

1. *How will you maintain balance?* A local initiative can be so multifaceted that it loses a focus. Or it can become so focused that it fails to move forward in several areas simultaneously. The challenge in planning is to maintain a balance among the many options and possibilities for action.

2. *What sort of financial base will the efforts need? How can it be secured and maintained?* Some communities have begun with volunteer-only efforts. Others have sought grant money for start-up. Some communities rely primarily upon resources within the community, while others seek grants and gifts from outside the community. It's not clear which approach or combination of approaches has the most success. But it is important that a decision be made early about these issues, and then planning be done accordingly.

3. *How will you resist the temptation to create new programs?* Because most responses to youth issues in recent decades have been programmatic, intentional energy is needed to avoid simply developing another short-term program to respond to a specific need. The most important tasks for the "vision bearers" for asset building are to keep the vision of a healthy community alive and to prompt individuals and institutions to discover ways in which they can integrate asset building into their own mission and commitments.

The season of preparing the soil often ends with submission of the plan to funders or partners for approval and buy-in. Many communities find this an important milestone to celebrate publicly. In traditional language, completion of this stage marks the end of the "planning." Next comes "implementation," with appropriate levels of funding and commitment.

Season 3: Planting the Seeds

As I write this chapter, springtime is emerging in Minnesota. Days are getting warmer and longer. The first buds are appearing on the trees. Neighbors have emerged from winter hibernation to tend to their yards and plant seeds in their gardens.

The time of planting seeds for a healthy community initiative has the same kind of energy that we experience every spring in Minnesota. A vision is ready to guide the efforts, and dozens of ideas are ready to be planted to see how they will take root.

Yet—just as spring gardening is a demanding time—there are a number of important tasks that, if attended to, help ensure a strong growing season for the initiative. A report from the Pew Partnership for Civic Change, based on interviews with civic leaders engaged in forming coalitions, suggests that three qualities guide effective coalitions:

1. *Continuity:* "A community coalition must have a core group that keeps it moving ahead, provides it with a sense of history and stability, and serves as the anchor of lasting networks for change."
2. *Flexibility:* "A community coalition must be ready to adapt to changes and circumstances, avoid rigid bureaucratic structures, and set, and then reset, expectations that make sense in these changing times."
3. *Openness:* "A community coalition must actively seek new members with fresh perspectives, join forces with existing and emerging organizations, come to understand the concerns of the entire community, and recognize and tap the full capacities within the community."[14]

Given the importance of these qualities, we suggest that the following tasks are critical as a local initiative is planted.

Cultivate Initiative Leadership. The quality and commitment of the leadership directly impacts the effectiveness of the healthy community initiative. There are many different ways to organize and structure leadership, depending on the particular dynamics and needs in a given community and the particular structure of the initiative (see "Develop an Organizational Structure" below). As we work with communities, we find it helpful to separate vision-focused leadership from planning and management. In addition, there is an important "coordination" function.

Vision-focused leadership. Communities often form a vision team to guide the effort. These groups are most effective when they are viewed more as keepers of the flame rather than primarily as the decision makers for the effort.

Though this group makes decisions for the initiative, its major role is to ensure that the vision of asset building remains the energizing focus for the work. In addition, it plays an important role in passing the flame to other organizations and individuals. This group typically consists of community leaders (formal and informal), other stakeholders (particularly those not in the community's power structure), and other residents (including youth, parents, and youth workers). This group should include a core of people with a long-term investment in asset building as well as individuals who bring fresh perspectives.

When they are most effective, vision teams see their role as more facilitative or process-oriented than top-down and controlling. As the Pew Partnership for Civic Change report asserts: "Changing times have brought about a recognized need for leadership which empowers people throughout the community to make choices through openness, trust, and consensus—thereby allowing participants to determine their own future."[15]

Planning and management. As the visionary leaders focus on the broad vision and future, the strategic leadership develops and implements concrete plans for moving toward that vision. Different people bring different strengths to each of these emphases.

Many communities develop committees or task forces to oversee various parts of the planning and implementation. Some communities have structured task forces around specific areas of assets (for example, constructive use of time). Others have developed task forces for each sector (business, education). Still others have focused on the type of work involved (such as marketing, fundraising, program planning).

Young people and adults cochair committees that are developing asset-building plans in LaCrosse, Wisconsin. The effort gives both groups the chance to spend time together and to develop asset-building plans.

One of the challenges for initiatives is to help the planners and implementers focus on empowering existing organizations or groups within the community to build on their existing strengths and take responsibility for specific strategies, instead of creating many new programs and activities. There is a tendency to want to directly meet needs and interests rather than connect those needs and interests with existing resources in the community.

Coordination. Some communities have been able to coordinate their efforts with volunteers, but most find that hiring a paid coordinator is an important investment. However, because of the focus on passing on the asset-building vision to existing organizations and structures, most healthy community initiatives do not hire staff to implement programs. Instead, the work is undertaken by volunteers or by individuals whose organization builds a commitment to the initiative into their job descriptions.

The primary tasks of the coordinator are not program development or event planning but information sharing, helping people network, and connecting people with opportunities for involvement. This person must resist the temptation to take over the community's asset-building work, and focus instead on equipping and empowering others to get involved themselves.

As communities begin developing their understanding of community leadership, it is important to emphasize that many, many people can be—and are— leaders in different capacities and spheres, whether or not they have participated in "communitywide leadership" in the past or will in the future. In commenting on current views of public leadership, Michael K. Briand writes: "The institutional concept of leadership, assuming an elite few can know best what to do, contrasts markedly with the democratic conception, assuming the community as a whole possesses the only capacity to respond effectively to public problems. The institutional conception of leadership is thus inappropriate for a society of democratic communities composed of citizens who have the capacity as well as the responsibility to act effectively in response to public problems. It is inappropriate because it replaces the role of citizen with the roles of consumers, clients, and victims."[16]

A person can be an important asset-building leader simply by becoming a vocal advocate for and friend to children on her or his block. This filter is an important reminder that the "leadership" in a vision team is not an elite group but the way people with certain gifts (networking, connections, etc.) can provide leadership for asset-building efforts in the community.

Develop an Organizational Structure. The structure put in place for the visioning process may not be the most effective structure for ongoing implementation. Therefore, an early task is to evaluate the existing structure and create one that fits the dynamics and needs of the initiative.

Because asset-building initiatives are not designed to create extensive programming but instead to prompt a movement in the community, the initiative's structure should be designed to empower or unleash the community to participate in the vision, instead of being designed to develop and implement massive programs. This distinction suggests several important characteristics:

- The structure needs a clear decision-making process built around the vision and mission. Decisions should be made through a filter of empowerment, not one of control.

- Clear communication channels should be established to communicate with active partners in the effort while also reaching out to the community. People need to know where to call to share information about what they are doing and to learn what others are doing.
- A structure for volunteer involvement should be developed beyond the vision team. One model is to have multiple committees or task forces that focus on specific components of the vision or on specific task areas (see Figure 7.1).
- Mechanisms can be developed for communication and support among the various committees. One model for addressing this need is to form a coordination group that consists of two members from each committee. Another model is to use the vision team for this purpose; however, this approach runs the risk of bogging the vision team down in day-to-day issues, rather than keeping the vision central.
- Leaders should be trained in process or facilitative leadership, since the style may not be familiar to many of them, particularly if they have official leadership roles in organizations.[17]

FIGURE 7.1. POSSIBLE CONFIGURATIONS FOR WORK GROUPS IN AN ASSET-BUILDING INITIATIVE.

1. A structure in which each work group or task force focuses on strengthening each type of asset in the community, i.e.:

- Support Task Force
- Empowerment Task Force
- Boundaries and Expectations Task Force
- Time Use Task Force
- Commitment to Learning Task Force
- Positive Values Task Force
- Social Competencies Task Force
- Positive Identity Task Force

2. A structure in which each work group focuses on competencies in specific task areas, i.e.:

- Communications Work Group
- Evaluation Work Group
- Celebrations Work Group
- Training Work Group
- Fundraising Work Group
- Cross-Sector Initiatives

3. A structure in which each work group focuses on mobilizing and equipping a particular sector in the community, i.e.:

- Youth Committee
- Business Committee
- Neighborhoods Committee
- Congregations Committee
- Media Committee
- Family Committee
- Schools Committee
- Community Agencies Committee
- Health Care Committee
- Cross-Sector Initiatives

Broaden Involvement and Ownership. One of the challenges that coalitions face is in remaining open to, and providing opportunities for, broad involvement by community members. Furthermore, coalition members become frustrated with the difficulties of engaging the public and keeping people engaged.[18]

The challenge, then, is first to find appropriate ways to involve people within the structure of the initiative (office volunteers, task force members, special event volunteers) and second to connect them with other asset-building opportunities in the community.

Part of the potential power of the developmental asset paradigm is its capacity to unite people currently polarized along economic, political, religious, or racial or ethnic lines. That is, the assets often become a language of the common good. However, as change agents readily admit, sustaining dialogue and action around the common good requires ongoing attention to process so that many voices are heard and respected.

Too often, power and privilege and their traditional vestiges corrupt the process. How dialogues are organized, who leads them, and where they are held are judgments that can either impede or advance community building. The inclusiveness of an asset-building initiative can be greatly enhanced by including people charged with the role of creating and maintaining an inclusive process. In every city, there are wise and seasoned change agents who can play this crucial facilitation role.

Plan for Early, Visible Successes. Every gardener knows that it can take weeks before you see the first sprigs of seedlings cracking through the soil into sunlight. To keep up the enthusiasm and interest, the gardener may put in some already-growing plants from a greenhouse or some seeds that germinate more quickly, such as radishes.

The same approach works in creating a healthy community. Some initiatives can have immediate, visible results (for example, a community festival), while others may take years to see the true impact (for example, helping youth-serving organizations focus their mission around asset building).

Although the overall initiative focuses on long-term growth, it is also important to plan for some early successes to energize and motivate people. This may include sponsoring existing activities or programs (for example, Children's Sabbath from the Children's Defense Fund) or beginning efforts that bear fruit quickly (writing a column in the local newspaper).

Many communities begin their efforts with a highly publicized town meeting that introduces people to the idea of developmental assets and provides opportunities to get involved immediately.

Keep Activities and Expectations to Manageable Levels. One of the dangers in the spring is planting a larger plot than you can tend. In healthy-communities work, the danger is setting in motion so many activities in the community that they become impossible to maintain. Similarly, there is a danger of setting expectations so high ("We're going to raise the asset profile of every young person by ten assets within five years") that people quickly become discouraged when they do not see rapid progress.

When an asset-building effort moves into a large metropolitan area, an immediate challenge is how to focus energy. Do you seek to reach everyone in the whole area? Or do you focus in a specific neighborhood where you can do more intensive work? Our sense is that the answer to both questions must be yes. Urban initiatives must develop a balance between broad dissemination of key messages while also working intensely and intently in more narrowly defined areas and networks.

Public awareness campaigns should be targeted broadly to reach all or most residents, with multiple exposures per year to developmental assets and calls for personal capacity and responsibility. In so doing, communication mechanisms should encompass a wide spectrum of resources, including neighborhood newspapers and preexisting networks of leaders and residents organized around language, race or ethnicity, and interests.

At the same time, encouragement and assistance is needed to help regions of a city (neighborhoods or planning districts) go "deep" with the movement. Urban neighborhoods have the capacity to interconnect many socializing systems, and with the right resources they can self-determine how to build redundant socializing experiences for children and adolescents. In these neighborhood movements, preexisting entities such as community-based organizations have the capacity and networks to catalyze the movement. In some urban centers, efforts are under way to link each of the deep movements with a citywide vision team. This urban model recognizes that within large and diverse populations there are communities within community.

Raise Awareness and Increase Knowledge. Once the basic planning has been done, many communities use this opportunity to go public regarding their initiative. Often they work with the media to feature stories based on youth surveys of developmental assets. They also share their vision and strategies with the community, suggesting ideas for simple asset-building action.

Sharing the findings from research on youth assets can also be a powerful tool for raising awareness. In one community, high school students studied the findings from the local portrait of assets based on Search Institute's *Profiles of Student Life: Attitudes and Behaviors* survey and then shared the results with civic, parent, student, religious, and other groups in the community. In another, young people developed a drama that depicted their experiences of assets in their community.

In addition, communities quickly discover an ongoing need to share the paradigm of developmental assets and its implications for different audiences within the community. Town meetings can be effective forums through which community members are invited to be part of the vision and initiative.

How One Community Used a Community Event to Engage Residents

The city of Mankato, Minnesota, used a community gathering as a catalyst event to unite the community for asset building. The Council for Health Action and Promotion (CHAP) and Region 9 convened community leaders to combine energy in preparation for the town meeting. "Each organization knew how to tap into the media in its own way," says event organizer Barb Maher. "And each could leverage four to ten people in his or her organization to get the word out."

The committee carefully planned to make the event attractive and accessible to a cross-section of the community. They offered signing for the hearing impaired, free baby-sitting, and free bus service. They ended up running four bus routes and recruited eight child care volunteers from the local technical school to run the child care service.

Much to their delight, twenty-three hundred people attended the town meeting, including everyone from youth to senior citizens.[19]

Perhaps what is important as an initiative begins is to identify and shape key messages and strategies for specific constituencies within the community based on the strategic plan. For example, the message to business leaders is quite different from the message to parents or young people. Chapters Eight through Eleven give a framework for how to shape these messages to individuals, families, and organizations.

Messages that introduce the asset-building paradigm and vision need to be coupled with opportunities to learn about the approach in more depth. Without this depth, asset building never becomes a transforming force in the community. Depth can be added in a number of ways:

- Provide opportunities for people to dialogue about the assets and their implication for their organizations or families.
- Host training events or conferences for leaders as well as parents, youth, and other residents. (There are people in the community who can offer expertise in specific areas of asset building.)
- Work with individual organizations in understanding the framework and developing their own vision for asset building within the context of the larger initiative.

- Provide people with more in-depth information about the assets and how to build them. This may include a variety of print or video resources that can be distributed or loaned to interested individuals.[20]

One tool to explore in meeting information-sharing and networking needs is computer-based civic networking. The ultimate impact of the Internet on community life and relationships is still unclear. On the one hand, critics contend that sitting at a computer screen sending cryptic messages to faceless e-names only takes away time from opportunities for true relationship building. On the other side, advocates describe the potential for virtual community that is not limited by geography or national boundaries.

According to a Millennium Communications Group report, civic networking— a term used for local efforts designed to provide citizens with information and connections to each other through computers—is growing rapidly across the country. And there's a growing interest among community activists in using the Internet as a tool for organizing.[21]

Civic networks typically provide information on activities and services in the community and offer access to the Internet in public places such as libraries, youth group facilities, and mall kiosks. According to the report, "The hope with these civic networks is not only to spur access to information but to create, electronically, places of conversation, engagement, and action."[22]

Civic networking has potential as a tool in an asset-building initiative at a number of levels:

- It can be an opportunity in which youth take the lead in building the information infrastructure because of their abilities with computers.
- A civic network can support many areas of an asset-building initiative, including sharing information, helping people link with each other, and learning ideas and innovations from the community itself.
- Electronic networks also provide a forum through which people within a particular sector can dialogue with each other without having to always convene meetings.
- It can provide a safer environment in which people begin discussions of community life and community issues.
- It can link community initiatives to one another for sharing ideas and information.
- It can provide an ongoing link to resources outside the community to enhance local efforts.

In thinking about the potential of civic networking for asset building, it is intriguing to conceptualize a community network that is built around the community's vision for its youth. It could, for example, be intentional in providing information on developmental assets, and people could exchange ideas and stories about how they are taking positive action. Furthermore, the network could become a forum for dialogue and communication across sectors within a community. Although these networks may engage relatively small percentages of a city's population right now, all signs suggest that their influence will continue to explode.

Monitor, Coordinate, and Celebrate Action. Asset building is a long-term vision, not a quick fix. But as communities embark on this journey, it is important to plan for, notice, celebrate, and talk about the landmarks along the way: the new awareness of young people, the shifts in conversations, the shared enthusiasm and commitments. These stories renew energy and refocus commitment.

The first challenge, then, is to provide low-risk, immediate, and visible opportunities for involvement that point people toward the larger vision. Thus, there may be a need for hosting events in the community (marches, rallies, festivals) that provide visibility and engage people in action.

Just as important is to help people begin seeing many existing activities within the community as asset-building activities. One strategy for achieving this is for the local initiative to cosponsor existing activities within the community. Or organizations can begin tying their activities to the larger community initiative in their announcements.

In addition to providing opportunities for concrete involvement, it is also important to tell the stories of how people are getting involved and making a difference. These stories generate interest and also provide people with concrete ideas and a sense that "I can do that too."

Initiative newsletters or columns in the local newspaper can be effective vehicles for sharing and celebrating stories. The monthly *Children First* newsletter from St. Louis Park, Minnesota, includes a page of paragraph-long descriptions of what people are doing to build assets as well as specific opportunities to get involved. Electronic networking has potential for similar sharing.

Draw in Existing Institutions. At this season in growing a healthy community, a major task becomes reaching out to additional networks and institutions. If the initiative had broad initial support, many are probably already interested. Once an initiative begins, efforts are needed to shift that interest to active involvement. Here are several strategies:

- Continue to raise awareness by using people who are already committed and involved as ambassadors in their own spheres of influence, hosting informational events for organizations from each sector, and distributing information to organizations.

- Engage organizations in shaping their own vision for asset building. What would this specific company look like and do if it focused on being an asset-building force in the community and in the lives of youth?
- Provide or broker training or resources to organizations to increase their effectiveness in specific areas of asset building. For example, Ozarks Fighting Back, an asset-building initiative in Springfield, Missouri, surveyed local companies about flexible work options for families; it then developed a brochure highlighting the value of flexible options and the cost—to both workers and the companies—of not having options available.

For more information on engaging and mobilizing organizations in the community, see Chapters Ten and Eleven.

Embrace Innovations from the Community. Once people are aligned with the vision of asset building, their creativity in finding ways to nurture assets can be startling. Encouraging this innovation is key to breaking out of old patterns and discovering fresh approaches to rebuilding community for kids.

Fill Gaps with Communitywide Activities. The ultimate vision for healthy communities could be that caring for children and adolescents is taken as second nature for all residents. However, such a vision by itself is too idealistic. There need to be structured opportunities where people can learn (or relearn), practice, and be reinforced in doing the kinds of activities and behaviors that are essential to a healthy community. The hope is that these behaviors do indeed become second nature, then, and permeate all areas of community life.

A number of programs and strategies—some of which have well-established track records—have potential for building assets and contributing to healthier communities for children and adolescents. Here are four samples of community-wide emphases that can be launched or coordinated by a healthy community initiative. There may be others more appropriate to certain communities. More than prescriptive, these ideas are illustrative of the kinds of ways a community can work together on focused projects related to asset building.

• *Seeking shared values, boundaries, and commitments.* Before a community can truly unite to provide its young people with consistent and redundant expressions of boundaries and positive values, that community must first come to an understanding of those things that people hold in common. Culture wars and mistrust between the left and right have polarized and divided the nation, making unity around shared values seem like an overwhelming challenge.[23]

Several communities that have engaged in an asset-building process decided early on to focus on identifying and promoting shared values. For example, the initiative in Fridley/Hilltop/Columbia Heights (suburbs in the Twin Cities in

Minnesota) calls itself Values First. Through community meetings and a survey in the community newspaper, the initiative identified seven values that are held in common in the community: responsibility, nonviolence, self-control, citizenship, integrity, caring, and respect.

Now the communities are focusing on each of these values for one month in communitywide awareness and activities, schools, congregations, and other institutions. In addition, the community sponsored a Values First Week, featuring a wide range of activities, including workshops, school activities, and community celebrations.

Another movement focuses on recovering and building "civic values" in communities. As expressed in the work of the Institute for the Study of Civic Values, this approach focuses on the values articulated in the Preamble to the U.S. Constitution. The organization's president, Ed Schwartz, writes: "If the major purpose of the Constitution was to define the structure and powers of the government that would enable 'we the people' to achieve these goals, the Preamble was a statement of shared values and goals that the government and the American people were expected to uphold."[24]

To rebuild a commitment to these civic values, the Philadelphia-based institute focuses uniting communities around a social contract built upon "mutual obligations to promote the general welfare of their communities." The process seeks to engage residents from all walks of life in assessing their own conditions, defining how the public and private sectors can work together "to promote the 'general welfare' in relation to safety, the physical environment, children, and economic opportunity," and committing to a social contract for the community.[25]

A final, albeit overlapping, movement to rebuild shared commitments to the common good focuses on "civic engagement" and the citizenship skills of residents "to engage in public discourse, to deliberate, discuss, disagree, and negotiate."[26] This approach can take many forms:

Study circles, in which five to fifteen people form groups to break down complex issues and work through dilemmas.[27]

Community conventions, which build on the model of the New England town meetings. Often these conventions begin with multiple rounds of small forums throughout the community at which participants select a representative for future rounds of discussions.[28]

Issue forums, in which local organizations in a national network select three issues for deliberation and public dialogue for a year.[29]

Although these approaches (and others) each have unique emphases, they all contribute to identifying things community members hold in common and equipping people to reengage in community life. The framework of developmental assets can bring to these efforts a vision, focus, and motivation that tap people's shared concern and commitment to young people in the community.

• *Programming across generations.* We have noted throughout this book the prevalence of age segregation in society. This lack of contact across generations not only isolates children and adolescents from the rich resources of older generations, but it perpetuates stereotypes and competition among generations.

Rebuilding relationships and a sense of shared responsibility across generations remains an important challenge in asset-building communities. There are certainly many specific strategies to address this need, but at least two broad approaches merit consideration: intergenerational activities and mentoring relationships.

Because intergenerational relationships do not occur naturally in this culture, intentional opportunities must be created to begin the process of relationship building. A number of efforts are under way to develop programs with an intergenerational focus. These include intergenerational choruses and music and theater groups, intergenerational retreats, and day care centers that serve both senior citizens and young children. The goal is to find mutually beneficial ways to match the generations for growth and learning. According to a report by the National Association of State Units on Aging, several intergenerational group homes are being explored and developed as alternatives to traditional institutional care.[30]

On another level are efforts for existing organizations and programs to develop intergenerational activities that bring youth and adults together for learning, fun, and relationship building.

Ideas for Intergenerational Activities

What Groups of Adults Can Initiate

1. Eat lunch with young people in the school cafeteria. Try to have two adults sit at each table.
2. Recruit senior citizens to wait with children at school bus stops throughout your community.
3. Start a book club where adults take turns reading books to children for a half hour every Saturday.
4. Bring healthy treats to a practice for young people playing on a football, tennis, soccer, or other team.
5. Whenever you plan an intergenerational event, always include one fun question that gives everyone a chance to talk.

What Groups of Young People Can Initiate

6. Plan a neighborhood art show. Display children's and adults' artwork, crafts, and hobbies.

7. Put up holiday decorations for people who otherwise wouldn't have them.
8. Set up a bicycle or walking club for youth and adults. Get together once a month to take a trip.
9. Organize a group of youth and adults to decorate a yard, several yards, or a whole block for a holiday. Then have a party.
10. Plan a grandparent party. Invite a grandparent (either yours or borrowed). Then celebrate grandparents and grandchildren.[31]

Intergenerational activities often include certain components:

- Concrete, shared experiences in which all ages can participate
- Group tasks related to the shared experience
- Opportunities for young people and adults to reflect and share based on their experience

There are clearly other ways to build and enhance intergenerational relationships. Some involve informal efforts in neighborhoods and other associations. However, intentional programs and activities can provide the structure and impetus needed to begin the process of rebuilding relationships—a process that continues in informal ways once relationships are established.[32]

Another widely touted approach to enhancing intergenerational connection involves forming mentoring relationships between adults and youth wherein the adult becomes a resource to the young person.

Although mentoring is usually equated with a one-to-one, long-term relationship between an adult and a young person, a Search Institute report suggests that there are five types of mentoring relationships, all of which can benefit both young people and adults:

1. *Traditional:* this category encompasses programs that many think of as typical: one adult in a friendship-oriented role-model relationship with one child.
2. *Long-term, focused activity:* these programs focus on a particular goal or outcome, over and above friendship or role modeling. They are sometimes remedial in nature, as in tutoring programs for underachieving students, but they are often designed to build on existing skills and abilities to encourage or promote academic progress or career exploration and skills.
3. *Short-term, focused activity:* programs in this category also focus on a particular area such as school or careers but do not require mentors to make more than a six-month commitment.
4. *Team mentoring:* team mentoring occurs when more than one adult volunteer works with a young person. This may be a family, or two (or more) unrelated adults, working together.

5. *Group mentoring:* group mentoring occurs when one adult volunteer works with a small group of young people. Girl Scouts, for instance, are beginning to view their volunteer troop leaders and assistants as mentors.[33]

Expanding the understanding and definition of mentoring opens new opportunities for adults to connect with young people in meaningful ways. With appropriate screening, training, and matching, these relationships can be laboratories for how a whole community reaches out to care for all of its children and youth.

Related to adult/youth mentoring relationships is the opportunity to train adolescents to be mentors to younger children and to play an active role in children's lives. This emphasis has the potential to broaden the volunteer base for children's programs (such as child care centers, in-school tutoring, etc.), and also provide adolescents with much-needed opportunities for leadership and responsibility.

• *Providing opportunities for service for all ages.* While social activities, block parties, and other opportunities of helping people form relationships play an important role in an asset-building community, they cannot alone cultivate the deeper bonds and commitments out of which true community emerges. A key strategy for moving people to a deeper commitment to the community is to engage residents of all ages in service to the community. These experiences can be powerful in providing assistance to others and enhancing a person's own relationships and competencies.[34]

Most communities already have a number of service-related efforts under way: service-learning programs in schools, volunteer programs for seniors and other adults, volunteer centers, numerous agencies that rely on volunteers, and active service emphases in religious congregations, to name a few. Yet these efforts often are not seen within the larger framework of community building. Nor are they coordinated in ways that engage as many residents as possible in some sort of volunteer or service efforts.

We envision communities undertaking a major strategy under the umbrella of asset building that focuses on providing a cross-sector, multigenerational network of service opportunities in the community, combined with easily accessible systems through which individuals can tap into the opportunities. These may include:

- Service-learning opportunities for elementary through college students that bring educational institutions and community agencies into partnership.[35]
- Opportunities for families to engage in service together, beginning when children are in preschool and continuing through at least adolescence. These service opportunities can be powerful in strengthening family life and relationships. They can be offered through agencies, schools, youth organizations, congregations, and others.

- A consistent emphasis on service opportunities in nonschool programs for children and youth, including community clubs and organizations, and congregations.[36] These programs, too, should be offered in partnership with community organizations dedicated to providing services.
- An ongoing program to engage adults (particularly senior citizens) in service to children and youth. This may include school volunteer programs and a volunteer clearinghouse for youth-serving programs, parks and recreation programs, and congregational youth programs. Integrated into these opportunities should be training in asset building and opportunities to build skills in relating to youth.
- An often untapped and overlooked service opportunity is intentionally designed intergenerational service projects. These may be special projects that involve all generations in developmentally appropriate tasks. Or it may involve coordinated activities among some of the previously described approaches.

In addition to direct service to people in need, an emphasis on service in the community can engage people in community planning and community enhancement opportunities. For example, many communities use volunteer energies (from all generations) to create child-friendly playgrounds and parks. Others actively engage volunteers in identifying resources and needs in the community. In these ways, the service opportunities not only enhance people's bond to the community but also contribute substantively to its betterment.

- *Recreating spaces for children and adolescents.* For all practical purposes, young people have been designed out of many parts of communities. Safe sidewalks for children's bicycles have been replaced with wide streets for cars. Youth have fewer and fewer safe, enriching places to hang out, and they are increasingly viewed as nuisances in malls and other retail areas.

Even homes have been taken over by adults. David Elkind notes, for example, that until recently basements in middle-class homes were most often reserved for children's play areas. Today, however these spaces "have been allocated . . . to the needs of adults rather than children"—library, in-home office, artist's studio, etc.[37]

The impact of these changes is compounded by the fact that communities have fewer and fewer places for public gatherings. Ray Oldenburg argues that "[Americans] are encouraged to find their relaxation, entertainment, companionship, even safety, almost entirely within the privacy of homes that have become more a retreat from society than a connection to it."[38] An asset-building perspective challenges communities to find ways to create structures and spaces that are conducive to enhancing relationships and building connections within the community.

A consistent message we hear from young people is that there are few places for them to spend time in their community. School often ends early in the afternoon, and parents do not come home until the supper hour. Malls and other stores are often unwelcoming, and there is a growing call for laws against loitering and curfews to keep youth out of crime.

Even though some of these efforts may be necessary, the net result is that young people have fewer and fewer places to spend time. Furthermore, many of the remaining options (public parks, street corners, unmonitored homes) become breeding grounds for negative activities. In short, we have failed to provide the kind of constructive activities and spaces that can contribute to young people's healthy development.

There are probably two different needs to be addressed here. One is to provide structured opportunities for growth for children and youth. These may include well-structured after-school programs, community clubs and athletic activities, and congregational youth programs.[39]

A major initiative in this area is the MOST Initiative (Making the Most of Out-of-School Time) funded by the DeWitt Wallace–Reader's Digest Fund. Coordinated by the Center for Research on Women at Wellesley College, the $6.5 million project is designed to stimulate systematic change to improve the quality and availability of out-of-school care for children. The communities involved are Boston, Chicago, and Seattle.[40]

The other need is for what Ray Oldenburg calls "third places." These are safe places where young people can "hang out." He identifies a number of characteristics of such informal settings of public life:

- They need to offer neutral ground where people can gather and come and go, where no one plays host, and where everyone feels comfortable.
- They need to be "levelers," that is, inclusive and accessible to the general public.
- The main activity is conversation. There may be games and other activities, but they should only be a backdrop to the conversation. (A synagogue on Long Island, New York, has a youth room equipped with games that require at least two people to play, thus reinforcing relationships and social interaction.)
- These places must be accessible and accommodating to the people who gather.
- There are a core of "regulars" who make the place come alive and give it its character.
- The facility isn't the focus; the relationships are. The building should have a low profile and not attract attention to itself.
- The mood is playful; laughter and acceptance are norms.
- The third places are like homes away from home in that people feel connected, feel a sense of ownership, relaxed, and warm.[41]

Establish Mechanisms for Evaluation. Too often, people do not think of evaluation as a task until it is too late to set up the mechanisms by which to effectively evaluate the effort. Yet evaluation can have several important purposes in an initiative. These include providing information about the initiative to assess progress and make changes, examining whether the initiative is meeting its goals, holding people accountable to funders and other stakeholders, and promoting public relations capacities. In addition, evaluation activities can also build new skills and relationships as people in the community participate in the process.[42]

Evaluation can be relatively straightforward or very complex, depending on its purpose. The range of possibilities, each with its own strengths and limitations:

• Gathering stories and examples that show what seems to be working and what is not is the simplest and least costly technique. These stories can be powerful and helpful in creating energy, identifying problem spots, and encouraging replication, but they are not adequate in and of themselves for systematic evaluation.

• Holding focus groups, interviews, site visits, and other approaches to gather qualitative information that can point to patterns and needs. These groups are invaluable in identifying key issues, but they are less useful in giving hard numbers or generalizing to the whole community.

• Gathering cross-sectional data from youth and adults regarding assets, activities, and attitudes. This typically involves telephone polls or written surveys of a representative group of people (all high school students, for example) at two different times, perhaps three to five years apart. This approach is valuable in looking for changes, but it is difficult to assert causal relationships between the initiative and specific changes in youth asset levels or adult attitudes. This approach tends to be more costly and requires involvement of qualified evaluation professionals.

• Gathering longitudinal and comparative data by tracking individual adolescents and adults across time. Ideally, this approach would match communities having asset-building initiatives with others that do not have similar efforts. This approach is very costly and complex, but the results are the most credible and precise.

Each of these evaluation techniques (and others) has a place in a healthy community initiative. Selecting the type depends on the community's needs and resources. Making decisions early on about the appropriate methods and then building systems to support the approach helps guide and support the community effort.

Documenting Progress in Creating a Healthy Community

What would be the signs and symbols that an asset-building movement uniting citizens and systems was taking hold? It could be documented at a number of levels:

- There would be longitudinal evidence that assets are increasing.
- There would be measurable change in the percentage of adults who accept this responsibility and capacity, and who take action.
- Policy makers (city council, school board, county commissioners, congregational councils) would use the asset framework to inform decisions.
- Conversations around water coolers, on the sidewalk in the neighborhood, and at office parties would more often focus on spending time and building relationships with children and adolescents.
- Youth would become more visible when people are discussing civic affairs and community life.
- On school board issues, as many people without children as those with children would support efforts to improve the education of that community's children.
- Property values would increase as word spread that this community is a place whose heart and soul has moved to placing young people first.

Season 4: Tending the Growing Garden

Spring turns to summer. The enthusiastic energy of spring planting gives way to the slow growth of summer. Other, newer activities deflect energy. And, frankly, some of the work of cultivating isn't much fun. Many gardeners stick with it in anticipation of the harvest, but others become distracted, and the garden can quickly be taken over by weeds.

The same thing can happen in a healthy-communities initiative. Indeed, one of the most common questions we hear is, "How do you maintain momentum after you get started?" Just as the summer is an essential part of the growing cycle, so too is this stage an essential part of developing the initiative.

Keep the End in Mind. When gardening, some people are motivated because they enjoy the day-to-day tasks. But if that is not always the case, at least they remember what results from their toil at harvest time.

The same principle holds true for asset building. Keeping the vision front and center is vital to keeping the initiative alive. Each new opportunity should be evaluated in light of the vision, and activities should be monitored to determine how they are moving the community toward its vision. Furthermore, it is also important for that vision to become deeply understood and embedded in the lives of individuals and the structures of organizations within the community.

Do Not Neglect Maintenance Tasks. The major trait needed for a spring planting might be energy and eagerness, but the most important traits for the summer months are patience and perseverance. Dozens of maintenance tasks need to be done in tending the growing plants to ensure that they have optimal growing conditions. A healthy community initiative includes some of these maintenance tasks:

- Communicating regularly among different people involved in asset-building efforts
- Continuing to raise awareness of the initiative, its activities, opportunities, and successes throughout the community
- Prompting new individuals and organizations to get involved in the initiative (from participation in the vision team to volunteering in an asset-building effort in a specific organization)
- Drawing new people and organizations into implementation
- Training individuals and leaders in the skills they need to be effective in asset-building efforts
- Pulling "weeds" by addressing potential traps, conflicts, and resistance to the initiative[43]
- Improving the system for involvement so that it is easier and more enriching for people to get involved and stay involved
- Building financial support to sustain the initiative, and leveraging new resources (financial, human, in-kind) to support the vision
- Promoting cooperation among organizations in communitywide activities

Network with Other Communities. One of the pleasures of gardening is talking with other gardeners. Sharing secrets to success. Bragging about the earliest or biggest or most bountiful harvest. These over-the-fence conversations both share useful information and have a way of keeping interest and enthusiasm alive.

Although many communities have begun asset-building initiatives, the vision is only in its infancy. No one knows all the answers, and no one knows how everything will work. But each community is learning something new every day.

Renew the Energy. Gardeners keep their energy going through the summer in different ways. Some regularly meander through their patch admiring what they see. Some get together with neighbors to share in the tasks. Others enjoy nibbling on the first vegetables and fruits as they ripen on the vine.

Renewing energy in a community initiative can occur in several ways. Here are some suggestions:

- Integrate new leadership into the initiative at many levels, particularly as early leaders rotate out of leadership roles. Work to bring new people's ideas, perspectives, and energy into alignment with the vision.

- Highlight the hidden benefits of initiative. For example, remind people of the many benefits of cross-sector communication that extend beyond asset building.
- Add incentives or awards for people and organizations that become active in the initiative. Some communities have begun naming an "Asset Builder of the Year," who is honored at a community celebration. Others are developing "membership" programs through which businesses and other organizations can qualify to become an asset-building organization for that community.

Season 5: Harvest

In some ways, it is inaccurate to place harvesting as a different season and as the final season. It gives too much of a sense of closure and finality, when, in fact, harvesting begins early and can continue for decades. Perhaps a better image is of the traditional annual garden as a patch of perennial flowers that bloom year after year, particularly if properly cared for.

The question emerges in healthy-communities work: How do you know when the efforts bear fruit? The question is best answered if efforts are made early to name goals and outcomes and then document progress along the way.

Doing a formal evaluation of initiative outcomes requires an in-depth knowledge of evaluation methods. However, less formal information gathering can be important and useful as well. Gathering stories of what has happened, listening to people say how the efforts have affected them, adding up numbers of activities and people involved, and reflecting on the process can all be fodder for evaluation and sources for celebration.

In addition to evaluation, there are specific tasks to be addressed at "harvest time." First, it is important to celebrate and share the harvest. Similarly, it is important to honor and affirm the people who have been involved. Finally, harvest time means bringing closure to efforts that are no longer needed as central to the initiative and preparing the soil for new efforts so that the growing cycle can continue.

Gardening Is Not an Exact Science

Careful soil analysis, meticulous planting of seeds, and careful tending of garden patches do not guarantee a bountiful harvest. Conversely, a hastily planted and then neglected garden can yield delicious vegetables. The odds are better for the garden that is appropriately cared for. But there are no guarantees.

The same is true for healthy-communities work. There are tools, processes, strategies, and resources that have been useful in many communities. Many of them have been tested and found to be effective. Yet there are no guarantees.

Furthermore, we are only in the early seasons of understanding asset building and healthy communities. People in communities continue to experiment with new ideas and new techniques. They will develop hybrids that have their own unique characteristics. They will learn methods that greatly improve on the methods we know today.

The task, then, is to use the skills and knowledge we have today, but be on the lookout for other ways of doing things. The result is ever-improving ways to ensure a better future for the children and adolescents in our communities.

CHAPTER EIGHT

THE POWER OF ONE

Engaging Individuals

Virtually every major social movement in this nation has begun with individuals making a personal commitment to addressing a need or a cause in their own lives, their community, or their world. The seeds for public schools, libraries, civil rights, and many other important traditions in our society were planted by individuals who saw a need and took personal responsibility for action, mobilizing others, and creating needed change.

Building young people's foundation of assets is no different. In fact, personal commitments to building relationships with youth is critical to the success of the movement. No matter how much money is spent, how many elaborate programs are initiated, how many laws are passed, or how many professionals are hired, the experiences of young people do not fundamentally change unless individuals—parents, youth, neighbors, friends, grandparents, and others—take personal responsibility to contribute to young people's healthy development.

In calling for a strategic focus on mobilizing individuals, it is important to caution that few communities using the asset approach have systematically addressed engaging individuals in widespread action over a sustained time. Therefore, the framework in this chapter primarily relies on translating for asset building the significant theoretical and practical work that others have done in mobilizing individuals for action. As our efforts continue and communities implement these strategies, we learn a great deal more about the specific opportunities and challenges of asset building for mobilizing individuals to make long-term, life-transforming commitments to youth.

The Challenges of Engaging Individuals

Calling for individual responsibility and action sets a more challenging agenda than simply calling for institutional and government action. Although institutions and government are struggling with insufficient resources and deep-seated inefficiencies, at least they are organized to take concerted action—if, of course, that action is undergirded by ample financial resources.

In contrast, individuals have gotten used to not taking responsibility and action, and there are few efficient mechanisms (such as grant money) that promote their taking action. Several realities stand as barriers to widespread commitments to asset building by individuals. We note several in Chapter Five, in discussing critical shifts in thinking and culture that are necessary for asset building. These include a sense of disempowerment in the face of overwhelming problems among youth, an individualistic culture that encourages people to say, "They're not my kids," and a broad sense of civic disengagement. In addition, other realities also merit mention.

Time Constraints

A frequently heard reason people do not get actively involved in young people's lives is a perceived lack of time. Many youth programs struggle to find volunteers to work with youth. Several social trends likely contribute to this, including the increased involvement of women in the workplace and increasing work or commuting hours for many workers.

Discomfort with Youth

Compounding the time problem, adults who have little or no interaction with children or adolescents are at best uncomfortable with them, and in many cases afraid of them. Part of the difficulty is also that young people are largely portrayed as problems. Several years ago, a poll of Minnesota youth found that two-thirds of young people believe adults in their community hold negative views of them.[1]

Different Perceptions of Need

Another reason adults may not be actively engaged in young people's lives is that their views of societal issues are very different from those of professionals who care for children and therefore seek to engage others in caring.

In its focus groups with a cross-section of American adults, Public Agenda found that people are deeply concerned about kids, but they define the problems very differently from how child advocates do. "Although our respondents do express concern about children," the researchers write, "no one spontaneously defines the problem as the child advocates do. What concerns them most are quite different problems: crime, sex and drugs in schools, consumerist values in society and lack of discipline in the home."[2]

Breakdown of Trust

In the end, perhaps the most difficult barrier to individuals' getting involved is the breakdown of trust in our culture. Fear keeps doors locked and neighbors apart. Instead of living in a communitywide culture of care, children are taught not to talk to strangers or eat cookies received from a neighbor. Many adults are afraid to show affection to children because of fears of accusations of abuse. Others are afraid to volunteer in youth programs because of fear of litigation if a tragedy occurs "on their watch." The result is that people do not feel safe to reach out, risk, get involved.

Characteristics of Asset-Building Adults

Before we can examine specific ways to overcome these barriers to action, it is helpful to examine what asset-building adults are like in terms of their attitudes and actions, for changes in adults' attitudes and behaviors are essential to the success of asset-building efforts. Marian Wright Edelman puts the need this way:

> It is time for adults of every race and income group to break our silence about the pervasive breakdown of moral, family, and community values, to place our children first in our lives, and to struggle to model the behavior we want our children to learn. Our "youth problem" is not a youth problem, it is an adult problem, as our children do what they see us adults doing in our personal, professional, and public lives. They seek our attention in negative ways when we provide them too few positive ways to communicate how to get the attention and love they need.[3]

This discussion opens up possibilities and suggests a vision toward which we seek to move people, individually and collectively. It is also an important reminder that just as we seek to build internal assets in youth, there are values and character issues that shape adults' actions and commitments related to children and adolescents. Sustained behavioral changes and action (doing) are thwarted if attention is not also paid to the personal qualities (being). We look at two categories of "being" characteristics and two categories of "doing" characteristics in Table 8.1.

TABLE 8.1. CHARACTERISTICS OF ASSET-BUILDING ADULTS (SUMMARY).

	"Being" Characteristics
Attitudes Toward Youth	• Values young people for who they are, not just who they will become • Has a sense of hope and optimism for young people and the future • Recognizes personal responsibility for youth in the community • Celebrates the gifts, commitments, and zeal of the adolescent years
Character and Competencies	• Has a personal foundation for healthy growth and development • Personally experiences assets (e.g., support, appropriate boundaries, self-restraint, self-esteem) • Has relational skills (conversation skills, skills for dealing with conflict, etc.) • Is trusting and trustworthy
	"Doing" Characteristics
Relationships with Children and Adolescents	• Takes the initiative in building relationships with young people • Respects and affirms young people; seeks to understand them • Spends time with young people; is actively engaged • Builds long-term relationships with young people • Balances protecting the young person with need for independence in ways that are appropriate to the young person's age and development • Models healthy attitudes and choices, including service, lifelong learning, civic involvement, and self-restraint • Never violates or takes advantage of a young person's trust
Other Actions	• Makes caring for children and adolescents a lifelong priority • Looks out for the best interests of children and adolescents in the community and the nation through advocacy, civic engagement, and political action

Attitudes Toward Youth

The lenses through which an adult views young people greatly influence his or her ability to build assets. If youth are viewed as problems, the adult is much less likely to treat youth with respect. At best, a problem-focused worldview leads to a condescending, paternalistic attitude under which young people chafe.

In contrast, asset-building adults show respect for and confidence in young people consistent with the young person's developmental stage. They value young people for who they are, not just who they are becoming. They celebrate the gifts, commitments, and zeal of the adolescent years, rather than dismissing it as an "idealistic phase."

Character and Competencies

One of the things that have become clear in our discussions with people in this area is the importance of building the asset base for adults so that they are equipped to build assets for and in youth. (See Chapter Four on assets for adults.) Adults who lack adequate support in their lives, for example, may be unable to provide healthy support to young people. Adults who do not have their own sense of boundaries have difficulty in monitoring and enforcing boundaries for children and adolescents.

Since relationship building is at the core of asset building, core competencies for asset-building adults are relational skills. One of the first concerns we hear as we talk about the importance of building relationships with youth is a concern that "I can't relate to youth" or "I don't know what I'd say or do." Building those basic skills must be part of any asset-building effort.

Finally, and most importantly, asset-building adults must be trusting and trust-worthy. A fundamental task of young children is to discover whether the world and the significant people in it are trustworthy. Too many young people have had their lives thrown into disarray by adults who took advantage of them, abused them, or otherwise undermined their trust. A William T. Grant Foundation report stated that "young people . . . do not tend to seek out adults whom they perceive to be highly judgmental or adults whom they believe will not respect their confidences."[4]

Relationships

Out of these internal qualities emerge quality relationships with youth and other actions on behalf of children and adolescents. The key here is that adults become proactive in seeking, building, and sustaining relationships.

Being proactive is vital for a number of reasons. First, being proactive is part of taking personal responsibility for young people's well-being. Second, many young people may not be interested in forming caring relationships with adults. This is due, in part, to the developmental changes of adolescence. Young people greatly want and benefit from relationships with adults, but they are also forming their own identity and independence. The Grant commission report summarized the tension this way: "At the core of the relationship between youth and adults lies a tension between the young person's need to experiment and to take risks and the adult's efforts to keep them from making mistakes. Yet, for young people, developing responsibility is partly an experience of having the chance to make mistakes from which they can learn powerful lessons. Keeping this tension in a delicate balance, allowing young people to grow in their capacity to be responsible without overprotecting them, is a difficult obligation that adults must assume."[5]

We should be quick to note, however, that this tension is not adequate reason to disengage from young people's lives. Much more important is finding appropriate ways to maintain a growing, changing, and sustained relationship with a maturing young person.

Adults may find many different opportunities for building relationships with youth. Some may be relationships in the extended family, neighborhood, social networks, the workplace, volunteer activities in youth-serving programs, or vocational commitments to serving youth.

Other Actions

In addition to building relationships with individual children and adolescents, an asset-building adult is also involved in other activities that affect young people's well-being. (These activities are often motivated and energized by personal connections with young people.) They may take the form of involvement in youth-serving organizations as well as civic or political action on behalf of youth.

What Is Left Out

Several widely assumed characteristics are intentionally left out of this list. Embedded in our culture are several stereotypes about the kinds of people who can best build relationships with children and adolescents. These myths come through in some of the excuses people give for not getting involved:

- "I don't have kids, so I really can't relate to them." (Having children is not a prerequisite for forming a caring relationship.)
- "Kids don't want to spend time with old folks like me." (Older Americans are an undervalued and underutilized resource for children and youth, and rich relationships form across generations. You don't have to be young to relate to youth.)
- "I'm not athletic or anything." (Neither are some young people, who need relationships, not high-achieving heroes.)

The point here is that the things young people need from adults do not depend on family status, age, abilities, income, or similar issues. Rather, young people need caring, principled people who are committed to them. To be sure, there are adults who have not developed these qualities—and there are adults with negative, harmful qualities who should be isolated from children and youth. But with the appropriate commitment, support, and encouragement, most adults can cultivate the capacity to make a tremendous difference for young people.

Moving Individuals Toward Asset-Building Lifestyles

Whereas the focus on everyone's power and potential as an asset builder is both hopeful and empowering, it also raises critical questions about how to engage people in this movement. People who seek to mobilize residents of their communities ask:

- How do we break through the barriers that keep people from getting involved?
- With people already feeling overwhelmed by responsibilities, how will they react to another call for something they "should" be doing?
- How do we overcome the fears people have about getting involved?
- How do we deepen commitments to asset building so that people do not stop with individual, infrequent action?

The emerging field of social marketing has much to offer in thinking about these questions. According to Alan R. Andreasen in *Marketing Social Change*, social marketing seeks to apply the technologies of commercial marketing to solving social problems that involve behavioral changes.[6] Unlike other approaches to social change that focus specifically on education, persuasion, or behavior modification, social marketing provides a more comprehensive framework that addresses change dynamics on several levels. Andreasen identifies four stages of personal behavioral change that provide a helpful framework for this discussion: precontemplation, contemplation, action, and maintenance.

Precontemplation

Many people in communities are unaware of the important role they can play in young people's healthy development. Even those who are involved daily in young people's lives may not be conscious of their own potential, and responsibility, as asset builders. Furthermore, their views of children and adolescents may interfere with their abilities to form positive relationships.

Moving people from little knowledge or personal investment toward active contemplation of their role primarily involves exposing people to the message so that they pay attention, getting them to like or become interested, and then comprehend what is said. This process involves using educational techniques and tools of awareness raising that are carefully aimed at the *real* needs, concerns, and perceptions of community members. Andreasen writes: "Social marketers' interest is not in telling customers everything that they could tell them or trying to change every value that could be changed. They focus on those educational and propaganda elements that are likely to influence behavior—or move potential customers on to the next stage in the behavior-change process."[7]

Several tasks are central at this early stage. Fundamental to social marketing is an emphasis on listening to people's views of themselves, young people, and the community. Without this clear understanding, messages are unlikely to communicate. For example, is the reason for noninvolvement fear, or apathy, or paralysis, or lack of opportunity? The answer dramatically shapes the messages and the approaches.

Fifteen Ways to Show Kids You Care

One way to motivate people to take initial action is to provide concrete, simple things they can do. The following ideas (excerpted from an awareness-raising pamphlet) suggest some of the ways people can start building assets.

1. Notice them.
2. Learn their names.
3. Remember their birthdays.
4. Ask them about themselves.
5. Play with them.
6. Listen to their stories.
7. Ask them for their opinions.
8. Delight in their discoveries.
9. Contribute to their collections.
10. Laugh at their jokes.
11. Keep the promises you make.
12. Meet their friends.
13. Help them become expert at something.
14. Write a chalk message on their sidewalk.
15. Love them—no matter what.

Source: Excerpted with permission from *150 Ways to Show Kids You Care.* Copyright © 1996 by Search Institute, Minneapolis, Minnesota.

The second key task is to make connections between asset building and the targeted audience. These connections, of course, vary considerably depending on the audience. Connections need to be made at several levels:

• The benefits for the specific audience of getting involved. The initial messages must include appeals to self-interest and perceived needs, not just altruism.

- How asset building connects to the audience's values and the values of their peers. This task is one that can be enhanced through endorsements from respected people in the community.
- How asset building connects with their own power and potential. Perhaps the most common response we receive when we speak to community members about assets is energetic enthusiasm that, finally, there is something concrete they can do that makes a difference.
- How asset building connects with their daily lives and world. This may involve showing the opportunities they have every day to interact with youth.

The third key task at the precontemplation stage is to focus the message on the areas that move them to the next stage, not necessarily to a full commitment yet. This means starting small and not overwhelming people with all the implications, costs, risks, and possibilities.

This task of focusing can be particularly challenging with a comprehensive framework of assets that has profound implications for many areas of people's lives. When we began some of our early asset-building work with one organization, we presented reams of paper filled with ideas and possibilities and implications. About thirty minutes into the discussion, someone stopped the discussion and said: "I'm totally confused with all these pieces. I need to know what these assets are. Maybe later we can talk about the other stuff."

Contemplation

Once you've gotten people's attention and they see the potential of asset building, they begin to evaluate the place of asset building in their own lives. What are the pros and cons of getting involved? How does it fit with other responsibilities and commitments? What could I really do? Andreasen writes: "At the beginning of the contemplation stage, they may have limited information and will have formed only vague intentions. However, as they progress, they will become more and more involved in the issue, gather more and more information, and take a reasonable length of time before deciding to go ahead."[8]

The key task in the contemplation stage is to change the cost-benefit balance for asset building in comparison to its "competition"—most importantly, the status quo. "Other things being equal," Andreasen writes, "behavior is likely to occur if and when . . . consumers conclude that, on balance, it is better to go ahead with the recommended behavior than with its competition."[9] Andreasen outlines five possible strategies that the social marketer (or change advocate) can employ at this stage:

1. Increase the expected gains.
2. Decrease the expected costs.
3. Increase the present social pressure.
4. Improve the consumer's ability to act.
5. Decrease the desirability of competitive alternatives.[10]

The asset-building approach can be promoted through all of these strategies. However, Andreasen cautions against trying to do everything at once. He notes that few efforts have the kind of resources necessary to undertake all the strategies simultaneously and effectively. In addition, using multiple strategies can confuse the audience. Finally, the strategies may be incompatible and send mixed messages.

So how do you decide which approaches to take, and when? The answers to several questions help shape your choices.

1. Which is a greater barrier: perceived benefits or barriers? In some cases the benefits may be obvious, but the costs are high. In others, the costs may be low, but the perceived benefits are not strong enough to move people out of the status quote and into action.

2. Where are people in the contemplation process? The importance of an emphasis on the benefits and costs shifts across time. Early in the contemplation stage, the benefits are most important. But as people come closer to making a commitment, they focus more attention on the costs. So knowing where people are in their thinking is critical in selecting a strategy.

3. How much is the audience's behavior influenced by others? In some situations, influential leaders can have tremendous impact on whether people change their behaviors. For example, a supervisor can have considerable influence on how an employee performs a job. Whereas influential leaders can shape a *community's* commitment to asset building, they are less likely to wield such influence over an *individual's* daily commitment to caring for youth.

At the same time, virtually all adult behaviors are shaped by perceived social norms and pressure. For example, we have become a society that does not expect— and even opposes—neighbors to say something to a parent when a child misbehaves. We expect each other to have a jaded view of adolescence. In many circles, it is taboo to talk about the values that we hold and share. Addressing these forms of social pressure, though difficult, is an important part of the community change process.

Thus influential people can help reshape social norms through their public commitments and advocacy for asset building. Some communities have developed a phased-in campaign that first communicates the asset-building vision to opinion leaders in the community, who in turn communicate to specific target constituencies. For example, presentations to service organizations (such as Lions

Clubs, Rotary, Kiwanis) can help reach community and business leaders who become champions for asset building within their own spheres of influence.

4. Does the audience believe it has the power and capacity to act? Because people have become paralyzed by the overwhelming problems they associate with children and adolescents, many do not feel they can make a difference in young people's lives. Creating this sense of personal power is often the final task in moving people from contemplation toward action.[11]

A sense of powerlessness can come from two general sources, both of which may need to be addressed. The first is that of internal components: a person does not perceive that she "has the skills and knowledge to take the proposed action." Second are the external factors: she does not feel circumstances are such to allow the action to happen.[12] Feelings of powerlessness may be particularly strong among people who have become disenfranchised in society, such as those with low incomes or limited education.

We encounter feelings of powerlessness coming from both of these sources when we talk with people about asset building. Many adults, for example, do not feel they have the skills or abilities to interact effectively with children or youth (particularly when they think of all the problems associated with youth). Furthermore, they are often at a loss for where to find opportunities to take action. The tasks of the asset-building advocate in this area are to help individuals see that they can, indeed, do things to build assets, while also providing opportunities to enhance their skills and comfort levels (by practicing, observing, or simulating the skills), and to make available concrete, low-risk, low-cost opportunities to take the first steps of action.

Bridget Gothberg, president-elect of the National Community Education Association and an advocate of asset building, sees addressing these issues as critical. "Adults today, because they are so busy, need two things in place before they commit. One, they need to be asked. I can't tell you the number of people who say to me, 'Nobody ever asked me before.' And, two, adults need to know exactly what the time commitment and what the expectations are."[13]

Action

Though it is important to answer all the questions in the contemplation stage, this does not guarantee that people who intend to act will actually do it. Complicating the problem, Andreasen writes, is the fact that there is scant research on the triggers for action. Thus he focuses on what is known about the barriers to action and suggests that each can be overcome with straightforward strategies. Table 8.2 depicts the barriers and strategies for an asset-building strategy, based on Andreasen's framework.

TABLE 8.2. OVERCOMING BARRIERS TO ACTION.

Barrier	Strategy	Asset-Building Strategies and Examples
Action is impossible	Make the impossible possible	• Encourage asset building as a part of everyday interactions that people already do. • Make opportunities for asset building readily available with little extra effort. • Advocate free or low-cost asset-building activities, or find ways to subsidize (or find sponsors for) activities that cost money.
Action is too complex	Make the complex simple	• Identify simple things people can do that get them started ("Look at and acknowledge young people when you see them on the street.") • Introduce actions in stages. Start with low-risk, low-commitment actions and gradually provide opportunities to increase the commitment.
Action requires too much time	Minimize the time inconvenience	• Highlight asset-building actions that add value to existing commitments and activities. • Bring training and education into people's existing schedules. For example, offer parenting workshops during lunch breaks at work.
Action isn't a priority	Increase the urgency	• Get people to make a personal commitment to specific asset-building activities as early as possible. • Have influencers, family members, and friends support and encourage action. • Tie action to specific dates, events, or celebrations.
Action is forgotten	Abolish forgetting	• Regularly remind people to take action and fulfill their commitments, particularly in places where they can actually take the action on the spot. (Placemats or table-top displays in fast-food restaurants with asset-building conversation starters could serve this purpose.) • Use posters, refrigerator magnets, bumper stickers, public service announcements, and other devices as reminders.

Note: This chart is based on Andreasen's description (pp. 277–280) of the barriers to and strategies for moving people from contemplation to action. Andreasen, A. R. (1995). *Marketing Social Change.* San Francisco: Jossey-Bass.

In moving people into action, it is important also to note the different types of action that may be appropriate for different people. Some people may be ready for long-term commitments, while others may only be ready to take one-time action or action that requires no extra commitment of time or resources. Once again, the goal is not to plunge individuals immediately into long-term, sustained commitments to asset building but to nudge them in that direction. The task, then, is to identify concrete action at different levels of commitment and a strategy for building commitment and involvement over time.

There are a number of concrete ways that you as an individual can take action for asset building. Here are some kinds of action a community initiative can encourage by community residents:

- View youth and youth issues through an asset-building lens. Whether you're reading the newspaper or talking with friends, interpret youth issues not in terms of problems but by identifying strengths you can help build or opportunities you can offer.
- Build sustained relationships with youth. Identify two or three young people with whom you would like to develop a lasting relationship. They may be through your extended family, social networks, or neighborhood. Or link with a young person through a formal mentoring program.
- Rebuild connections and commitments in your neighborhood. Get to know your neighbors, including their children. Organize informal get-togethers. Encourage people to watch out for kids. If your neighborhood has an organized association, identify creative ways to use this network to build assets.
- Get involved in youth-serving programs. Many programs struggle with inadequate resources. Volunteering in and donating to these programs strengthens their ability to build assets in youth.
- Influence organizations and networks. Share your perspectives with a group of friends who get together informally to watch football or play cards. Or encourage a corporation or organization to contribute some of its philanthropic resources to asset-building efforts.
- Advocate on behalf of youth. Attend a neighborhood meeting or caucus to encourage a proactive approach to addressing the needs of young people. Speak out about concerns that are raised about young people. Meet with or write to a public official to support legislation that can contribute to asset building.

Maintenance

Some asset-building actions are one-time commitments (attending an event, participating in a service project, sharing information with a friend). Others may involve longer commitments, even if they come to an end (volunteering in a youth program, helping build a youth center, being a mentor for a young person).

However, there are also asset-building behaviors and actions that need to become a way of life. They involve permanent lifestyle changes (such as forming ongoing relationships with young people and spending discretionary time and income in ways that benefit young people) or actions that you want people to carry out when they are in particular situations (how they treat youth who come into their store, how they vote on children's issues). These last two types require not only moving people to action but helping them maintain their involvement and commitment. Prochaska and DiClemente describe the maintenance stage in the change process (based on a therapeutic focus) this way: "Maintenance is the stage in which people work to continue the gains attained through action and to prevent relapse to their more troubled level of functioning. Maintenance is thus not an absence of change but a continuance of change. . . . Maintenance tends to be a rather lengthy stage, usually lasting at least six months before the person no longer fears relapsing, but frequently lasting years and even a lifetime."[14]

Andreasen's analysis suggests seven key strategies for helping maintain action and involvement; they parallel some of the issues in the precontemplation stage.[15]

1. Monitor satisfaction. People choose to act based on their perceptions of benefits, costs, social influence, and sense of personal ability to make a difference. As people act, they compare their expectations with their experience. As Andreasen writes, "The outcome of this evaluation will play a very strong role in influencing whether they are likely to repeat the behavior."[16] Unless the change advocates know whether the expectations were met, they cannot develop strategies that respond to disappointment or inertia. Thus, ongoing evaluation of people's satisfaction with their asset-building experiences is an essential and central task of maintaining involvement.

2. Keep expectations realistic. Take care not to set expectations so high that people get discouraged or disappointed. Being a mentor can be difficult in some cases. Building assets is not a cure-all for everything in communities or families. Controlling expectations involves being sure that the benefits promoted are realistic as well as being clear about the costs as people contemplate and undertake action.

3. Highlight hidden benefits. Sometimes benefits are hard to measure or see. Sometimes it takes years to bring them to fruition. The advocate's task is to highlight the hidden benefits and progress toward the goals. Providing checklists to monitor changes, telling success stories, and other such tactics can be effective in this task.

4. Improve the system. Sometimes dissatisfaction comes simply because it is difficult to access opportunities or work through bureaucracies. Responding to this feedback, improving systems and resources, and being flexible with how people get involved are important components of a maintenance plan.

5. *Enlist the support of influencers.* Another reason people can get discouraged is that they experience negative reactions to what they are doing from those around them. Employers react that they are putting too much energy into their volunteer work. Friends question why they are spending all that time with kids. Community members complain that asset building is taking away from other important issues and needs. Thus, an asset-building effort must continue to reach out to and gain the support of influencers in the community who can reinforce individuals' commitments.

6. *Emphasize ongoing skills building.* People do not continue taking action if they do not feel successful at it. Failure only reinforces their sense that they do not have the capacity to take action for young people. Thus, a community and its organizations and leaders must continuously provide opportunities to reflect on and learn from experiences while also learning new skills.

This skills building can take place in many settings. Workshops in schools, family resource centers, community centers, congregations, senior centers, and other settings have a role. Doctors, counselors, teachers, social workers, parent educators, youth workers, clergy, and other professionals can teach skills one-to-one with their constituencies (once they have been trained). In addition, publications, support groups, online bulletin boards, and other tactics should be explored.

7. *Add extrinsic incentives and rewards.* For lasting change to occur, the primary rewards of asset building must always be intrinsic, integral to the activity itself. So caution should be used in developing other incentives and rewards. However, public recognition, awards, gifts, discounts, contests, and other incentives can have a place in overcoming inertia, getting people started, and maintaining momentum, particularly when the intrinsic rewards take a long time to reap.

Extrinsic rewards also raise ethical questions in that they can entice people to take action simply to get the reward. Andreasen suggests three criteria for choosing to add extrinsic rewards that minimize ethical concerns and reduce the likelihood that people's action ceases when the reward wears off:

1. The rewards should be used only to encourage people to get started with or maintain a behavior that becomes intrinsically satisfying.
2. They should only be used as one of many positive benefits of the behavior (that is, the reward should not overshadow the other benefits).
3. The actions taken to get the reward should be reversible if the person later chooses to do so.[17]

This framework of social marketing is conceptual, not based on experience in communities that have undertaken asset-building initiatives. Thus we are cautious about making bold claims about how it works. However, Andreasen's work (and others') synthesizes strategies that have proven to be highly effective in changing people's health behaviors in the United States and around the world. A few organizations, such as the Academy for Educational Development and the Kellogg Foundation, have begun applying social marketing to youth issues with promising results. In addition, Search Institute is developing a statewide awareness-to-action strategy in Colorado that tests and refines many of these ideas. This major effort, funded by The Colorado Trust, seeks to connect statewide awareness raising with concrete opportunities for action in communities and will include evaluation of the impact of the effort on adult attitudes and behaviors toward youth.

We believe the social marketing framework has considerable potential for use by communities in organizing their asset-building work. We must begin thoughtful, sustained efforts to try, and to evaluate, these strategies to learn what works and what doesn't. In addition, other approaches to engaging individuals in action must also be explored, piloted, and evaluated. Building on the strengths and addressing the gaps in different approaches result in even better understanding of how people move from inaction to action on behalf of children and adolescents.

Youth as Community Builders

To this point, the chapter has focused largely on adults' roles in asset building. This adult focus is necessary because adults are the ones who have often failed in their responsibility to provide the relationships, resources, and opportunities that young people need. A significant focus of asset-building initiatives is to change adults' attitudes and behaviors toward youth.

At the same time, we recognize the danger in this emphasis in inadvertently giving the message that youth are objects of, not actors in, asset building. It is important to break the inertia of adult action, but it is equally important to break the societal barriers to young people's own actions to strengthen their communities. One piece of the strategy is to involve them in communitywide action (Chapter Seven) and leadership within institutions (Chapters Ten and Eleven). But it is also important that they be encouraged and equipped to take the individual actions that strengthen community and build assets in themselves, their peers, and people of other ages.

Most of the literature on youth empowerment focuses primarily on involving young people in organizational structures and leadership roles in society. Less has been written about how to shape young people's actions on an individual level. However, the social marketing model applies effectively to youth. Thus, as planners identify target audiences, listen to people's needs and perspectives, identify benefits and costs, connect with values, apply social pressure, and undertake all the other social marketing strategies, young people need to be part of the mix. In other words:

- What are young people's perceptions of their communities and their own needs?
- What are the benefits of asset-building involvement for youth? What are the barriers and costs?
- How does asset building connect with their values, and what social pressures can be brought to bear?
- What are simple asset-building actions that can get young people started?
- How do young people evaluate their own experiences in community building, and how can those experiences be strengthened and reinforced?
- How do you translate the early actions into long-term commitments?

Answering these questions requires not just efforts to involve youth in organizations and systems but also examination of the role of asset building in their everyday lives. Particularly important is shifting the social norms that make young people invisible and passive. This involves ongoing efforts to change adults' attitudes and behaviors combined with efforts to change young people's views of their own capacity to act and make a difference.

One concrete way of engaging young people in creating healthy communities is by training youth in peer helping skills. These are "a variety of interpersonal helping behaviors assumed by nonprofessionals who undertake a helping role with others."[18] We see a number of specific ways that peer helping can build many skills young people need to contribute to each other and to their community.

First, peer helping is a concrete and proven strategy that focuses on the heart of asset building: relationships. It equips young people (as well as others) with basic skills to offer caring, support, and guidance—the very skills that have been neglected in our fragmented society.

Second, and related to the first, peer helping has been a leader in moving away from a professionals-only approach to young people's needs and concerns. Indeed, by emphasizing the professional's role in equipping *others* to provide care and support, peer helping is a valuable model of how the entire culture needs to move.

Third, peer helping actively engages young people as resources in their schools, congregations, and the community. They learn social competencies such as conversational skills, decision making, and building one-to-one relationships.[19]

Fourth, peer helping has the potential to build bridges across youth-serving sectors because it already has a strong presence in public education, community youth organizations, and religious congregations. That same kind of shared understanding, commitment, and mutual respect across turf lines is needed in broader youth-serving systems. Peer helping can be a model and guide in making that happen.[20]

Making a Difference One by One

Mobilizing individuals for action may seem inefficient and time-consuming. It is harder to show progress on a grand scale. But, one by one, individuals can have a tremendous impact. In every community that begins this work, we hear the stories of how one person has made a difference. It took one person to turn around Deon Richardson of St. Louis Park (Minnesota), the first community to embrace asset building as a framework for community action.

Ninth grade wasn't a good year for Richardson. Every day he would skip class. He would write graffiti on the walls and the school lockers. He got into fights. By the end of the school year, he had only earned half an academic credit.

One of his teachers, Tom Bardal, a health and driver's education teacher, noticed. He sought out Richardson and talked with him. He noticed that when Richardson skipped class, he often headed to the gym to shoot baskets with his peers who were also skipping class.

"I could see how basketball was very important to him," Bardal says. "He had potential not only as an athlete but as a student as well." Bardal also happened to be the varsity basketball coach, and he often encouraged Richardson to try out for the team. But Richardson kept turning him down.

"I never had time for it," Richardson says. "I never wanted to play [on a team]."

Bardal didn't give up, however. "He would talk to me during my freshman year, and I would just push that all to the side," Richardson says. "But then my sophomore year came around . . . and he said I could be one of the best if I would really try."

Despite Richardson's skepticism, he decided to try out for the team. He made it. "I never had anybody tell me I was good," he says. "He was the first coach who told me I could be somebody. He was the first one. And that's why I think I will thank him right now for being there. Otherwise I would still be on that wrong path."

Bardal took an interest in Richardson's playing ability but also in his school work. He checked on him every day to see if he was attending class. He talked to his other teachers. When he found out that Richardson was skipping study hall, he brought him into his room to help him with his homework. "I saw a kid with potential and that's what teachers are all about," Bardal says. "We can talk about curriculum and teach it day in and day out, but sometimes that's not as important as turning a kid's life around."

Still, Bardal credits Richardson for making most of the changes. By his junior year, Richardson had caught up on all his academic credits by going to summer school and attending after-school classes. Today his favorite subjects are English, math, and chemistry, and he's getting A's and B's. He's now comparing colleges. "I want to go into business," he says. "I want to have my own business. I think it would be cool have your own business. And basketball is something I can fall back on."

Where does Richardson think he would be now if he hadn't changed? He figures he would be in jail. Or he would have seriously hurt someone by now.

"When he was a ninth grader, I thought, 'This kid isn't going to make it,'" says John Headlee, assistant principal of St. Louis Park High School. "Now he is one of the leaders on the basketball team. All the kids respect him. He's a success story."

The respect is far-reaching. When the junior class voted to choose two or three peers to be on the Natural Helpers Committee (a program that provides peer support for students), Richardson was chosen.

"Kids now say, 'Hey, if Deon can do it, anybody can do it,'" he says of himself. "There's good stuff in everybody. And I tell them, instead of going out looking for trouble, go home and read a book. And they look up to me. They admire me for that."[21]

CHAPTER NINE

CRUCIBLES OF CARE

Strengthening Families

Without a strong family, it can be very difficult to nurture a solid foundation for development in children and adolescents. As Maggie Scarf writes, "It is within the family that we imbibe and incorporate the skills and knowledge that will one day enable us to live outside it. . . . The family is the earliest, most basic environment in which we learn about what things we are—or are not—entitled to, and about whether people are reliable and trustworthy."[1]

Extensive research by many scholars has shown that a strong, healthy family has a significant impact in insulating a young person from risky behaviors, even in communities with serious environmental risks such as violence, poverty, or neglect.[2] Thus, asset-building communities must pay attention to strengthening the asset-building capacity of families, particularly parents.

At the same time, strong individual families do not, in themselves, make strong communities. In a report titled *Healthy Communities, Healthy Youth*,[3] my colleague Dale A. Blyth analyzed the differences between communities where youth are more likely to engage in risky behaviors (less healthy communities) compared to those where youth are less likely to engage in them (healthier communities). In a summary of this study, he writes: "Our research finds relatively small differences in families between the healthiest and least healthy communities. In the healthiest communities, for example, 38 percent of youth experience caring and supportive families, compared to 34 percent in the less healthy communities."[4]

So a focus on strengthening families' asset-building capacity should be within the context of engaging all adults and all community institutions to play their own role in building assets for children and adolescents. In this chapter, we examine the dynamics of asset building within families and how communitywide initiatives and organizations can support and equip families as part of their asset-building strategies.

Challenges to Families

Nurturing strong, asset-building families needs to be a high priority in communities committed to children and adolescents. Yet several challenges and obstacles hamper families' ability to be effective in their role.

The Focus of Blame

Parents are often blamed for all of young people's problems, saddled with all the responsibility for ensuring that their children grow up successfully, and hit with a barrage of conflicting messages about what they should or shouldn't do.

Parents are blamed for either neglecting or overindulging and failing to discipline their children. For example, when Public Agenda conducted focus groups about the problems facing America's children, participants most often came to the conclusion that "the real explanation [for the problems] was the irresponsibility, low motivation and lack of education of many parents (especially in the inner cities)."[5] Nontraditional families (especially single-parent families) are most likely to feel the brunt of the attacks. Instead of receiving support to help them cope with additional challenges they face as parents, they are often set up for failure.

Unrealistic Expectations

While blaming families for all the problems, society also has tremendously high expectations for families as the primary solution to the nation's economic, social, and moral ills. Sylvia Ann Hewlett puts it this way: "We expect parents to expend extraordinary amounts of money and energy on raising their children when it is society at large that reaps the material rewards. The costs are private; the benefits are increasingly public. If you are a 'good' parent and put together the resources and energy to ensure that your child succeeds in school and goes on to complete an expensive college education, you will undoubtedly contribute to 'human capital formation,' enhance GNP, and help this nation compete with the Japanese, but in so doing, you will deplete rather than enhance your own economic reserves."[6]

Lack of Support for Families

These high expectations are not matched with equally high support. As society has become more mobile and individualistic, the nuclear family has lost many of its sources of support: extended family, long-term relationships with neighbors, and deep relationships in civic and religious organizations. Further, more and more families have cut ties with social institutions (community centers, congregations, civic organizations, etc.) that supported families in the past.

Urie Bronfenbrenner tells the story of being interviewed extensively by NBC in the late 1970s to be part of the network's show that would usher in the Year of the Child in 1979. Bronfenbrenner spent most of his interview talking about the critical need for society to surround the family and its children with care and support. "I spent practically all of my time trying . . . to marshal evidence and argument showing that the capacity of a family to stay together, let alone function effectively, depends on how it is treated by the rest of society," he writes. "I explained how parents, while still feeling and being held responsible for their children, were increasingly becoming powerless to influence their own child's experience."

Despite his efforts, however, none of this information was included when the TV show aired. The message that made it to the airwaves, from him or anyone else, focused exclusively on the inner workings of the family. He concludes: "It is significant that the rest of the society was not on the program, neither as individuals or nor as institutions. . . . Three hours, and not a word about the circumstances under which the families lived, the conditions that needed to be changed, the actions that had to be taken at the national or local level. 'That's the way it is,' said the media message. 'It's up to these people themselves to come to terms with their problem; some do, more don't.'"[7]

Family Isolation

Many families, particularly in urban areas, have become disconnected from more traditional supports including extended family, cohesive neighborhood, congregation, or civic organizations. In addition, they often mistrust the institutions within communities (police, service agencies, and so on) that might otherwise be sources of support and connection.

In his study of families in dangerous neighborhoods in Philadelphia, Frank Furstenberg found that a downward spiral occurs in these neighborhoods as community institutions leave or become less effective. As this occurs, the more competent and resourceful parents seek help from beyond the neighborhood, further hastening the decline and withdrawal of local institutions and "fueling a spiral of demoralization among residents." Completing the spiral, the decline of the formal institutions weakens informal networks as people end participation in school and neighborhood meetings. The result is increased isolation, alienation, and fear among neighbors. Furstenberg concludes: "These changes at the community level help to bring about the disengagement of the family from the community. The family becomes less and less embedded in formal and informal structures that reinforce parental standards. Other adults in the community are no longer relied upon to supervise and sponsor children. And systems of formal and informal control are attenuated. As the family becomes separated from the community, parents resort to more individualistic strategies of managing the external world. They are disinclined to delegate authority to other parents or, reciprocally, to assume responsibility for other children."[8]

Problem-Centered Parenting Resources

Where supports are available for families, they tend only to be available to families that are experiencing problems or crisis. Indeed, the only way many parents can qualify to take advantage of some sources of support is to show that they have serious problems and are inadequate.[9]

On a more subtle level, almost all parenting resources (training, support groups, printed materials) are marketed with an emphasis on a specific problem (particularly after one moves beyond the parenting-a-baby books), even when the content focuses on the proactive skills and life patterns that are truly asset enhancing. The subtle, unspoken message is that parents who attend workshops or support groups must be having trouble with their kids. Unless parents are willing to withstand those preconceptions, they are unlikely to seek support and help until the problems reach crisis proportions.

Changes in Families and Parenting

Finally, dramatic changes in families and parents' view of their role have altered the family's ability to provide a foundation for young people. Many of the obvious changes—two-career families, single-parent and blended families, and other family structures—shift roles, expectations, and resources.

However, these visible changes are only part of the story. Indeed, other social forces and values may have an even greater impact on how families care for their children. In his provocative book *Ties That Stress: The New Family Imbalance*, David Elkind suggests that the modern nuclear family is being replaced by a "permeable" family. Although he sees advantages in this shift, he argues that many of today's parents "do not think of children and youth as requiring a full helping of security, protection, firm limits, and clear values, and many of those who still believe in the goodness of those things no longer have faith in their ability as parents to provide them in today's complex world."[10]

In analyzing the problem, he suggests that much of the blame lies in a shift in family values away from the best interest of the children to the emotional needs of adults. He writes: "Our most binding family ties are the emotional ones—the feelings that attach us one to the other. In the modern nuclear family these binding sentiments were largely child-centered in the sense that they gave preference to the well-being of children and required the self-sacrifice of parents. In the post-modern permeable family, however, the sentimental ties have been transformed and are now more likely to be adult-centered to the extent that they favor the well-being of parents and adults and require self-sacrifice from the young."[11]

It is difficult to know what role each of these forces plays in handicapping families in their efforts to be healthy, nurturing environments for children and adolescents. Indeed, efforts to place blame or to return to an idyllic past do little to improve the situation for young people. A more fruitful approach is to ask the question: Given current realities, what can be done to strengthen today's families in their ability to raise healthy children and adolescents?

The Potential of Asset Building for Families

The asset-building paradigm offers a framework for answering that question. Parents and family-serving professionals who have begun using the asset-building approach find that it gives a concrete, sensible perspective for thinking about parenting and family life, beginning at birth and continuing through adolescence. Rather than offering a laundry list of "stuff you should do," it suggests priorities and perspectives to shape the parenting task. The framework offers several benefits, as the following sections reveal.

A Focus for Parenting

The asset-building framework reminds parents of the bottom line in their child-rearing. Rather than focusing on getting ahead or avoiding problems, the assets help parents see that their primary role lies in raising caring, competent, and responsible young people. "The asset-building approach gives our family a language to talk about what we're trying to do in our family," says Beth Allen of Minnetonka, Minnesota. "It's nice to be able to look at the list of assets and realize how important some of the things we do really are."

Affirmation and Motivation

Asset building affirms parents' important role in their children's lives. It reminds them that what they do makes a big difference. Furthermore, it motivates them to stay actively involved in their children's lives throughout childhood and adolescence, rather than assuming that teenagers no longer need their parents when they begin becoming independent.

A Positive Perspective

Many parent educators say they struggle to get parents to come to workshops because parents are afraid of being labeled as having problems with their kids. By emphasizing the positive things all young people need, asset building can break down the barriers and reduce the stigma of seeking support and guidance.

When Brenda Holben, a prevention coordinator for the Cherry Creek School District in Englewood, Colorado, gives parenting workshops, the assets provide a positive focus that reshapes the way parents look at themselves and their children. In one exercise, she has participants each fold a paper in half four times to make a grid of sixteen rectangles. She then gives them each sixteen small Post-It notes. Participants go home and hold a family meeting; as a family they identify sixteen family assets, writing each one on a Post-It note. Then they organize the notes on the grid in ways that highlight the family's strengths.

It's one of the few homework exercises that everyone does. By the end of the six-week course, Holben sees a big shift in the way the parents talk about their kids. "Parents are now saying, 'My kids have assets. We are building on strengths' instead of 'My kids really need help.' "

Partners in Parenting

Because asset building seeks to nurture a shared responsibility in the community for raising the youngest generation, this approach promises to provide families with a supportive, caring network of partners in raising their children. In short, it begins to recreate the kind of informal community that previous generations of parents depended on for support and guidance.

Asset-Building Ideas for Families

What are the implications of the asset-building paradigm for families? While the possibilities are endless, the underlying shift is that parents become proactive and engaged, focusing attention, energy, and resources on the things their children need to grow up healthy. Here are some specific ways parents can and do build assets:

- Developing a family mission statement that focuses on building assets, then using it as a guide for family decisions and priorities.
- Modeling and talking about the values and priorities the parents wish to pass on to their children.
- Taking time to nurture their own assets by spending time with supportive people, using their time constructively, and reflecting on their own values and commitments.
- Regularly spending time with their children doing things that they all enjoy, which might include tasks around the house, recreation activities, and service projects.
- Actively seeking support from the extended family, neighbors, a congregation, and others in their networks of friends.
- Eating at least one meal together every day.
- Limiting television watching.
- Being active in their children's education through school activities, monitoring homework, and talking with the children about school and learning.
- Negotiating boundaries and consequences for behavior for the whole family.
- Modeling involvement in structured activities in the community or in a congregation. In the process, they keep a balance so that activities do not overwhelm the parents' ability to meet other needs.[12]

Reshaping Services for Families

Given parents' central role in providing a healthy foundation for young people's development, an emphasis on parent education, empowerment, and support has an important place in an asset-building initiative. Indeed, the positive focus on asset building dovetails nicely with the growing body of literature on family strengths, parent education, and family empowerment.

As communities examine the opportunities for supporting, educating, and empowering parents, attention must be paid to the varying needs and interests of parents from different cultures and at different stages in their child's development. Often, available support and education focuses primarily on the first years of life, which is when it is often easiest to engage parents. These resources for early childhood are appropriate, but there is a similar need for parent education as children enter adolescence.

A Search Institute study of family support programs found that most of them do not explicitly address adolescence, yet they see a growing need to help parents at this stage in life. Furthermore, many of the people in these programs do not have an adequate understanding of adolescence to be as effective as they would hope in helping families through this important developmental period.[13]

Shifting Perspectives

As initiatives and organizations seek to involve families, it is important to address some false assumptions about the relationship between the family, the community, and family-serving organizations. These assumptions shape the way organizations work with families as well as the expectations that families have of organizations in the community. Here are some of the shifts in thinking that need to be addressed:

Shift From Believing . . .	*To Believing . . .*
The purpose of involving families is to get more support for the organization's programs and activities.	The purpose of involving families is to support them in their primary role as asset builders for youth at home.
Efforts are most successful if a lot of people show up for activities.	Efforts are most successful when you see a positive difference in family life.
Teenagers don't want to be with their parents.	Teenagers and parents need to learn new ways to relate to each other as the young person grows up.
If a lot of people don't show up for an activity, they must not want support.	If a lot of people don't show up, perhaps they are too busy, or perhaps the time was bad, or perhaps the topic didn't really address their needs, or perhaps. . . .
Asset building is something families need to add to their already busy lives.	Asset building is a tool to help parents examine priorities and be more effective in their role as parents.

Each of these shifts in thinking affects the way organizations and community initiatives develop strategies for working with families. For example, instead of focusing on "getting a lot of parents to come to a workshop," the focus should be on finding the best ways to support and equip families to address a topic. Perhaps a workshop is a great strategy, but there may be other ways that are more effective in serving families.

Benefits of Supporting Families in Asset Building

In addition to the potential impact on families and youth, there are also other reasons for equipping families as part of asset-building efforts within a community or organization. These include:

- *Consistency.* An intentional focus on equipping families for asset building provides the opportunity to develop consistent, mutually reinforcing messages and opportunities to youth related to asset building and healthy development throughout the community. Establishing community norms regarding use of alcohol and other drugs is much more likely to have an impact when that message is reinforced—and enforced—at home.
- *Parental involvement.* Extensive research has underscored the value of parental involvement in school. Similar principles likely hold true for parental involvement in other youth- and family-serving systems. Young people are more likely to internalize and apply what they learn through other youth programs and activities when their parents are involved.
- *Parental support.* Finally, connecting with parents builds their support for asset-building efforts in the community or organization. When they know about and support what is happening, they can be influential in broadening support throughout their neighborhoods, social networks, and other spheres of influence. If, however, they misunderstand the goals and become antagonistic, they can seriously undermine efforts.

Strategies for Equipping Families

Below are four broad approaches for equipping families for asset building: supporting parents, educating parents, providing opportunities for families together, and advocacy on behalf of families. The strategies present some significant opportunities for communitywide initiatives. In addition, they provide guidance to youth- and family-serving systems in communities, including family resource centers, parent education networks, corporate human resource services, schools, parent-teacher organizations, congregations, and social service providers.

Supporting Parents

The goal of providing family support is to empower families to build their own strengths and resources, not to make them dependent on a service organization or professional. Unfortunately, some efforts to support parents have actually undermined the family's own capacity by taking away its control and fostering dependency on the help giver. Efforts are more successful when, among other things, they do not undermine the family's own capacity and responsibility, are reciprocal in nature, help parents feel successful, promote cooperation, and build parents' skills.[14] (See the text "Effective Family Support Programs" for characteristics.)

Effective Family Support Programs

A Children's Defense Fund report identified the following characteristics of effective family support programs:

- They emphasize the family unit.
- They build on family strengths.
- They make participation voluntary.
- They address family needs comprehensively.
- They develop parenting skills.
- They provide nurturing connections with others.
- They respond to individual and community needs.
- They work to prevent crises.
- They respect individual and cultural differences.
- They coordinate and cooperate with other agencies.[15]

It is particularly critical to build support for families that have become isolated, disconnected, or alienated from traditional supports, including extended family, cohesive neighborhood, congregation, or civic organizations. As one response to this challenge, Mayor Sharon Sayles Belton of Minneapolis suggests creating a network of "point people," at least one per neighborhood, to become neighborhood-based conduits for the asset-building paradigm as well as first points of contact for advice and counsel on available resources to assist families in locating and utilizing available services.

Research on various types of help has identified a number of factors that contribute to empowering help.[16] These factors are highly consistent with an asset-building approach. There are numerous important themes in developing support efforts for parents. Here are several issues and ideas to keep in mind.

Identifying support networks. In the past, parents received much guidance and support from their extended family and long-time neighbors. That is less true in this mobile society. The result is that many families feel isolated and alone in their parenting task. The challenge is to develop systems that promote and enhance the family's natural support networks instead of replacing them with professional services. This may mean, for example, that parents connect with other parents in their neighborhood, a parent association, a congregation, or a civic organization rather than starting new networks.

One way to keep from overprofessionalizing family support is to recognize that parents are themselves valuable resources for supporting and educating each other. Peer-led parent groups using parents' natural networks of support build on existing resources and enhance a sense of community.

As part of the parent support efforts, intentional strategies could tap the wisdom of elders in the community who may be eager to help support the parents of the "grandchildren" of the neighborhood. In addition, particular attention should be paid to weaving a web of support and structure for families under severe stress who have isolated themselves and feel powerless against external circumstances.

Providing needed and wanted support. It is also critical that the support offered be help that the parents want and need, and that it be extended when they want and need it. For support to meet needs, it must not only be consistent with their culture but also meet the everyday needs they are experiencing with their children. If parents are struggling with curfews, for example, the support should help them address those issues from an asset-building perspective.

One way to engage parents effectively is to do it when they are most open: during critical transition periods, including preparation for the birth of a child, preparation for kindergarten, the child's onset of adolescence, and the transition from high school to college or school to work. These teachable moments become opportunities to set new life patterns.

Reaching fathers is a key challenge in identifying the appropriate kind of support to provide. Fathers play a critical role in a child's development, yet it can be difficult to engage fathers in parent education, particularly if it does not address their specific needs. Developing creative approaches to educating and supporting fathers can be a pivotal strategy for enhancing parent education.

Enhancing competency and capacity. A key to avoiding creating patterns of dependence, it is important to continually enhance parents' capacity and sense of accomplishment. Such an emphasis equips parents with positive behaviors and skills that decrease the need for help and increase their own competence. This might include training parents in how to talk with their teenager and how to use positive discipline. Another strategy is regularly to encourage parents to reflect on their progress and affirm each other.

These guidelines give some broad parameters for the kind of support that communities, service providers, and other organizations can provide families as part of their asset-building efforts. They provide an important filter for evaluating the various support opportunities for families to determine if these activities are truly empowering parents or making them feel dependent.

Educating Parents

Saying the family is a critical asset builder is only the beginning of the conversation. Many families lack skills to be effective in their role. As a report from the Children's Defense Fund asserted: "In today's complex world no family has within itself all of the knowledge and resources necessary to meet all of its members' needs. Parents in different circumstances need different kinds of help and different kinds of support, but all parents need some kind of help at one time or another."[17]

The asset framework is filled with specific themes to address in parent education. An obvious possibility is a class that explores the parenting implications of each of the eight types of assets. Or there may be specific assets that parents feel a need to examine.

Another approach is to identify some of the underlying themes and skills for asset building and focus sessions on building these skills. For example, communication is a parenting skill that is necessary for building many of the assets. Similarly, an understanding of basic adolescent development allows parents to be more comfortable with, and build assets during, the changes occurring in their family as their teenager grows up. And by tying educational opportunities to the asset framework, parents see, for example, how a workshop on positive discipline relates to a class on helping their teenager choose a college.

In thinking about educating parents, keep in mind the many ways you can help them learn new skills and perspectives:

- Classes or workshops with many parents together
- Small groups of parents who might study a book, watch a video, or have some other form of ongoing, peer-led discussion
- Resources (tip sheets, newsletter articles, bulletin boards, videos, books, etc.) given to parents for self-learning at home[18]
- Along with sponsored educational events for parents within the organization's network, alerts to parents about other education opportunities in the community

Providing Opportunities for Families Together

When we talk about supporting and educating families, often the first things that come to mind are parent education classes and support groups. Opportunities for parents play an important role in an overall system, but it's perhaps even more important to find opportunities to support and educate families together, through parent-youth events, activities, classes, and so forth. These family events are important for several reasons:

- They keep the family together rather than pulling them apart.
- They give families an experience that everyone shares.
- They provide a safe environment where parents and their children can develop new understandings of each other.
- They give families practice in communicating with each other in safe ways.

Here are some of the kinds of opportunities organizations and community-wide efforts can provide for parents and their children together:

Learning together. There are dozens of asset-building topics that can be addressed to parents and their children together. These might range from positive family communication to effective decision making; they can occur in many environments, from a workshop to a special event or a family retreat setting.

Your education could focus on asset-building themes and family relationships, but another approach to consider is offering classes and workshop on hobbies and interests that parents and teenagers can learn together. A colleague writes: "One of my fond memories as a teenager was taking a photography darkroom class with my dad. Neither of us knew anything about photo development, but we were both interested. Our relationship grew as we learned side by side, compared notes, and practiced together."[19]

Service and action. Family service projects can be powerful shapers of young people's values. Yet family service is a rare experience. Designing service opportunities that allow parents and their children to spend time together, talk about what motivates them, and share their values has tremendous opportunity for both enriching family life and also strengthening young people's commitment to caring. The challenge is helping parents see that service is not "just for kids," but can be a formative experience for adults as well.

Celebration and fun. One of the best ways to strengthen relationships in a family is to have fun together. Family sports teams, game nights, camping or canoe trips, and dozens of other activities can be effective, nonthreatening ways for parents and teenagers to spend time together, particularly if they are noncompetitive. Competitive activities can be problematic. If parents and teenagers are on the same team, the parent may revert to the role of a pushy coach. If they are on opposite teams, fierce competition can drive them apart.[20]

Advocacy on Behalf of Families

Support and education are at the heart of an asset-building approach to supporting and nurturing families. However, community initiatives and organizations committed to asset building can also play an advocacy role in the community to address issues that get in the way of parents' abilities to build assets. Here are some ways to be advocates for families:

- Advocate for policies that increase parents' abilities to build assets. These may include advocacy for flexible work schedules and family involvement opportunities in schools, youth-serving organizations, and congregations.
- Attack the social stigma that attaches to parents who seek services or support. Efforts might include public awareness campaigns that challenge negative messages about parenting and highlight ways parents seek support simply to increase their effectiveness.
- Call on businesses and corporations to provide flexible work schedules, on-site day care, and other family-friendly policies for parents.
- Lobby for public policies that make it easier for families to build assets.

Surrounding Families with a Web of Support

We note at the beginning of this chapter that families are a critical focus for asset-building efforts, but it would be a serious mistake to put all the responsibility for asset building on families. Indeed, this chapter devotes considerable space to outlining the role of community initiative and organizations in supporting families for asset building.

In addition, the asset-building vision needs to move into the heart of organizations and systems in the community in order to have a significant impact on the community's culture. Therefore, the next two chapters explore the potential roles of primary and secondary socializing systems in creating a healthy, asset-building community.

CHAPTER TEN

THE FIRST RING OF SUPPORT

Youth-Serving Systems

In addition to mobilizing and equipping individuals and families for asset building, creating healthy communities also involves engaging many socializing systems in a community in the vision and effort. By engaging them (instead of creating new institutions and structures to try to do the work), the community-building effort increases its potential reach and impact at relatively low cost and without unnecessarily duplicating programs in the community. Indeed, these organizations may be instrumental in reaching, equipping, and maintaining involvement in asset building by individuals and families.

Involving organizations in the community-building effort does not necessarily mean they need to collaborate on programming or even be part of community-wide planning (though many will want to be). Rather, it calls on institutions to play to their own strengths, develop asset-building strategies within their own arenas of work, add their own improvisations to the vision, and take a lead role when it's appropriate. There are at least five ways organizations can contribute to communitywide asset-building efforts:

1. Present the asset-building concept to employees, constituents, or members in newsletters, workshops, or other forums. Share practical ideas for how individuals can build assets.
2. Highlight, develop, expand, or support programs that build assets, such as mentoring, peer helping, service learning, parent education, or youth empowerment.

3. Provide meaningful opportunities for young people to contribute to others in and through the organization.
4. Develop employee policies that encourage asset building, including flexible work schedules for parents as well as other employees so they can volunteer in youth development programs.
5. Use organizational newsletters, press releases, or events to recognize employees, constituents, or members who make special efforts to build assets for youth in the community.

Virtually every institution and organization in a community can contribute to creating a healthy community, either through its specific mission or through its community leadership and responsibility. In addition, the asset-building vision has important implications for systems change and reordered priorities within institutions that serve children and adolescents. This chapter examines the roles of several youth-serving organizations and systems—those that have regular, direct contact with community youth—in asset building, focusing on specific possibilities in the different institutions.[1] We focus attention on the following institutions and networks:

Schools

Community youth organizations

Religious congregations

Neighborhood organizations

In addition, the chapter addresses how community organizers can engage these organizations in asset-building efforts. Then, in Chapter Eleven, we shift to the roles of institutions and systems that have less direct, regular, relational contact with youth, such as government, health care, and the media.

The Roles of Youth-Serving Systems in Creating Healthy Communities

Many of the tasks of asset building are informal and relational; however, asset-building efforts are difficult to maintain and sustain without support and involvement from organizations within a community. Without tapping the existing organizations, a healthy-communities initiative must create systems and structures that provide the context, education, coordination, and opportunities to sustain and grow the efforts.

Organizations can be involved in asset-building efforts in several ways. Indeed, many are already committed to asset-building activities, even if they do not use that language. Here are some principle ways organizations can get involved in creating healthy communities.

Integrate asset building into their own mission and operations. As we note throughout this chapter, many organizations see asset building as a helpful framework for understanding their core mission. Thus they reshape or reframe their mission in terms of building assets. When this occurs, the commitment becomes an anchor in the shifting tides of community needs. In addition, these organizations may integrate asset-building strategies into their internal policies and procedures, including family-friendly employment practices, employee relations, and youth involvement in the organization.

Partner in communication and education. As part of integrating asset building into their own mission, many organizations are the key communicators to youth, parents, and the community at large regarding asset building. Virtually any organization that communicates with the public has the potential of communicating the healthy-communities message. Furthermore, many organizations are the resources needed to provide the expertise and the structures that offer training and education to support and equip individuals for their asset-building role.

Provide a gateway for individual commitment. Throughout this book, I emphasize that asset building is not a program but a vision and philosophy. The goal is to get people to integrate asset building as an everyday part of their lives and commitments. Yet, as we suggest in Chapter Eight, systems need to be in place that provide individuals with structured opportunities for action as they move from awareness to action and commitment.

Youth-serving organizations can be an important part of this behavioral change process. As people become aware of their own potential as asset builders, youth programs become a natural, structured place where people can volunteer and receive support and training as asset builders. Through this volunteering, individuals assist in meeting program goals and also internalize commitments and skills for asset building that carry over into other areas of their lives.

Expand programs to serve the whole community. Many community organizations have extensive and sophisticated programs that focus on internal needs or a specific constituency. These foci are often quite appropriate. In addition, these programs or emphases can be offered to others in the community at little or no extra cost.

For example, a youth-serving organization may invite youth workers from other institutions to participate in a training event. Or a congregation may make a particular asset-enhancing opportunity open to other congregations in the community. Or a business may invite adults from other businesses in the office building or surrounding area to participate in parent education during the lunch hour. The underlying principle is recognizing and building on existing resources that can be shared by many people or institutions with similar needs and a shared focus on asset building.

Engaging Youth-Serving Organizations

Many times, organizations undertake asset-building action before a community unites for a healthy-community initiative. Indeed, communitywide efforts often have their impetus from one of the youth-serving sectors (schools, community youth organizations, congregations). However, as a local initiative begins, strategies must be developed to engage multiple sectors within the community as partners in the vision. Let us look at several strategies to use in nurturing their interest in and commitment to the asset-building vision.

Identify Needs and Self-Interest

Take time to listen to each sector about its needs and interests. Strategies must be based on the organization's own interests and priorities. Making an appeal based on commitment to the community may garner initial support, but it is unlikely to elicit long-term involvement unless the business already has deep commitments to the community.

Assess Readiness

Different organizations are at different stages of awareness, interest, and involvement. For example, reaching out to a business that has an active mentoring program is very different from trying to engage a similar business that has no previous commitment to or interest in youth. Similarly, some schools may have a long history of positive youth development, while the concepts are new to others. Knowing those differences is an essential part of identifying appropriate messages for getting the organization involved.

Hand Off the Vision

The goal of asset building is not simply to get the organization to buy in to and support an existing program. The goal is to create a shared vision and commitment that becomes internalized within each organization in the community. Although this vision calls organizations to work together on some things, it's more important that the vision draw each organization to explore its own asset-building potential and then develop strategies for how it contributes to the communitywide vision. In this case, the role of the asset-building advocate is to be vision bearer, supporter and resourcer, and prompter for action.

Address Costs and Benefits

Just as you must help individuals see both the benefits and costs of getting involved in a healthy-community effort, the same principle applies to organizations. There certainly are many benefits to organizations for getting involved, but there are also costs. Being open with both can help leaders know whether and how they can commit.

Build on Capacity and Strengths

As noted throughout this chapter, each institution in the community brings particular strengths and capacities to a community asset-building effort. For example, schools may bring access to families. Congregations may bring opportunities for informal intergenerational relationships. Businesses may bring financial resources or skills in marketing. In each case, seek to engage the organizations in their areas of strength, not where they struggle or have little to offer.

Increase Social Pressure

Just as individuals can be swayed to take action based on what they hear other people saying, organizations can be heavily influenced by what they hear from their customers, constituents, and peers. For example, when public officials hear about asset building in every public hearing, they pay attention.

Offer Training, Tools, and Support

Each organization brings skills or resources, but they also need assistance to help them succeed in their efforts. A partnership between school and business can fail miserably without appropriate planning and coaching. Congregations may need additional training to learn how to capitalize on or build caring relationships between youth and adults. Youth-serving organizations may need guidance in assessing whether programs are truly responsive to the young people being served. Providing opportunities to build these skills involves not only a network of resources and expertise upon which to draw but also current information from the organization about its needs and any stumbling blocks it faces in the effort. Here are some strategies that can help build organizational capacity and commitment:

- Provide workshops in the asset paradigm for organizational leaders and staff.
- Provide training in how to develop and implement a plan for organizational change.
- Create an asset-building team to create the plan. (The planners and the actors should include youth.)
- If they do not already exist, consider creating citywide networks of organizational leaders representing particular sectors.

Challenge Organizations to Move Toward Transformation

Perhaps one of the greatest challenges in engaging youth-serving institutions is to ensure that the asset-building efforts are not just "painted over" existing programs, creating an illusion of buy-in and support without any real transformation of the programs and services of the institutions. In this context, asset building offers both an affirmation and a challenge.

The affirmation comes in identifying and highlighting the many programs and services organizations offer that, by their nature, build assets. These may include skills-building activities, youth groups with supportive relationships, service opportunities, values education, and many others.

But it is a misinterpretation of the asset-building framework to identify one or two assets that a program builds and rest on that knowledge without examining the overall impact of the program on young people's development. For example, a program aimed at increasing youth involvement in homework might backfire if the environment is unsupportive, judgmental, and disempowering to the young people who participate.

A more useful way to think about asset-building programs is to examine how the basic framework of assets can be infused into programs and services in ways that enhance the ability of those activities to build the overall developmental foundation.

Take, for example, the area of service to others (volunteering, community service, etc.). Sometimes people note that service to others is, in itself, one of the forty assets. But service involvement doesn't just build this one asset. Indeed, if designed well, it can contribute to building all eight types of assets:

1. Doing service with peers, parents, and other adults can cement relationships of *support* and caring between peers and with parents and other adults.

2. Young people become *empowered* through service as they contribute to their world and are seen as valuable resources for their congregation and community.
3. *Boundaries and expectations* are reinforced as service activities include ground rules for involvement and as adults and peers become positive role models for each other.
4. Service projects should be careful to provide opportunities for youth to *use their time constructively*, not just do make-work.
5. Many service activities can unleash a new *commitment to learning* as youth apply their knowledge to real-world issues and problems and as they are exposed to questions that challenge their worldview and thinking—particularly if a framework of service learning is used.[2]
6. Through service, young people express their *positive values* and have opportunities to affirm and internalize the values that are important to them.
7. Many skills and *social competencies* are nurtured as young people plan their activities, take action, and build relationships with their peers, adults who serve with them, and service recipients.
8. Finally, service learning becomes an important catalyst for shaping *positive identity* as young people discover their gifts and their place in the world through their acts of service and justice.

The same kind of analysis could be done with many other types of programs and services, including classroom learning, counseling, youth group activities, sports and recreation, arts activities, and many others. The asset framework contributes a helpful perspective that can move youth-serving activities beyond business as usual.

Add Incentives, Recognition, and Celebration

Finally, many organizations respond well to added incentives that recognize their efforts. These may include awards for asset-building efforts, articles in the local newspaper, or banquets for participating groups. These incentives, however, should be used with care so that they do not overshadow the intrinsic rewards of their involvement in asset building.

We turn now to look at each sector's unique asset-building potential, focusing first on the organizations that directly serve children and youth: schools, youth-serving organizations, and congregations. In addition, we address the immediate context in which young people live, namely, neighborhoods. Chapter Eleven then focuses on the secondary support systems that surround youth in the community.

Schools

Schools are natural allies for communitywide asset-building initiatives. Not only do schools have a great deal to offer to these efforts, but integrating asset building into a school's mission has tremendous potential for helping schools achieve it. Researchers who study effective schools find, for example, that among other things they:

- Are safe places with consistent rules and boundaries
- Adopt a core set of values for behavior
- Engage young people's minds
- Nurture positive relationships within the school
- Develop connections with other parts of young people's world, including their families[3]

Asset building embraces and provides a framework for each of these tasks, giving an opportunity to reexamine all areas of school life to determine how they contribute to a goal of equipping young people to be active, responsible, engaged, and productive citizens and workers. In a report on effective middle schools, Peter Scales connects asset building to school reform and other educational challenges. Among other conclusions, he writes: "All the dropout prevention and school reform literature can be reduced to a single conclusion: Young people are more likely to stay in school and do well there (or in any other program) if they like it there. And they are more likely to like middle schools if they feel safe there, if they have successes there, if their friends, neighbors, and family are proud of what they do there, if they have fun there, and if they feel someone in school cares for them."[4]

Asset building can inform virtually every aspect of school life, from classroom management to budget priorities to cocurricular activities.[5] (See "Asset Building Ideas for Schools" later in this section.) Here are some of the areas where asset building can have a clear impact on school policies and practices:

- Providing a caring, nurturing environment in which young people can effectively learn (assets of support). This includes policy issues of limiting classes to manageable sizes and allowing students to build relationships with teachers and peers through such strategies as block scheduling, team teaching, and cooperative learning strategies. (One of the assets that is consistently lowest in surveys of communities is caring school climate, which is experienced by only 36 percent of youth in the Search Institute survey.)
- Developing intentional ways to build partnerships with parents (support).

- Ensuring that school is a safe place for all students (empowerment).
- Involving young people in contributing to their school through leadership, decision making, and service (empowerment).
- Having clear expectations and behavior guidelines in school, ones for which young people take part in developing, monitoring, and enforcing (boundaries and expectations).
- Setting expectations for learning that are challenging for students of all abilities (boundaries and expectations).
- Providing strong connections to and opportunities for community-based after-school and cocurricular programs (constructive use of time).

Several school districts have found asset building to be a natural tool for effective parent education. In St. Louis Park, Minnesota, for example, the school district's asset-building committee chose to tackle the issue of inadequate parent-child communication through an initiative they called "Catch 22." "We invited parents to 'Catch 22' minutes to spend each day with each child," says Karen Atkinson, coordinator of the community's citywide Children First initiative.

Local educators put together tip sheets for preschool, elementary, and secondary school students suggesting activities for parents and children to do together. The district's staff embraced the idea with enthusiasm. Tip sheets found their way home in backpacks and conference materials. In the days preceding Valentine's Day, children suggested their own ideas of activities they most enjoy doing with adults.

"We are always talking about the importance of parental involvement," Atkinson says. "But sometimes we need something in hand, something concrete to build upon."

Asset-Building Ideas for Schools

- Make it a priority to provide caring environments for all students.
- Train support staff, teachers, paraprofessionals, administrators, and other school staff in their role in asset building.
- Provide additional opportunities to nurture values deemed crucial by the community.
- Expand, diversify, and strengthen cocurricular activities for all youth.
- Develop mentoring relationships between teenagers and children.
- Provide opportunities for staff to share "best practices" for providing support, establishing boundaries, nurturing values, and teaching social competencies.
- Integrate service learning, values development, relationship building, development of social competencies, and other asset-building strategies into the curriculum.
- Use the schools' connections to parents to increase parental involvement and to educate parents in their asset-building roles.

Community Youth Organizations

Many youth-serving organizations across the nation are discovering that asset building provides a new focus, rationale, and demand for their services. Amid increased national interest in the potential of youth-serving organizations for young people's healthy development,[6] the concept of healthy communities adds a framework for thinking about the potential for and impact of nonschool organizations dedicated to developing healthy youth.

Although there are more than seventeen thousand nonprofits in the United States with youth as their focus,[7] far too few young people participate in these programs. Nationally, we find that only 41 percent of sixth-to-twelfth-grade youth participate in these activities.[8] In addition, analysis of the 1988 National Education Longitudinal Study (NELS 88) found that 83 percent of eighth graders from upper-income families participated in out-of-school activities, compared to 60 percent of low-income youth. Much of the difference can be attributed to upper-income families' ability to pay for lessons, clubs, and other enrichment activities.[9] Access to transportation may also be a factor. Furthermore, many youth organizations struggle with declining involvement of both youth and adult volunteers.

There are dozens of kinds of programs in youth organizations that have potential for building assets. (See "Asset-Building Ideas for Youth Organizations" later in this section.) A Search Institute report titled *Making the Case: Measuring the Impact of Youth Development Programs* surveyed the extant literature on youth development programs to find the positive outcomes associated with involvement in each type of program. According to the research consulted in the report, here are some of the potential positive outcomes related to asset development of several types of youth development programs:

- *Sports and recreation:* improved self-concept, increased interest in community activities, and increased success in school.
- *Camps:* development of specific skills, goal-setting abilities, reduction in recidivism of adjudicated youth, and increased self-esteem.
- *Service:* academic improvement, problem-solving skills, leadership development, and positive relationship with peers and adults.
- *Mentoring:* decreased alcohol and other drug use, reduced violent behavior, increased success in school, and improved relationships with adults and peers.
- *Drop-in centers:* decreased alcohol and other drug use, and establishment of places where youth feel comfortable seeking adult advice and support.[10]

When communities adopt an asset-building vision, one of the first things they discover is the need to strengthen and expand the availability of out-of-school activities for youth. The challenge is to develop a web of activities within a community that meet the diverse needs of young people. The Carnegie Council on Adolescent Development put the challenge this way: "Community programs for youth—regardless of sponsorship—should view themselves as part of a services network and engage in joint planning and coordination at the local and national levels. Whether they are new or expanding efforts, such networks should take an inclusive approach, enlisting the participation of both established and emerging organizations."[11]

In addition to the challenge of networking across the community, there is the challenge of integrating the asset-building vision throughout an organization's programming. This includes everything from selection of programs to initiate or sustain, to priorities for staff development, to expectations of staff and volunteers. Some of these strategies bump into issues of funding priorities and guidelines, which often demand that a funded program combat a particular "problem." Thus the need for advocacy and change among private and public funders (see Chapter Eleven).

An additional challenge for youth-serving organizations is to find innovative ways to measure the impact of their programming using the asset framework. Search Institute is working with National YMCA in developing strategies for program evaluation based on the framework of developmental assets.[12] This approach opens new strategies for accountability and funding based on positive outcomes. Such policy changes lay the groundwork for other changes necessary to enable community youth organizations to integrate a long-term strategy for asset building.

Asset-Building Ideas for Youth Organizations

- Involve youth in leadership and program planning.
- Provide a range of structured activities for youth with diverse interests and needs.
- Provide programs and opportunities where young people feel supported and safe.
- Develop expectations, boundaries, and consequences with youth who participate in programs; enforce appropriate consequences when boundaries are not respected.
- Train volunteers, leaders, and coaches in asset building and in young people's developmental needs.
- Focus on asset building in programming, including building social competencies, engaging youth in service, and nurturing personal identity.
- Support young people's educational development through tutoring, computer skills, literacy programs, and other forms of academic enrichment.
- Develop strategies for actively involving parents in their children's activities and personal growth.

- Coordinate activities and priorities with other youth-serving organizations.
- Advocate for young people in the community.
- Maintain programming for youth of all ages.

Religious Congregations

Congregations have many qualities that can be significant resources for asset building, including intergenerational community, programs that promote healthy values and choices, and a commitment to service. As the Carnegie Council on Adolescent Development noted, "For many adolescents, their religious organization and its leaders are often as trusted as family. This sense of familiarity, combined with the commitment adult church leaders have to nurture young church members, lends strength to church-based youth programs."[13]

Congregations may be particularly valuable as resources in inner-city communities, according to Henry G. Cisneros, former U.S. secretary of housing and urban development. He notes four characteristics of congregations that, when drawn together, make them a unique resource:

1. "Faith communities are still there." While many congregations did leave cities for the suburbs, some stayed and new ones have formed, making them one of the strongest institutions in some inner-city areas.
2. "Community is central to the mission of charity." All of the major faith traditions share a commitment to service, charity, or justice. Many congregations live this out in community development efforts.
3. "Faith communities have unique resources." They may not have financial resources, but they often have links outside the community (through their denominations), and their leaders have important organizational skills.
4. "Faith communities touch the soul." This quality allows congregations to focus on the values and commitments that there are things worth living for. It is a quality that emphasizes supportive relationships, caring, and nurturing.[14]

Yet too often congregations are unrecognized as resources in their community. Furthermore, many congregations focus so much energy on "our kids" and their own institutional needs that their potential for youth in the community is largely unrealized.

Some observers have suggested that it is virtually impossible to get religious leaders to work together across faith traditions, since those traditions are often hostile to one another. However, Search Institute research suggests that religious youth workers across faith traditions share a commitment to many goals related to asset building. This includes a commitment to helping youth make wise decisions, providing a safe and caring place for youth, developing young people's skills and values, building caring relationships among youth, building caring relationships between youth and adults, and nurturing a commitment to service.[15]

The challenge for congregations, then, is to tap the latent potential of these communities of faith in the lives of youth. That work is beginning at the community level and nationally. Leaders see asset building offering new credibility and a constructive framework through which they can evaluate and strengthen their programming, which, too often, is haphazard and unfocused.

A number of national religious organizations, including Jewish, Catholic, and Protestant denominations, are now exploring how asset building can be integral to their work with youth.[16] In addition, with a major grant from the DeWitt Wallace–Reader's Digest Fund, Search Institute is involved in a four-year initiative to equip religious youth workers and congregations to build developmental assets. Called Uniting Congregations for Youth Development, the initiative offers youth workers opportunities to participate in interfaith networks of other youth workers in their own community, access to quality training and practical resource materials to strengthen their congregation's work with youth, and communitywide activities for youth and youth workers that build assets. The goal is for these networks of youth workers to become partners and resources in community efforts for asset building.

Asset building has the potential to shape congregations' work in at least four contexts or spheres of influence, according to Eugene Roehlkepartain, project director for Uniting Congregations for Youth Development:[17]

1. *Within the youth program.* The framework of developmental assets gives a focus and sense of direction for an array of youth programming. It challenges congregations to ensure that youth have a leadership role in shaping the activities, and it highlights key developmental needs to be embedded into youth programming (such as providing a safe, caring, challenging, and open environment for youth).

2. *In reaching families.* Congregations have natural opportunities for reaching families of youth (many of whom already view the congregation as a trusted resource). These opportunities open doors for developing consistent messages for youth between home and congregation, while also equipping parents in their roles as asset builders. The challenge is to find ways to support and educate families who may not see congregations as natural allies in their parenting tasks.

3. *In the congregation as a whole.* Although congregations have the potential of being intergenerational communities for youth, too often they are as age segregated as the rest of society. Roehlkepartain writes: "As reflected in the majority of resources and training for youth work, the typical congregation has a distinct structure

[for youth work] that runs essentially independent of any other congregational activities. Youth rarely, if ever, interact meaningfully with more than a handful of adults who are designated to work with youth. Connections to other areas of congregational life are coincidental or serendipitous. Almost the only time the youth program is discussed by the congregation's board is when there is a problem."[18]

Roehlkepartain suggests that there are at least four important themes for integrating youth into the whole of congregational life, comprising congregational planning and leadership, worship, religious education, social activities, congregational care, and service in the community:

- Nurturing a welcoming climate for children and youth throughout the congregation.
- Encouraging individual commitments to youth and asset building by members of the congregation.
- Developing intentional strategies and structures for building intergenerational relationships.
- Reshaping congregational leadership so that it no longer segregates or excludes youth and youth issues from other areas of congregational planning.[19]

4. *In community outreach.* The asset-building vision calls congregations to reach into the community to serve and advocate for young people. It also opens doors for cooperation in the community (with other congregations as well as other youth-serving and youth-influencing institutions) if congregations focus on the shared concern for youth, rather than parochial or sectarian concerns.

When Rob Rose, former senior high youth minister at Trinity Lutheran Church in Town and Country, Missouri, learned about developmental assets, he connected with the school to develop the approach. "I made it clear to the school that my goal was not to convert the world to being a Lutheran," he says. "I was there for all kids regardless of their religious affiliation. My job and the school's job have very similar goals: we want the betterment of kids. So we worked on our similarities rather than our differences."

The church and the Parkway School District began developing a community-wide initiative to build assets in the community, which is still in the initial planning stages. "There was a time in which schools, communities, and businesses worked together," he says. "Today if you can work together, you can accomplish a lot more than if you're working individually and in a lot of different directions. Part of our church's philosophy is that Trinity needs to be a community center. We need to be more than just a building. We need to go out into the community and work in the community to make it better. That's what we're doing with assets."

Asset-Building Ideas for Congregations

- Intentionally foster intergenerational relationships by providing activities for all ages within the congregation.
- Listen to what youth say they want.
- Regularly offer parent education as part of the congregation's educational programs.
- Focus attention on values development.
- Make community service a central component of youth programming.
- Network with other congregations and other institutions in the area for mutual learning, support, and programming.
- Maintain year-round connections with youth. Don't lose contact over the summer.
- Involve youth in caring for and teaching younger children.
- Emphasize maintaining strong programs for youth throughout middle school and high school.
- Sponsor celebrations of children and families.
- Provide many opportunities for youth to be leaders in and contributors to the congregation.[20]

Neighborhoods

When we go to communities to talk about the relational nature of asset building, the issue of neighborhoods inevitably surfaces. Some neighborhoods maintain the kind of social interactions that the word *neighborly* connotes, but the reality is very different for most people in the United States. Often we ask: How many kids are there on your block or in your apartment complex? If people know the answer, the next question is: Do you know their names?

For many people, neighborhood has become little more than a place to sleep at night, and it would be unrealistic to expect nostalgia for a bygone era to guide efforts to rebuild a sense of neighborliness. At the same time, apartment buildings, blocks, and neighborhoods offer a unique opportunity to provide community and support for young people.

There has been something of a revival of neighborhood organizations in recent years. Many have been motivated by a fear of crime or deteriorating property values. For example, on a national level, the annual National Night Out for Crime is organized through police departments and "block captains" to build relationships among neighbors and a shared sense of responsibility for the block.

The asset-building focus has the potential to unite communities not around a shared enemy but a shared commitment. It may begin as simply as getting to know the names of the children on the street or neighbors looking out for neighborhood children as they play outside. It may grow to be more formal as neighborhood organizers arrange for shared intergenerational activities from picnics to service proj-

ects to community gardens. Or it may involve businesses in the neighborhood working together to support a teen center or a youth-run business. (See "Asset-Building
Ideas for Neighborhoods" below for specific ideas.)

Many efforts are under way to rebuild neighborhoods. Although they do not
all focus on children and youth, making neighborhoods good places to raise children is always an underlying subtext. One systematic effort to organize neighborhoods is led by the Institute for the Study of Civic Values in Philadelphia. A
key strategy is to work with neighborhood residents to develop a social contract
that addresses many, interlocking needs in the block or neighborhood within the
context of the civil values outlined in the U.S. Constitution. Among the commitments in the "Block Club Social Contract," which residents sign, is: "We will create an atmosphere of trust that strengthens families and enables all residents of
all generations to work together. To this end, we will make a special effort to ensure
that the spirit of cooperation that we promote on our blocks extends to our young
people. We will encourage them to join neighborhood clean-up improvement projects as junior block captains, as well as participate in block social activities.
Through a variety of efforts, we will place a high priority on helping families provide adequate support to secure quality education for our children."[21]

Another effort is the Caring Neighborhoods with Youth project, a joint effort
of the Junior League, the Marion County Commission on Youth, and Community Partnerships with Youth, in an inner city neighborhood in Indianapolis. The
effort seeks to assist "local residents of all ages and walks of life to work together
to provide a safe environment for all."

One component of the effort is a youth-adult council that provides leadership in the neighborhood. Says the project's site coordinator, Dax Gonzales,
"These kids are bright and ambitious. They are determined to create change and
bring pride back to their neighborhoods."

An early project was to begin reclaiming a house near a park that had been
donated to the effort. The young people cleaned up the property and are now
working with the Junior League to assess whether to turn the house into a youth
center.[22]

These and other neighborhood efforts have the potential of reconnecting
young people with the adults who live around them and to see youth as a major
resource in rebuilding neighborhoods. In the process, these efforts may ease some
of the mistrust and insecurity that undermine neighborhood stability and connections.

Asset-Building Ideas for Neighborhoods

- Create neighborhood service projects linking adults and children.
- Make asset building a criteria for setting priorities for action in the neighborhood.

- Coordinate residents to provide safe places where young people can go after school if they would otherwise be home alone or if they feel unsafe.
- Organize informal activities (such as pickup basketball) for young people in the neighborhood.
- Use neighborhood meetings and other settings to educate people about their responsibility and power for asset building.
- Work with children and teenagers to create a neighborhood garden, playground, or park.
- Mobilize to promote a safe and drug-free neighborhood.

Extending the Reach

Each of the systems outlined in this chapter—from schools to youth organizations to congregations to neighborhoods—has a tremendous amount to offer young people from an asset-building perspective. Yet each faces unique challenges in terms of other agendas that cry for attention, the dynamics of integrating change into an established organization, and other external challenges, such as decreases in funds for doing more work.

For these reasons, it is important to note that an asset-building vision does not necessarily mean that each of these systems has to add a lot of new programming to its already stretched resources. Rather, the asset-building vision helps provide a lens for setting priorities, celebrating strengths, enhancing current practices, and using untapped potential as the larger vision within the community unleashes new resources and commitments that can extend an organization's reach and impact.

The efforts of these primary socializing systems is greatly enhanced when they are undergirded by a commitment to asset building by other sectors and influencers in the community (which may become the channels for both volunteers and financial resources for youth development programs). Chapter Eleven turns attention to how other sectors in the community can reinforce asset building with their commitments.

CHAPTER ELEVEN

UNITING THE VILLAGE

The Roles of All Sectors in the Community

I f this book ended with Chapter Ten, it might give the impression that the organizational expression of and commitment to asset building is largely programmatic: the kinds of important opportunities already offered by youth-serving
programs. That involvement is a crucial part of the effort, but lasting change requires that the vision be broad, reaching out to every sector and system within the
community to determine if and how that sector or system can support the asset-
building vision.

In addition to the organizations having regular contact with youth, numerous other institutions also play important roles in communitywide strategies. We
choose the phrase *secondary socializing systems* as a convenient way to differentiate
these systems from the schools, congregations, youth organizations, and neighborhoods that were the focus of Chapter Ten.

In many cases, though, these organizations also have direct contact with many
youth, if not as frequent or widespread. Employers, for example, are major influences in the lives of older youth. Health care providers have families as core constituencies. But these systems also have a broader leadership role in shaping the
priorities, culture, and tone of community life. Without the involvement and buy-
in of these systems, an asset-building effort faces an uphill battle in shaping community life around asset building.

In this chapter, we look briefly at some of the roles secondary socializing systems can play in growing a healthy community. Then we illustrate how six specific

sectors can contribute, knowing that there are many other sectors that also have much to offer.

Major Roles for Secondary Socializing Systems

Many of the roles outlined for primary socializing systems in Chapter Ten have parallels for secondary systems, particularly those that have direct and ongoing contact with youth. In addition, there are specific roles that are more heavily weighted to the kinds of strengths and resources that the secondary systems can offer an initiative:

Shaping programs and services to advance the vision. Though these systems may have less direct contact with youth, many do touch young people's lives occasionally or through specific programs and strategies. Whenever this is the case, the asset-building filter likely has something to offer.

Examining internal practices. How do the organization's internal policies either encourage or detract from an asset-building focus? For example, does the company have family-friendly employment policies that give parents time, flexibility, and support for their needs? In what ways does the organization support (and offer incentives for) employees' getting involved in asset building? How does the organization promote an asset-building climate? And how does it ensure that the perspectives of youth are represented in planning and other deliberations?

Providing impetus and leadership. In all of the communities that have begun this work, the impetus and vision of creating a healthy community has emerged from one or more organizational leaders within the community. Sometimes it's the school superintendent or the mayor. Other times it may be a business leader or a religious leader. Whatever the specific case, these leaders of community institutions have had the ability to convene the stakeholders in the community and provide the initial leadership and management for an initiative.

Eventually, the leadership becomes less dependent upon a specific organization or sector as the vision is shared and internalized by others. In fact, it can be detrimental for a communitywide initiative to become too tightly identified with one sector or organization within the community, because that can reinforce preconceptions that the initiative is "a school program" or "a government program," rather than a communitywide movement that has support and involvement from local institutions.

Lending expertise and access. A community initiative is strengthened by tapping into the existing networks, expertise, credibility, and resources within a community. For example, advertising and marketing agencies can be key resources in helping to shape messages and get the word out to the community. Many nonprofit organizations, health care firms, and businesses have training systems that could be used to support the effort. The challenge is to break out of traditional program-matic thinking that says everything has to be done using resources within a particular organization, instead to unleash new possibilities for volunteer com-mitments and in-kind services.

Engaging in advocacy. In addition, many organizations can play pivotal roles in shaping policies (both public and corporate), advocating for appropriate changes and increased asset-building opportunities within the community.

Providing financial support. Finally, although asset building does not need to have tremendous financial resources, it does need some funding to carry out basic strategies. Many organizations within the community have access to resources that could be extended for these purposes.

Business and Industry

One of the areas of surprisingly strong interest in asset building is the business sector in communities. Indeed, the first communitywide asset-building initiative (in St. Louis Park, Minnesota) was underwritten by business leaders who saw the potential and importance of the framework for their community.

The interest is not all altruistic. Al Ernest of Owens-Corning in Newark, Ohio, describes the self-interest of business this way: "We have a major stake in nurturing asset-rich kids. Currently, many job applicants do not have the skills and values we want in our employees: empathy, team skills, goals, and a sense of pur-pose. As a major employer in the community, we need to ensure the quality of our workforce down the road."

Businesses can contribute to asset building in a number of ways (additionally, see the text "Asset-Building Ideas for Business and Industry" below):

- Make it possible for employees (including parents) to engage in asset-building efforts by offering flexible scheduling, on-site child care, and other family-friendly policies.
- Develop employee volunteer programs that encourage employees to partici-pate as volunteers in youth-serving organizations and schools.
- Use the asset framework as a resource for employee training and development programs.
- Frame corporate giving programs to focus on programs that promote devel-opmental assets in the community.
- As part of the company's efforts to build goodwill and corporate responsibil-ity, assume a leadership role in communitywide asset-building efforts. Also, sup-port the efforts through appropriate in-kind contributions.

With eight thousand employees, American Express Financial Advisors has begun using asset-based materials in its work and family division. According to Sharon Klun, work and family coordinator for the corporation, the approach has been empowering to their employees. She says a number of employees have shared the information about assets with their local parent-teacher organizations, congregations, communities, clients, and youth coalition groups. The materials "give people building blocks that they can work with," Klun says. "Giving it to our people empowers them to see what they can do."

From a corporate point of view, providing information about assets is essential. "It improves our bottom line," she says. "And it helps on all those fronts for retention, recruitment, absenteeism, stress reduction, you name it. . . . If people can be better parents and not be so stressed out at home, they can be better employees."

Asset-Building Ideas for Business and Industry

- Develop family-friendly policies that allow parents to be active in their children's lives.
- Provide opportunities for employees to build relationships with youth through mentoring and other volunteer programs, flexible scheduling, and internships for youth.
- Be intentional about nurturing assets (such as support, boundaries, values, and social competencies) in the lives of teenagers employed by the company.
- Become partners in and advocates for initiatives designed to create healthy communities for children and youth.
- Provide resources (donations, in-kind contributions, etc.) to youth development programs.

Health Care Systems

Health care systems are going through rapid change, driven in part by economic realities and competition for market share. Whether hospital, clinic, managed care, or insurance provider, interest is building in both advocating health promotion strategies and developing a community presence. As a manual from the Healthcare Forum Leadership Center advocates: "To address health in a meaningful way, we must start by redefining health and by considering the relationships between wellness and key components of our living and working environments."[1]

These strategic developments, when combined with the missional commitment to health, position health care systems as valuable allies in building asset-rich communities. Indeed, it could be argued that it is in the self-interest of health care systems to support and advocate communitywide asset-building initiatives, if on no other grounds than that developmental assets likely reduce some of the health-compromising behaviors that often require costly medical treatment.

One of the asset-building capacities of health systems is the delivery of services to children and families. We now know of hospitals, for example, that give a kit of asset-building materials to new parents as part of the birthing experience, and physicians who do the same with expecting parents.

Imagine the capacity of pediatricians to use the language and concepts of asset building with parents, children, and adolescents. Ultimately, pediatricians advance health by incorporating these kinds of inquiries with youth: "How many adults in your community do you know?" "What clubs, teams, and organizations do you belong to?" "How often do you spend time helping other people?" As a voice for asset building, pediatricians sow seeds for both effective parenting and promoting proactive asset building among youth.

Health care systems and their leaders also have significant power to serve as advocates for communitywide asset-building initiatives. Hospitals, clinics, and managed care systems have unique capacity—as catalysts, conveners, and networkers—to unite and equip many sectors of a community. Mercy Medical Center in Nampa, Idaho, is a prime example. This hospital took the lead in convening and supporting the community dialogues that ultimately birthed a long-term city commitment to asset building and incorporated it into the city's strategic plan.[2]

Asset-Building Ideas for Health Care Systems

- Serve as visionary leaders in reshaping public consciousness about the health and well-being of children and adolescents.
- Offer information on asset building to parents and teenagers when they seek care.
- Emphasize integrating asset building into health care facilities. For example, are the facilities providing a supportive, caring environment for children and adolescents?
- Provide financial and in-kind support to initiatives within the community that seek to strengthen developmental assets.
- Involve youth as volunteers in hospitals and other health care facilities.

Community-Based Organizations

In every town and city in America, community-based organizations provide vital services and resources that enhance the quality of life. Whether these organizations are volunteer-driven or have large staffs, they are on the front lines in building community strengths and providing important services.

In several places throughout this book, I note that our society has become overdependent on social services to provide care for children and adolescents. Despite overemphasis, they do have important roles to play in a communitywide commitment to asset building. Indeed, in a time of "devolution" of social services, the asset-building vision may help provide a focus for making decisions under mounting pressure to provide more and more services with less and less public-sector support. Furthermore, if a community takes seriously and is able to implement the vision of a healthy, connected, and caring community, the need for crisis intervention and remedial services may become more manageable than is currently the case.

As with other organizations, the asset-building vision calls community organizations to examine their mission and internal practices. This assessment should include an examination of employee practices to ensure that they encourage asset-building commitments among staff members, and an assessment of organizational climate to determine whether the culture models or undermines healthy community.

In addition, the vision of asset building can be integrated into the programs and services provided by the agency. These may include programs that directly involve youth in asset building (such as mentoring or providing child care and after-school care) and programs that support and educate families.

In addition, other organizations having less direct contact with youth can also integrate the framework into their activities. For example, programs that provide food, housing, and emergency assistance can ensure that they are providing a supportive, caring, and empowering climate for the families using their services. In addition, they can build skills and relationships that help people form social networks to help, over time, in providing stability, trust, and informal sources of support.

The asset-building vision also calls upon agencies to find their appropriate place in community partnerships for youth. This may include informal networking, forming partnerships with other organizations related to asset building, or being a catalyst for change in the community.

One example of potential partnership is in the area of service learning. As schools and other youth-serving organizations seek to engage youth in service, there are natural opportunities for agencies to tap a pool of young, competent volunteers. Yet too often, schools scramble on their own to find good service opportunities for youth, while agencies struggle to find adequate volunteer help to accomplish their mission. Forming creative partnerships can help both institutions in their agendas and also strengthen asset-building opportunities in the community.[3]

Asset-Building Ideas for Community-Based Organizations

- Involve youth as volunteers and leaders in the agency.
- Provide information on asset building to families and others who participate in programs and services.
- Train agency staff and leaders in their role as asset builders.
- Examine all programs in the agency to determine the best ways to involve youth.

- Integrate an intergenerational perspective into programming so that you are intentional about connecting people across generations who use services.
- Advocate for asset-building approaches in the networks and communities you serve.
- Provide leadership, in-kind contributions, and other support to community asset-building initiatives.[4]

Government

From Capitol Hill to state capitols and city halls across the United States, policy makers and analysts are reexamining government's role in society. It's unclear how much this examination actually promotes change (and whether the changes will be for the better); nevertheless, the current climate provides openings to frame policy making in the positive terms of asset building and positive youth development. We have begun seeing changes at many levels of government.

City and County Government

City hall is an active partner in many of the existing local asset-building initiatives. In some cases, public officials (mayors, police chiefs, city managers, etc.) become important conveners of stakeholders in the community. In others, they implement specific asset-building strategies through their public works, parks and recreation, public awareness, community education, and other program areas.

In Winona, Minnesota, for example, the asset framework has influenced the county's child protection services, according to Connie Blackburn, coordinator of the county's asset-building initiative, Community Connections. When a family gets involved in child protection, the child protection worker goes through the list of assets and has the family start identifying the positive things that they're doing in their family. The child protection worker then helps the family identify some activities that would help them build additional assets in their children's lives.

Another issue for local government is the role of city planning in either promoting or inhibiting asset building. Examining all the issues involved in city planning is beyond the scope of this book.[5] However, communities involved in asset building are beginning to think about what the implications are for city development and planning, regarding relationships and opportunities for youth.[6]

Asset-Building Ideas for Local Government

- Through policy, training, and resource allocation, make asset development a top priority in the city.
- Become a champion of asset building throughout the city. Convene stakeholders to begin efforts to coordinate a neighborhood or citywide vision for asset building.

- Initiate communitywide efforts to name shared values and boundaries.
- Partner with other organizations in creating child-friendly public places, and safe places for teenagers to gather.
- Build asset-building approaches into law enforcement and juvenile justice.
- Expand community education.
- Train service providers, police, parks and recreation staff, and other public employees in asset building.
- Help coordinate and publicize after-school, weekend, and summer opportunities for youth in the city.
- Preserve neighborhoods.
- Create child-friendly public places.
- Strengthen or develop ordinances that reduce or eliminate juvenile access to alcohol and tobacco.
- Develop ordinances to place day care centers, schools, and after-school programs where senior citizens live and spend time.[7]

State Government

Bringing resources together at a state level for asset building has the potential to shape state policy and funding. In Vermont, for example, a statewide network of twenty-five policy makers in the areas of education, health and human services, and nonprofits has been formed to build assets and create resiliency in the youth of Vermont. "In terms of policy making for children and families, this can have a big impact," says Sue Mahoney, planning specialist for the Vermont State Department of Education.

Currently the group is in the planning process. Yet the state has already changed its Safe and Drug-Free Schools Community Partnership Grants program to focus on assets and resiliency, distributing six grants to support communities in their efforts to build assets in youth. Mahoney sees great potential for her state even though Vermont's largest community is thirty-five thousand people and there are only one hundred thousand kids statewide. "Everyone needs to work on it," she says.

The asset framework also has potential within states' public health efforts, particularly as the field of public health is shifting from a disease-prevention model to one of health promotion, according to Susan Nalder, an epidemiologist in the public health division of the New Mexico Department of Health. "Here is information that tells us what our private and public agenda needs to be in order to successfully reduce—from a public health perspective—the important risk behaviors in our youth," she says. "But what was most compelling was seeing these risks in their proper context, in other words, in context with the youngster's support systems—assets, as they are called—as well as those things that may be considered deficits and risk behavior."

Nalder contends that studying young people's developmental assets provides much more useful data and information than surveys that focus mainly on problems, such as drugs, alcohol, and other risky behaviors. "The findings of the assessment provide an agenda for action that has implications for public health practice, for families, individuals, communities, neighborhoods, groups, and so on," she says. "That's why I find it ever so much more useful than our ability to name, count, and describe the distribution of risk-taking behaviors."

On a larger scale, asset building has the potential to help create a sense of an articulated agenda for children and youth. A study by the State Legislative Leaders Foundation showed that state legislators do not discern a clear agenda or constituency for children and families. Furthermore, many are unclear that state government can play a positive role in addressing needs.[8] The developmental asset framework and the healthy-communities focus have the potential of addressing both of these gaps.

Finally, the asset-building approach has important implications for how states make critical decisions regarding policies and funding. Recommendations from the Texas Commission on Children and Youth illustrate the potential. This commission identified "investment budgeting" as an essential strategy for moving beyond a short-term funding focus. "This approach," the commission contended, "enables policy makers to consider investments that may not yield a return within the current biennium, but will pay off handsomely in the long run—not only in dollars, but also in human potential."[9]

Furthermore, as part of this budgeting approach, the commission recommended that all legislation and policies affecting children include a Children's Impact Statement, which would outline the ways all proposed policies affect children and families. This approach is quite consistent with asset building. As policies and legislation are developed that affect young people, questions such as these need to be asked:

- Would this action increase or decrease asset-building programs and services for young people?
- Would this action reduce or increase barriers to having youth and families participate in asset-building activities or receive asset-building services?
- Would this action make it more or less difficult for communities to coordinate programs and services across sectors?

National Government

Although the language of developmental assets is only just entering the culture of Washington, D.C., recent years have seen a growing interest in and commitment to the language of positive youth development. For example, the 103rd U.S.

Congress passed the Youth Development Block Grant to authorize $400 million in the first year to expand community-based programs for children and adolescents. Other legislation has included extensive language that supports a positive youth development perspective.[10]

In a time when many programs are in danger of being cut to balance the federal deficit, the asset-building framework can help focus priorities. Unfortunately, many programs that have tremendous potential to build assets (such as youth recreation or youth service) are at risk in a climate that emphasizes getting tough and clamping down.

Several national youth-serving organizations are now calling for a national undertaking, in a document illustratively titled *Contract with America's Youth: Toward a National Youth Development Agenda*. Their call is compatible with the asset-building paradigm, though they emphasize programmatic goals with less emphasis on the informal opportunities and relationships that nurture assets in youth. They identify and make recommendations in three areas:

1. Strengthening national systems and federal programs that affect youth.
2. Strengthening community infrastructures.
3. Establishing national youth development goals.[11]

These programmatic emphases offer a beginning point. On a deeper level is a need to infuse national life, including the public sector, with a commitment to the healthy development of children and adolescents as a filter for crafting and passing legislation and for funding decisions.

There is a major obstacle in utilizing governmental entities to support communitywide asset-building movements. Such support requires a bold commitment to the transfer of power to communities. It requires the ideological belief that the people in communities can—when empowered—tackle and solve compelling social problems. And it requires moving government officials from this awareness to action steps that empower communities. This includes everything from providing financial assistance for local community-building initiatives to providing technical expertise in community change. As one county commissioner recently put it, "as much as public officials now speak of community empowerment in an era of devolution, we rarely have the courage of our convictions." Translated, this seems to imply that government, wedded historically to service provision and control, views community empowerment as threatening. Yes, enabling citizens to build community is in some sense a threat to the status quo. But the status quo, when it comes to how this society now raises its young, is untenable. Our view is that in the long run, the well-being of this society grows proportionally to the degree that all sectors—government and otherwise—trust and affirm that the people have the ultimate capacity to trigger and sustain healthy community.

Juvenile Justice

Much of this book is devoted to describing both the nature of healthy development and the dynamics of communities that promote it. The strongest utilization of these paradigms is in long-term initiatives on behalf of all children and adolescents. But all communities have in their midst troubled and troubling youth. Thus, there is growing interest in how to apply the asset development paradigm to the lives of young people who become visible to us as runaways, dropouts, or delinquents.

One perspective on this issue is to ask whether developmental assets can be built or rebuilt in lives already moving along a troubled path and often surrounded by social environments counterproductive to asset building. How well our work can function as a model for promoting second chances is currently unclear, but leaders in intervention systems are beginning to apply asset development ideas to their work. This is particularly evident in the field of juvenile justice.

Asset building has tremendous potential to reshape this system, according to Tom English, president of the Oregon Council on Crime and Delinquency in Eugene. He finds that the framework of assets and asset building has helped transform his training and consulting in juvenile justice and delinquency prevention across the country.

"This is the piece that resonates with the current juvenile justice research," he says. "And essentially that says we grow healthy kids in units of socialization sequentially, which is through the family, the school, the peer group, and the community. We need to offer kids opportunities to be successful, the skills to be involved successfully, and consistently reward them. If we do that we create attachments, commitment, belief, and prosocial kids.

"Asset building works for kids in the system," he says. "Instead of looking at these kids as law violators, which they are, we also need to take a look at the competency deficits and the skills deficits that brought them into the system. Those are asset deficits. How do we rebuild assets in these kids who didn't get them along the way so they can come back and be productive members of society?"

But the real impact of assets on the juvenile justice system, English contends, is connecting realities in the system with realities in the community. "We now know that building strong families, effective schools, positive peer groups, and open communities provides the resiliency and the protective factors to keep kids from falling into those negative pathways," he says. "We further know that even if kids come from highly dysfunctional families, we do have a way, through other environments to intervene, to bring them up to speed. And these interventions are low cost, are very effective, and have payoffs."

Currently under way are a number of practical applications. These include efforts by juvenile judges and probation officers in several states to case manage youth using the template of the developmental assets and deploying staff to teach the asset framework to young people and parents through school and neighborhood settings.

Reclaiming troubled youth continues to be an elusive enterprise; few social issues are of more importance. The template of developmental assets may provide a useful blueprint for strategy and action. It takes intense and innovative work in assessment, service design, case management, collaboration, training, and evaluation to make progress.

One innovation is occurring in Maine, where the Kennebunk and Kennebunkport police departments have used the asset approach to intervene early with juvenile offenders. Until now, if a juvenile got into trouble, up to a month might pass before a probation officer would contact the young person, who then had to report to a caseworker once every two weeks. Moreover, casework overload made many of these contacts superficial, and it could take up to a year to get a court date.

"We wanted to shorten up the time between the offense and the consequence," says Lt. Doug Sharlow of the Kennebunk police department. So he and another officer started the Jump Start program, which draws on the community's commitment to asset building.

With this program, any first-time, nonviolent juvenile offender must sign a contract, have a parent sign a contract, begin a three-month probation, do community service, make restitution, write letters of apology to the victims, and participate in an eight-week decision-making skills course through the police departments. Each offender is also assigned to an adult mentor through the whole program.

The eight-week program focuses on building assets, building relationships, and exposing youth to positive, caring adults. "They get a lot of positive feedback from the adults," Sharlow says. "We found that after eight weeks, the kids still want to show up for the course."

In the first fifteen months of operation, the program served fifty-seven youth, with only three repeat offenders (about a 7 percent recidivism rate, compared with a typical rate of 35–40 percent). Sharlow has seen other big changes in the youth involved in the program. Many have turned around their academic performance. Others have joined support groups for chemical dependency issues. "It's very positive," Sharlow says. "And we think we're building assets in our youth through this program."

Asset-Building Ideas for Juvenile Justice

- Use the framework of assets as a tool for case management for juvenile offenders.
- Build connections to positive youth organizations within their community for juvenile offenders.

- Educate parents and other support networks about the developmental needs of young people at risk.
- Explore how the asset framework may support innovative practices and programs in juvenile detention centers.
- Train police officers, probation officers, and others to understand their role in asset building with youth in the communities they serve.

Corporate and Philanthropic Foundations

Nearly all communities benefit from the philanthropy of community and corporate foundations. How foundations shape their giving guidelines often determines to a significant extent how communities pursue the public good. In this way, foundations shape public consciousness about what matters.

The role of foundations in expanding the asset-building energy within communities therefore has two parts. The first is to shift guidelines for giving, to encourage innovative thinking and strategy development for promoting developmental assets. The other is to support these innovations, via grant making and technical assistance.

The HealthSystems Minnesota Foundation now accomplishes both. By board action, it now places the list of forty assets on the cover of its brochure. In the narrative, the brochure instructs grant writers to name the developmental assets to be promoted, the strategies to be used, the evaluation efforts to monitor asset change, and the linkages the effort makes with other community asset-building efforts. In essence, this shift says: "Tell us which assets you will grow rather than which behaviors you will prevent." In addition to providing funding for asset-building innovations, this pioneering foundation also gives core funding and leadership to Children First, the long-term community movement for asset building in St. Louis Park, Minnesota.

In Search Institute's backyard of Minneapolis and St. Paul, we see other foundations expanding their vision to incorporate communitywide efforts to promote developmental assets. The corporate giving arms of Cargill, the nation's largest privately held company, now not only support asset-building community initiatives but also invest in educating employees about the asset-building paradigm.

Foundations affiliated with national corporations can leverage social change in many ways. A prime example is Lutheran Brotherhood, the fraternal benefits society that provides financial services, community service opportunities, and philanthropic outreach in communities nationwide. Just as significant as its role in providing a capacity-building grant to Search Institute to grow our asset-building work is its role of generating employee and volunteer commitment to the paradigm. Lutheran Brotherhood's board members, corporate employees, national sales force, and regional networks of volunteers are mobilized through training, workshops, national conferences, publications, and grant making to serve as ambassadors and resources in hundreds of communities across the country. The relational or people resources of such national corporations are as vital for promoting the social good as are its financial resources.

Asset-Building Ideas for Foundations

- Provide financial support and leadership to communities in their efforts to build assets.
- Revise grant-making guidelines to ensure that they encourage asset-building efforts, rather than promoting quick-fix responses to narrow problems.
- Encourage and equip employees to build assets in their own networks and spheres of influence.
- Work with asset-building initiatives to establish clear areas of accountability that are consistent with the asset-building approach.
- Include youth in grant-making roles within the foundation.[12]
- Examine how the foundation's practices model asset building in the community. For example, does the process for grant seeking empower residents, or does it make them become overdependent upon outside funding?

The Media

The media have a tremendous impact on society's norms, particularly since many children are heavily socialized by the mass media and because the media play a major role in shaping society's attitudes toward the young. Currently, the media largely portray young people in a negative light.

A survey of five hundred adolescents and one thousand adults sponsored by Lions Clubs International found that both groups believe the media's portrayal of young people is overwhelmingly negative. Given five options, Table 11.1 shows the percentages of teenagers (ages twelve to seventeen) and adults who say each phrase "most accurately describes how the media portray young people."[13]

Whether because of public pressure or economic realities, journalists and other media leaders are recognizing their responsibility to participate in efforts to create healthy communities and to address youth issues in a more balanced manner. To call on the media to become partners in efforts to create healthy communities is consistent with the commitment to "civic" or "public" journalism that has emerged in the past decade. A report from the Millennium Communications Group describe the movement this way: "Civic journalism essentially involves journalists—and the newspapers and broadcast outlets that are the institutional

TABLE 11.1. MEDIA PORTRAYALS OF YOUTH: ADULT AND YOUTH PERCEPTIONS (PERCENTAGES).

	Youth	Adults
• Mostly portrays them negatively.	39	40
• Conveys the feeling that there is no hope for the future.	22	18
• Portrays them with an even-handed balance.	16	18
• Conveys the feeling that there is a great deal of hope for the future.	15	12
• Mostly portrays them positively.	5	5

Source: ICR Survey Research Group. (1995). *Youth problems study.* New York: AUS Consultants.

structures behind journalists—in producing coverage that not only reports on problems but also promotes the education and discussion that leads to solutions. . . . Civic journalism thus engenders a media that is actively involved in re-engaging citizens in public life, in promoting and improving public deliberation, and in strengthening the connections between journalists and their communities."[14]

These civic journalism initiatives have taken many forms and have addressed many issues: crime, economic development, race relations, and others. These efforts are not simply altruistic; they provide opportunities for the media to engage with their audiences and help generate significant and relevant local news. In some communities with asset-building initiatives, the local media have become significant partners and leaders. For example, in Nampa, Idaho, the local paper helped to sponsor the study of youth assets and then dedicated a series of front-page articles (plus editorials) to covering the findings.[15]

According to the report from the Millennium Communications Group, the emergence of civic journalism offers new opportunities that move beyond pushing for coverage of a particular issue toward educating community members who can, in turn, advocate the media's involvement in civic affairs. "This is very different," the report insists, "from advocating for coverage, or asking for 'good stories.' It must engage local media outlets in problem-solving and dialogue-enhancing processes—either as initiators or as partners with civic institutions."[16]

Although there are natural connections between asset building and the news-oriented media, it is perhaps even more important to develop a consciousness of the asset-building paradigm in the entertainment and advertising industries. These media have tremendous impact—both positive and negative—and can also bring valuable skills and resources to asset-building efforts, particularly in awareness raising and educational efforts in the community. Furthermore, they can be active partners (through policy commitments and public service announcements, for example) in efforts to shape positive community boundaries, norms, and values for young people.

Asset-Building Ideas for the Media

- Recognize the media's responsibility and role in creating a community climate in which youth are valued, cared for, and supported.
- Pay attention to the hidden stories of people giving their time, energy, and creativity to improve the lives of children and youth.
- Listen and respond to the public demand for more balanced coverage of young people. Recognize the newsworthiness of how young people, families, and communities are starting to work together to create a better future.
- Seek out stories that highlight the ways young people contribute to society.
- In analyzing trends, policies, and legislation, emphasize their potential long-term impact on the positive development of young people.
- Monitor coverage to ensure that most stories about children and adolescents place them in a favorable light.

Everyone Is an Asset Builder

One of the dangers in surveying the ways specific sectors can be involved in asset building is that it may inadvertently give a feeling of exclusivity. Not every type of organization is highlighted. Why haven't we included libraries? labor unions? realtors? other social service providers and charities? higher education? All of these, and many others, potentially have much to offer asset-building efforts. Shouldn't they be included?

Yes! There are other players in communities with the economic, political, and social capital to unleash or support asset-building community initiatives. The United Way has immense capacity to catalyze unifying community movements for children and adolescents. Service organizations, such as Rotary, Lions, and Kiwanis, are already asset-building partners in many of the initiatives under way, providing leadership, advocacy, networking, visibility, and financial support.

This chapter does not intend to limit the scope but instead to hint at some ways in which different systems and sectors within a community can contribute to the vision. The ideas are more illustrative than exhaustive. We fully expect to continue being surprised at the innovative and creative ways people within communities find to partner together and make a difference in the lives of young people.

Take, for example, Gary Walker, who has been in real estate for more than thirty years and is chairman of the board for the housing developer United Development. He wants the planned community he is building to be a community with kids at its heart. By designing neighborhoods, a community center, and other programs with asset building in mind, the ten-thousand–resident community of Las Sendas hopes to be a place where children and youth are valued, respected, and cared for by all the residents. The framework of developmental assets is integral to the community's master plan. Here are noteworthy asset-promoting plans in the project:

- A coordinator for asset-building activities in the community
- A multifaceted community center where youth and adults can hang out and get involved in a wide range of activities
- An art gallery where young people can display their work, and music appreciation workshops for young people
- An ecology garden that youth plan, plant, and maintain
- Numerous child-friendly parks
- A voluntary directory of youth and adults' interests so people can connect with neighbors around common interests

"As developers, we can include the physical and architectural aspects that can accommodate, foster, and inspire things to happen, like safe gathering places," says Bob Williams, who works with Walker at United Development. "We've all agonized over the demise of the American community," says Williams. "When you think that there will be two thousand families or more living in Las Sendas, you realize you have a tremendous arena of influence."

POSTSCRIPT:
THE POWER OF COMMUNITIES

We are losing our way. Through a conspiracy of factors, the processes and dynamics of healthy human development during the first two decades of life are eroding. It is becoming the norm to segregate our cultural neophytes from the wisdom and experience of adults; treat children and adolescents as objects of community programs rather than as subjects in community; give mixed signals— or no signals at all—about what matters; ignore the young in public places or treat them with suspicion; deny them meaningful roles in civic life; fill their heads with images of conflict and mayhem; fuel an early lust for possessions; tolerate or even encourage self-indulgence; raise them in neighborhoods where few know their names; expect little responsibility for the welfare of others; and send them to underfunded, understaffed, and all-too-often inattentive, schools, day care, and after-school programs. Then we bemoan their fate, while blaming their families and holding the parents solely accountable.

Developmental assets are in disrepair in all communities, irrespective of family income or race. Underlying systemic factors such as economic inequality and exclusion exacerbate this rupture in the developmental infrastructure. The crisis we face is general and widespread inattention to the dailiness of healthy socialization. As Robert Bly cogently writes, "We must find and name that secret road that has led American society in such a brief time from a moderately disciplined, moderately respectful culture to a culture in which twelve-year-olds shoot each other [and] Calvin Klein uses children for sexually explicit advertisements."[1]

Into this developmental vacuum—into this moment when too many young are untethered to community or tradition—streams a susceptibility to sensation seeking and instant gratification, a desperate search for belonging, an overtesting of limits.

The way out of this morass begins with a massive shift in public will, with a resurrection of collective memory about the capacity and responsibility of citizens to envelop their young in supportive, attentive, and caring community.

The developmental assets, in the aggregate, approximate this collective memory.

It is difficult to paint a brief word picture of an asset-building community. Indeed, we expect our understanding to sharpen as we grow with and learn from the many communities now seeking to unleash their asset-building capacity. Here are some of the images we currently envision:

- All residents build caring relationships with children and adolescents and express this caring through dialogue, listening, commending positive behavior, knowing their names, acknowledging their presence, involving them in decision making, and doing things with them.
- Families elevate asset development to top priority for their own children and their children's friends.
- Religious institutions mobilize their capacity for intergenerational relationships, parent education, value development, quality structured opportunities, and service to the community.
- Schools place priority on becoming caring environments for all students, provide additional opportunities for the nurture of values deemed crucial by the community, strengthen cocurricular activities, and use connection to parents to escalate parental involvement and reinforce the importance of family attention to assets.
- Youth organizations train leaders and volunteers in asset-building strategies.
- Businesses that employ teenagers address the assets of support, boundaries, values, and social competencies. Employers develop family-friendly policies and provide mechanisms for employees to build relationships with youth.
- Through policy, training, and resource allocation, city government moves asset development to top priority.

Ultimately, rebuilding and strengthening the developmental infrastructure in a community is not a program run by professionals. It is a movement of people and systems that creates a communitywide sense of common purpose, places residents and their leaders on the same team moving in the same direction, and creates a normative culture in which all residents are expected—by virtue of their membership in the community—to promote the positive development of children and adolescents.

Emmet Carson, president of the Minneapolis Foundation and a lifelong advocate for children, echoes this call for comprehensive and multifaceted change. In his terms, we need to surround kids with three circles of care: family, community, and policy.[2] Each circle of care is a necessary factor in healthy development, but none working alone is sufficient. Good family, for example, is crucial. But good family is not enough. Asset-building community as well as policies enabling community mobilization are also crucial, even when family is strong, and doubly so when it is not.

Learnings from the Field

The paradigm of developmental assets has many applications. We know, for example, that the framework is used by:

> Probation officers and social service providers to case-manage troubled and troubling youth
>
> Youth organizations as a road map for guiding program development
>
> Schools and religious organizations as a call to action and a framework for goal setting
>
> Parents as a daily reminder of their capacity and responsibility
>
> Community educators as a template for parent education
>
> Foundations as guidelines for funding proposals
>
> Evaluators as a framework for defining program outcomes
>
> Park and recreation departments as a training device for volunteer coaches
>
> Mentoring programs as a way of defining the work of mentors

However, the paradigm reaches its fullest expression as a vehicle for unleashing a communitywide asset-building initiative. As Search Institute stays in touch with, and occasionally assists, the close to two hundred community initiatives under way, we hear testimony about the power of the developmental assets and healthy-community paradigms. In urban, suburban, and rural settings, efforts to mobilize citizens and systems around the vision of developmental assets have five noticeable impacts. They trigger action by individual citizens; stimulate action and policy development in multiple organizations and institutions; renew the enthusiasm and commitment of professionals who serve youth (teachers, community youth workers, religious youth workers); create alliances of cooperation that were, as one observer put it, "unthinkable" prior to the healthy-community initiative (for example, it is not uncommon for communities to mention collaborative networks occurring among religious, school, and business leaders); and serve as a catalyst for innovative methods for educating the public about its capacity and responsibility.

There are two other areas where we see an impact almost everywhere across these communities. One is the way the asset paradigm creates an umbrella of shared purpose under which preexisting collaboration and initiatives can join hands in pursuit of the common good. The second is about hope and possibility. It is profound to us to frequently hear community leaders and other residents describe how this work touches the heart: "It is a language of hope." "It reminds me that I make a difference." "It compels me to take action." "I can't stop talking about it with my friends and colleagues." "It tells us that change is possible."

These reactions are so common (and often deeply emotional in the telling) that there must be in many communities a despair for which the paradigm provides an antidote. Perhaps the paradigm of developmental assets hits the culture at an important moment, at a time when energy and commitment and common purpose are suppressed but are close enough to the surface to seek expression. As Michael Lerner asserts in the introduction to *The Politics of Meaning*, "At the same time that we are caught in cynicism, however, we are desperate for hope."[3]

We are now in the process of developing several statewide efforts to mobilize and network multiple cities beginning the asset-building journey together. This work provides the occasion to develop regional infrastructures to support their efforts, including statewide media campaigns to mobilize citizens around the capacity and responsibility to promote developmental assets, technical assistance, and training centers to assist community vision teams and schools, congregations, neighborhoods, families, and businesses to go deep in asset building. As these efforts are launched, and as the initial initiatives around the country mature into full-fledged movements of action, we will work to evaluate and document the impact of healthy-community initiatives on asset development and to discern how, when, and under what conditions momentum is sustained.

Developmental Assets in Social Context

With its accent on naming and pursuing healthy socialization for all children and adolescents, the paradigm of developmental assets addresses one of the dominant features of contemporary American life: the immobilizing and despair-inducing trend toward polarization. William Damon at Brown University describes our current plight this way:

Of all the distortions in today's public conversation about youth, the most disturbing is the unnecessary polarization of opinions about education and child rearing. Oppositional thinking rules the day. In education, we argue about whether we should make school playful or rigorous; whether we should teach reading through phonics or whole language; whether we should emphasize character or academics; and whether we should encourage children to acquire good habits or to develop their capacities for reflection. In the home, we argue about whether parents should emphasize freedom or duty, self-expression or discipline. In the community, some argue for increasing children's rights, others for increasing children's responsibilities, and firestorms are brewed over issues such as whether children should be directly told to abstain from drugs and sex or whether they should be given more detailed instruction about the nature of the risks.

Beyond the havoc that it wreaks with the truth, polarization around matters of child rearing leads to paralysis among the groups of elders who should be mobilizing to provide young people with guidance. The paralysis created by oppositional thinking has been a main contributor to the lack of direction that plagues so many young people these days. In order to combat widespread youthful demoralization, responsible adults need to show solidarity rather than discord with one another."[4]

The experience of communities that use the asset paradigm is that it is unifying, not divisive. It becomes a community vision that builds bridges across political, religious, and moral perspectives. This feature of the asset paradigm may be its greatest strength. It becomes a tool for naming the common good. This is a vital prerequisite for mobilizing and unleashing the power of community.

Much of the work of asset building occurs for free. It is the stuff people do in their everyday lives, but now supported by the intentional and planned efforts of organizations and institutions. Because asset building depends as much on relational energy as programmatic energy, if not more so, the initiatives are cost-effective. Given the escalating downturn in funding available for programs and professionals, this feature also makes healthy-community initiatives particularly timely.

There are, of course, costs for training, research, coordination, dissemination of resources, and other activities. To cover these, we advocate that community initiatives pursue a new kind of fundraising. Traditionally, communities turn to foundations or government agencies for a single grant. If indeed asset building is about being community, then it is both empowering and symbolic to spread the funding responsibility across many sources. In this model, dozens of businesses, congregations, and organizations should contribute, matched by small contributions from hundreds of individuals.

Much is now being made of the "disappearance of social capital and civic engagement in America."[5] Healthy society requires networks and norms supporting the coming together of citizens to pursue shared goals (social capital) and the meaningful participation of citizens in building and being community (civic engagement). Both of these dynamics are threatened and retarded by mistrust, cynicism, isolation, and the privatization of life. We suggest that asset-based community initiatives represent a powerful methodology for rekindling both social capital and civic engagement. They do so by creating a vision of the common good (developmental assets) and reminding citizens of their capacity to promote positive change, individually and in unison.

We note in many communities that advocates for the asset-building paradigm seek to find a term to categorize it. The three most common categories used are *prevention, resiliency,* and *youth development.* Asset building certainly overlaps with each of these three areas of inquiry and practice. But each, by itself, is limiting. Prevention tends to connote program, resiliency tends to be an approach aimed at some youth rather than all youth, and youth development tends to focus on the middle school and high school ages. Our work is about communitywide mobilizations to promote the healthy socialization of all children and adolescents. It does not fit neatly into any current box or category.

We do not seek to coin or franchise a term for this approach. If pressed, the term *community-based human development* comes to mind. Whatever the term becomes, it ought to connote a cross-sector, communitywide, long-term, and citizen-involved and citizen-led commitment to promoting the necessary building blocks of human development during the first two decades of life.

Given the power of the developmental assets and their current state of repair, a commitment to asset building should become top priority in all communities. It is not the only essential approach, however. Quality interventions, treatment systems, and service collaborations are needed. Forces that can destroy or thwart asset development in youth (such as adults who exploit them, overexposure to the mass media, abuse, violence, economic inequality, and racism) must also be vigorously combated. Indeed, the healthy city ideally pays attention simultaneously to the *reduction* of threats to healthy development as well as the *promotion* of developmental strength. But unless we place major energy in rebuilding developmental assets, the problems we now see will persist—and likely increase.

The communities whose asset development work is under way are on a journey. It is a journey we take with them, with lessons learned along the way and course corrections anticipated and made. It is my hope that this passion for placing children first leads to a national movement in which hundreds of places commit to long-term, sustained community transformation, bonding citizens in pursuit of the common good. As communities so unite, two discoveries will emerge. First, community-based efforts to raise healthy youth are handicapped by poverty. There just may be a public cry for humane public policy to ensure that no child will want, regardless of perceived family deservedness. Second, the responsibility and capacity of being community extends beyond children and takes unto itself a like commitment to the old, the lonely, and the marginalized. It is then that the image of healthy community reaches full expression.

Although communitywide initiatives may be the ultimate strategy for building assets, the effort most often begins with *a* family, *a* teacher, *a* neighborhood, *a* congregation that sees the vision and decides to act. Quiet, even solitary beginnings do make a difference. Over time, these quiet actions can become a steady drumbeat that transforms our nation, one young person and one community at a time.

APPENDIX A

SELECTED REFERENCES FOR THE FORTY DEVELOPMENTAL ASSETS

Prepared by Nancy Leffert and Peter C. Scales

_____

The authors wish to thank Judith L. Gibbons and Robin Pulver for their research assistance.

earch Institute's framework of developmental assets builds on the important
work of scholars and researchers in the fields of child and adolescent development as well as those who are leaders in articulating the domains of resiliency,
youth development, and prevention. (For more information on the assets, their
definitions, and their roots, see Chapter Two.)

The following bibliography presents some selected scientific references that
support the relation of each of the forty assets to:

- Enhancement of one or more indicators of thriving
- Promotion of other assets
- Reduction of adolescent at-risk behavior (such as sexual intercourse, alcohol
  and other substance use)

This list of sources is selective; it is neither representative nor exhaustive. A
comprehensive review of the literature relating to each of the forty assets is sched-
uled for publication by Search Institute in 1998. (Note: for some of the assets, we
have cross-referenced to other articles in the bibliography of this Appendix that
are useful but not central to the discussion of a particular asset. These articles are
listed under "Also see.")

Support

1. Family Support

Bronfenbrenner, U. (1991). What do families do? *Family Affairs, 4*(1–2), 1–6.

Jaccard, J., Dittus, P. J., and Gordon, V. V. (1996). Maternal correlates of adolescent sexual
and contraceptive behavior. *Family Planning Perspectives, 28*(4), 159–165.

Steinberg, L., Mounts, N. S., Lamborn, S. D., and Dornbusch, S. M. (1991). Authoritative
parenting and adolescent adjustment across varied ecological niches. *Journal of Research on
Adolescence, 1,* 19–36.

Youniss, J., and Smollar, J. (1985). *Adolescent relations with mothers, fathers, and friends.* Chicago:
University of Chicago Press.

Also see: Chase-Lansdale, Wakschlag, and Brooks-Gunn (1995).

2. Positive Family Communication

Grotevant, H., and Cooper, C. (1985). Patterns of interaction in family relationships and the
development of identity formation in adolescence. *Child Development, 56,* 415–428.

Collins, W. A. (1990). Parent-child relationships in the transition to adolescence: Continuity
and change in interaction, affect, and cognition. In R. Montemayor, G. R. Adams, and
T. P. Gullota (eds.), *From childhood to adolescence: A transitional period? Advances in adolescent development* (Vol. 2). Thousand Oaks, Calif.: Sage.

Freedman, M. (1992). *The kindness of strangers.* Philadelphia: Public/Private Ventures.

Also see: Rice and Mulkeen (1995); Lord et al. (1994).

3. Other Adult Relationships

Scales, P. C., and Gibbons, J. L. (1996). Extended family members and unrelated adults in the lives of young adolescents: A research agenda. *Journal of Early Adolescence, 16*(4), 365–389.

Rice, K. G., and Mulkeen, P. (1995). Relationships with parents and peers: A longitudinal study of adolescent intimacy. *Journal of Adolescent Research, 10*(3), 338–357.

Werner, E. E. (1993). Risk, resilience, and recovery: Perspectives from the Kauai Longitudinal Study. Special issue: Milestones in the development of resilience. *Development and Psychopathology, 5*(4), 503–515.

4. Caring Neighborhood

McLaughlin, M. W., Irby, M. A., and Langman, J. (1994). *Urban sanctuaries: Neighborhood organizations in the lives and futures of inner-city youth.* San Francisco: Jossey-Bass.

Garbarino, J., Dubrow, N., Kostelyny, K., and Pardo, C. (1992). *Children in danger: Coping with the consequences of community violence.* San Francisco: Jossey-Bass.

Werner, E. E., and Smith, R. S. (1992). *Overcoming the odds: High risk children from birth to adulthood.* Ithaca, N.Y.: Cornell University Press.

5. Caring School Climate

Carnegie Council on Adolescent Development. (1989). *Turning points: Preparing American youth for the 21st century.* Washington, D.C.: author.

Newmann, F. M. (Ed.). (1992). *Student engagement and achievement in American secondary schools.* New York: Teachers College Press, Columbia University.

Noddings, N. (1992). *The challenge to care in schools.* New York: Teachers College Press.

Zimmerman, M. A., and Arunkumar, R. (1994). Resiliency research: Implications for schools and policy. *Social Policy Report, 8*(4), 1–18.

6. Parent Involvement in Schooling

Eccles, J. S., and Harold, R. D. (1993). Parent-school involvement during the early adolescent years. *Teachers College Record, 94*(3), 568–587.

Epstein, J. L. (1992). School and family partnerships. In M. C. Aiken (ed.), *Encyclopedia of educational research.* New York: Macmillan.

Epstein, J. L., Coates, L., Salinas, M. G., and Simon, B. S. (1997). *School, family, and community partnerships: Your handbook for action.* Thousand Oaks, Calif.: Corwin Press.

Ooms, T., and Hara, S. (1992). *The family-school partnerships: A critical component of school reform.* Washington, D.C.: Family Impact Seminar.

Empowerment

7. Community Values Youth

Blyth, D. A., and Leffert, N. (1995). Communities as contexts for adolescent development: An empirical analysis. *Journal of Adolescent Research, 10,* 64–87.

Price, R. H., Ciocci, M., Penner, W., and Trautlein, B. (1993). Webs of influence: School and community programs that enhance adolescent health and education. *Teachers College Record, 94*(3), 487–521.

Wynn, J., Richman, H., Rubenstein, R. A., Littell, J., Britt, B., and Yoken, C. (1988). *Communities and adolescents: An exploration of reciprocal supports*. New York: W. T. Grant Foundation Commission on Work, Family, and Citizenship.

8. Youth as Resources

National Crime Prevention Council. (1990). *Changing perspectives: Youth as resources*. Washington, D.C.: author.

Petersen, A. C., Hurrelmann, K., and Leffert, N. (1993). Adolescence and schooling in Germany and the United States: A comparison of peer socialization to adulthood. *Teachers College Record, 94*(3), 611–628.

W. T. Grant Foundation, Commission on Work, Family, and Citizenship. (1988). *The forgotten half: Pathways to success for America's youth and young families*. New York: author.

9. Service to Others

Conrad, D., and Hedin, D. (1991). School-based community service: What we know from research and theory. *Phi Delta Kappan, 72*(10), 743–749.

Kraft, R. J., and Krug, J. (1994). Review of research and evaluation on service learning in public and higher education. In R. J. Kraft and M. Swadener (eds.), *Building community: Service learning in the academic disciplines*. Denver: Campus Compact.

Switzer, G. E., Simmons, R. G., Dew, M. A., and Regalski, J. M. (1995). The effect of a school-based helper program on adolescent self-image, attitudes, and behavior. *Journal of Early Adolescence, 15*(4), 429–455.

10. Safety

Earls, F. J. (1994). Violence and today's youth. *The Future of Children, 4*(3), 4–23.

Hechinger, F. M. (1992). *Fateful choices: Healthy youth for the 21st century*. New York: Hill and Wang.

Hingson, R., and Howland, J. (1993). Promoting safety in adolescents. In S. G. Millstein, A. C. Petersen, and E. O. Nightingale (eds.), *Promoting the health of adolescents: New directions for the twenty-first century*. New York: Oxford University Press.

Boundaries and Expectations

11. Family Boundaries

Benson, P. L., Williams, D. and Johnson, A. (1987). *The quicksilver years: The hopes and fears of early adolescence*. San Francisco: Harper San Francisco.

Henry, C. S. (1991). Family system characteristics, parental behaviors, and adolescent family life satisfaction. *Family Relations, 43*, 447–455.

Small, S. A., and Kerns, D. (1993). Unwanted sexual activity among peers during early and middle adolescence: Incidence and risk factors. *Journal of Marriage and the Family, 55*, 941–952.

Smetana, J. G. (1995). Parenting styles and conceptions of parental authority. *Child Development, 66*(2), 299–316.

Also see: Phelan, Davidson, and Cao (1991); Small, Silverberg, and Kerns (1993).

12. School Boundaries

Jackson, A. W., Felner, R. D., Millstein, S. G., Pittman, K. J., and Selden, R. W. (1993). Adolescent development and educational policy: Strengths and weaknesses of the knowledge base. *Journal of Adolescent Health, 14,* 172–189.

Phelan, P., Davidson, A. L., and Cao, H. T. (1991). Students' multiple worlds: Negotiating the boundaries of family, peer, and school cultures. *Anthropology and Education Quarterly, 22*(3), 224–250.

Small, S. A., Silverberg, S. B., and Kerns, D. (1993). Adolescents' perceptions of the costs and benefits of engaging in health-compromising behaviors. *Journal of Youth and Adolescence, 22,* 73–87.

13. Neighborhood Boundaries

Arnett, J. (1995). The young and the reckless: Adolescent reckless behavior. *Current Directions in Psychological Science, 4*(3), 67–71.

Brooks-Gunn, J., Duncan, G. J., Klebanov, P. K., and Sealand, N. (1993). Do neighborhoods influence child and adolescent development? *American Journal of Sociology, 99*(2), 353–395.

Duncan, G. J. (1994). Families and neighbors as sources of disadvantage in the schooling decisions of white and black adolescents. *American Journal of Education, 103*(1), 20–53.

Also see: Petersen, Hurrelmann, and Leffert (1993).

14. Adult Role Models

Bandura, A. (1977). *Social learning theory.* Englewood Cliffs, N.J.: Prentice-Hall.

Danziger, S. K., and Farber, N. B. (1990). Keeping inner-city youths in school: Critical experiences of young black women. Special issue: Persistent poverty. *Social Work Research and Abstracts, 26*(4), 32–39.

Also see: Price et al. (1993); Brooks-Gunn et al. (1993).

15. Positive Peer Influence

Hartup, W. W. (1996). The company they keep: Friendships and their developmental significance. *Child Development, 67,* 1–13.

Tobler, N. (1986). Meta-analysis of 143 adolescent drug prevention programs: Quantitative outcome results of program participants compared to a control or comparison group. *Journal of Drug Issues, 16*(4), 537–567.

Also see: Rice and Mulkeen (1995); Youniss and Smollar (1985); Price et al. (1993); Phelan, Davidson, and Cao (1991).

16. High Expectations

Carnegie Council on Adolescent Development. (1989). *Turning points: Preparing American youth for the 21st century.* Washington, D.C.: author.

Eccles, J. S., Midgely, C., Wigfield, A., Buchanan, C. M., Reuman, D., Flanagan, C., and MacIver, D. (1993). Development during adolescence: The impact of stage-environment fit on young adolescents' experiences in school and in families. *American Psychologist, 48*(2), 90–101.

Wheelock, A. (1992). *Crossing the tracks: How 'untracking' can save America's schools.* New York: The New Press.

Constructive Use of Time

17. Creative Activities

Esman, A. (1986). Giftedness and creativity in children and adolescents. *Adolescent Psychiatry, 13*(62), 62–84.

Halperin, D. A. (1988). Master and apprentice: The mentoring relationship in the development of adolescent creativity. *Adolescent Psychiatry,* 15, 279–287.

Rothenberg, A. (1990). Creativity in adolescence. *Psychiatric Clinics of North America, 13*(3), 415–434.

Also see: Goleman (1995).

18. Youth Programs

Carnegie Council on Adolescent Development. (1992). *A matter of time: Risk and opportunity in the non-school hours.* Washington, D.C.: author.

Dubas, J. S., and Snider, B. A. (1993). The role of community-based youth groups in enhancing learning and achievement through nonformal education. In R. M. Lerner (ed.), *Early adolescence: Perspectives on research, policy, and intervention.* Hillsdale, N.J.: Erlbaum.

Also see: Price et al. (1993); Blyth and Leffert (1995).

19. Religious Community

Blyth and Leffert (1995).

Donahue, M. D., and Benson, P. L. (1995). Religion and the well-being of adolescents. *Journal of Social Issues, 51*(2), 145–160.

Patterson, J. M., and McCubbin, H. I. (1987). A-COPE: Adolescent coping orientation for problem experiences. In H. J. McCubbin and A. J. Thompson (eds.), *Family assessment inventories in research and practice.* Madison, Wis.: Health Programs.

Thomas, D. L., and Carver, C. (1990). Religion and adolescent social competence. In T. P. Gullotta, G. R. Adams, and R. Montemayor (eds.), *Developing social competency in adolescence. Advances in adolescent development* (Vol. 3). Thousand Oaks, Calif.: Sage.

20. Time at Home

Benson, P. L., and Donahue, M. D. (1989). Ten-year trends in at-risk behaviors: A national study of black adolescents. *Journal of Adolescent Research, 4*(2), 125–139.

Costa, F. M., Jessor, R., Donovan, J. E., and Fortenberry, J. D. (1995). Early initiation of sexual intercourse: The influence of psychosocial unconventionality. *Journal of Research on Adolescence, 5,* 93–121.

Felson, M., and Gottfredson, M. (1984). Social indicators of adolescent activities near peers and parents. *Journal of Marriage and the Family, 46*(3), 709–711.

Fuligni, A. J., and Stevenson, H. W. (1995). Time use and mathematics achievement among American, Chinese, and Japanese high school students. *Child Development, 66*(3), 830–842.

Also see: Blyth and Leffert (1995).

Commitment to Learning

21. Achievement Motivation

Brooks-Gunn, J., Guo, G., and Furstenberg, F. F. (1993). Who drops out of and who continues beyond high school? A 20-year follow-up of black urban youth. *Journal of Research on Adolescence, 3*(3), 271–294.

Eccles, J. S., and Midgley, C. (1990). Changes in academic motivation and self-perception during adolescence. In R. Montemayor, G. R. Adams, and T. P. Gullotta (eds.), *From childhood to adolescence: A transitional period? Advances in adolescent development* (Vol. 2). Thousand Oaks, Calif.: Sage.

Wentzel, K. R. (1993). Motivation and achievement in early adolescence: The role of multiple classroom goals. *Journal of Early Adolescence, 13,* 4–20.

22. School Engagement

Ainley, M. D. (1993). Styles of engagement with learning: Multidimensional assessment of their relationship with strategy use and school achievement. *Journal of Educational Psychology, 85*(3), 395–405.

Connell, J. P., Halpern-Felsher, B. L., Clifford, E., and Crichlow, W. (1995). Hanging in there: Behavioral, psychological, and contextual factors affecting whether African-American adolescents stay in high school. Special Issue: Creating supportive communities for adolescent development: Challenges to scholars. *Journal of Adolescent Research, 10,* 41–63.

Connell, J. P., Spencer, M. B., and Aber, L. J. (1994). Educational risk and resilience in African-American youth: Context, self, action, and outcomes in school. Special Issue: Children in poverty. *Child Development, 65*(2), 493–502.

23. Homework

Elmen, J. (1991). Achievement orientation in early adolescence: Developmental patterns and social correlates. *Journal of Early Adolescence, 10,* 125–151.

National Education Goals Panel. (1994). *The national education goals report: Building a nation of learners.* Washington, D.C.: author.

U.S. Department of Education. (1988, 1992). *National education longitudinal study of American eighth-graders.* Washington, D.C.: author.

24. Bonding to School

Cernkovich, S. A., and Giordano, P. C. (1992). School bonding, race, and delinquency. *Criminology, 30*(2), 261–291.

Goodnow, C. (1993). Classroom belonging among early adolescent students: Relationships to motivation and achievement. *Journal of Early Adolescence, 13,* 21–43.

Jackson, A. W., Felner, R. D., Millstein, S. G., Pittman, K. J., and Selden, R. W. (1993). Adolescent development and educational policy: Strengths and weaknesses of the knowledge base. *Journal of Adolescent Health, 14,* 172–189.

Lee, V. E., and Smith, J. B. (1993). Effects of school restructuring on the achievement and engagement of middle-grade students. *Sociology of Education, 66,* 164–187.

25. Reading for Pleasure

Davidson, J., and Koppenhaver, D. (1993). *Adolescent literacy: What works and why* (2nd ed). New York: Garland.

Foertsch, M. A. (1992). *Reading in and out of school: Factors influencing the literacy achievement of American students in grades 4, 8, and 12 in 1988 and 1990* (Vol. 2). Washington, D.C.: National Center for Health Statistics.

National Education Goals Panel. (1994). *The national education goals report: Building a nation of learners.* Washington, D.C.: author.

Also see: Connell et al. (1995).

Positive Values

26. Caring

Chase-Lansdale, P. L., Wakschlag, L. S., and Brooks-Gunn, J. (1995). A psychological perspective on the development of caring in children and youth: The role of the family. *Journal of Adolescence, 18*(5), 515–556.

Chaskin, R. W., and Hawley, T. (1994). *Youth and caring: Developing a field of inquiry and practice.* Chicago: Chapin Hall Center for Children.

Hart, D., and Fegley, S. (1995). Prosocial behavior and caring in adolescence: Relations to self-understanding and social judgment. *Child Development, 66*(5), 1346–1359.

Also see: Estrada (1995); Eisenberg et al. (1991).

27. Equality and Social Justice

Beutel, A. M., and Marini, M. M. (1995). Gender and values. *American Sociological Review, 60*(3), 436–448.

Estrada, P. (1995). Adolescents' self-reports of prosocial responses to friends and acquaintances: The role of sympathy-related cognitive, affective, and motivational processes. *Journal of Research on Adolescence, 5*(2), 173–200.

McDevitt, T. M., Lennon, R., and Kopriva, R. J. (1991). Adolescents' perceptions of mothers' and fathers' prosocial actions and empathic responses. *Youth and Society, 22*(3), 387–409.

Also see: Eisenberg et al. (1991).

28. Integrity

Eisenberg, N., Miller, P. A., Shell, R., and McNalley, S. (1991). Prosocial development in adolescence: A longitudinal study. *Developmental Psychology, 27*(5), 849–857.

Westenburg, P. M., and Block, J. (1993). Ego development and individual differences in personality. *Journal of Personality and Social Psychology, 65*(4), 792–800.

McDevitt et al. (1991).

29. Honesty

Graham, S., Weiner, B., and Benesh-Weiner, M. (1995). An attributional analysis of the development of excuse giving in aggressive and nonaggressive African-American boys. *Developmental Psychology, 31*(2), 274–284.

Lamborn, S. D., Fischer, K. W., and Pipp, S. (1994). Constructive criticism and social lies: A developmental sequence for understanding honesty and kindness in social interactions. *Developmental Psychology, 30*(4), 495–508.

Pleck, J., Sonenstein, F., and Ku, L. (1993). Masculinity ideology: Its impact on adolescent males' heterosexual relationships. *Journal of Social Issues, 49*(3), 11–30.

30. Responsibility

Gonzalez, J., Field, T., Yando, R., and Gonzalez, K. (1994). Adolescents' perceptions of their risk-taking behavior. *Adolescence, 29*(155), 701–709.

Goodnow, J. J., and Warton, P. M. (1992). Understanding responsibility: Adolescents' views of delegation and follow-through within the family. *Social Development, 1*(2), 89–106.

Wentzel, K. R. (1991). Relations between social competence and academic achievement. *Child Development, 62*(5), 1066–1078.

Also see: Beutel and Marini (1995); Eisenberg et al. (1991).

31. Restraint

Brooks-Gunn, J., and Paikoff, R. L. (1993). "Sex is a gamble, kissing is a game": Adolescent sexuality and health promotion. In S. G. Millstein, A. C. Petersen, & E. O. Nightingale (eds.), *Promoting the health of adolescents: New directions for the twenty-first century.* New York: Oxford University Press.

Kirby, D., Short, L., Collins, J., Rugg, D., Kolbe, L., Howard, M., Miller, B., Sonenstein, F., and Zabin, L. S. (1994). School-based programs to reduce sexual risk behavior: A review of effectiveness. *Public Health Reports, 109*(3), 339–360.

Pentz, M. A., Dwyer, J. H., MacKinnon, D. P., Flay, B. R., Hansen, W. B., Wang, E.Y.I., and Johnson, C. A. (1989). A multicommunity trial for primary prevention of adolescent drug abuse. Effects on drug use prevalence. *Journal of the American Medical Association, 261*(22), 3259–3266.

Also see: Gonzalez et al. (1994).

Social Competencies

32. Planning and Decision Making

Beyth-Marom, R. (1989). *Teaching decision-making to adolescents: A critical review.* Working paper commissioned by the Carnegie Council on Adolescent Development, Washington, D.C.

Mann, L., Harmoni, R., and Power, C. N. (1989). Adolescent decision-making: The development of competence. *Journal of Adolescence, 12*(3), 265–278.

Weithorn, L. A., and Campbell, S. B. (1982). The competency of children to make informed treatment decisions. *Child Development, 53*, 1589–1598.

Also see: Kirby et al. (1994).

33. Interpersonal Competence

Elias, M. J., Gura, M., Ubriaco, M., Rothbaum, P. A., Clabby, J. F., and Schuyler, T. (1986). Impact of a preventive social problem solving intervention on children's coping with middle-school stressors. *American Journal of Community Psychology, 14*(3), 259–275.

Goleman, D. (1995). *Emotional intelligence.* New York: Bantam Books.

Vernberg, E. M., Ewell, K. K., Beery, S. H., and Abwender, D. A. (1994). Sophistication of adolescents' interpersonal negotiation strategies and friendship formation after relocation: A naturally occurring experiment. *Journal of Research on Adolescence, 4*(1), 5–19.

34. Cultural Competence

DuBois, D. L., and Hirsch, B. J. (1990). School and neighborhood friendship patterns in blacks and whites in early adolescence. Special issue: Minority children. *Child Development, 61*(2), 524–536.

Eder, D., and Sanford, S. (1986). The development and maintenance of interracial norms among early adolescents. In P. Adler (ed.), *Sociological studies of child development* (Vol. 1). Greenwich, Conn.: JAI Press.

Schofield, J. W. (1982). *Black and white in school: Trust, tension, or tolerance.* New York: Praeger.

35. Resistance Skills

Botvin, G. J. (1991). Personal and social skills training: Applications for substance abuse prevention. In R. M. Hubbard and B. J. Smith (eds.), *Strengthening health education for the 1990s.* Reston, Va.: Association for the Advancement of Health Education.

Minnesota Department of Education, Prevention and Risk Reduction Unit. (1992). *Promising prevention strategies: A look at what works.* Minneapolis: author.

Zimmerman, R. S., Sprecher, S., Langer, L. M., and Holloway, C. D. (1993). Adolescents' perceived ability to say "no" to unwanted sex. *Journal of Adolescent Research, 10*(3), 383–399.

36. Peaceful Conflict Resolution

Dryfoos, J. G. (1990). *Adolescents at risk: Prevalence and prevention.* New York: Oxford University Press.

Powell, K. E., Muir-McClain, L., and Halasyamani, L. (1995). A review of selected school-based conflict resolution and peer mediation projects. *Journal of School Health, 65*(10), 426–431.

Smith, M. (1993). Some school-based violence prevention strategies. *National Association of Secondary School Principals Bulletin, 77*(557), 70–75.

Positive Identity

37. Personal Control

Gamble, W. C. (1994). Perceptions of controllability and other stressor event characteristics as determinants of coping among young adolescents and young adults. *Journal of Youth and Adolescence, 23,* 65–84.

Masten, A. S., Coatsworth, J. D., Neeman, J., Gest, S. D., Tellegen, A., and Garmezy, N. (1995). The structure and coherence of competence from childhood through adolescence. *Child Development, 66,* 1635–1659.

Rutter, M. (1993). Resilience: Some conceptual considerations. *Journal of Adolescent Health, 14,* 626–631.

38. Self-Esteem

Harter, S. (1990). Processes underlying adolescent self-concept formation. In R. Montemayor, G. R. Adams, and T. P. Gullotta (eds.), *From childhood to adolescence: A transitional period? Advances in adolescent development* (Vol. 2). Thousand Oaks, Calif.: Sage.

Lord, S. E., Eccles, J. S., and McCarthy, K. A. (1994). Surviving the junior high transition: Family processes and self-perceptions as protective and risk factors. *Journal of Early Adolescence, 14*(2), 162–199.

Simmons, R. G., and Blyth, D. A. (1987). *Moving into adolescence: The impact of pubertal change and school context.* New York: Aldine deGruyter.

39. Sense of Purpose

Hayes, C. D. (1987). *Risking the future: Adolescent sexuality, pregnancy, and childbearing.* Washington, D.C.: National Research Council, National Academy Press.

Klaczynski, P. A. (1990). Cultural-developmental tasks and adolescent development: Theoretical and methodological considerations. *Adolescence, 25*(100), 811–823.

Levitt, M. Z., Selman, R. L., and Richmond, J. B. (1991). The psychosocial foundations of early adolescents' high risk behavior: Implications for research and practice. *Journal of Research on Adolescence, 1*(4), 349–378.

40. Positive View of Personal Future

Diener, C. I., and Dweck, C. S. (1980). An analysis of learned helplessness: II. The processing of success. *Journal of Personality and Social Psychology, 39,* 940–952.

Garmezy, N. (1993). Children in poverty: Resilience despite risk. *Psychiatry, 56,* 127–136.

Rutter, M. (1987). Psychosocial resilience and protective mechanisms. *American Journal of Orthopsychiatry, 57,* 316–331.

APPENDIX B

FINDINGS FROM THE
1990–1995 ASSETS SAMPLE

Since 1989, Search Institute has conducted in-depth studies of sixth-to-twelfth-grade students in public school districts across the country.[1] The first aggregate report, based on 112 school districts, was published in 1990. Titled *The Troubled Journey: A Portrait of 6th–12th Grade Youth,* this report documented the shape of the original thirty developmental assets, deficits, and at-risk behaviors among forty-seven thousand students. A companion volume, *Healthy Communities, Healthy Youth,* deepened the analysis of community dynamics related to enhancing or inhibiting assets.[2]

By early 1995, the number of public school districts conducting this research had grown to 460. This large sample, aggregated across school districts, constitutes the portrait of youth shared in this book.

In each school district, students were administered an anonymous 152–item survey called *Profiles of Student Life: Attitudes and Behaviors.* The instructions were standardized. Students place completed surveys in an envelope sealed and mailed to Search Institute for processing and generation of a school district report. Usually, those school district studies represent a complete census of all sixth-to-twelfth-grade students attending school on the day the survey is administered.

The survey instrument measured each of the thirty original developmental assets (see Table B.3) as well as a number of other constructs, including developmental deficits and high-risk behaviors. These high-risk behaviors include substance abuse (alcohol, tobacco, and other drugs), sexual intercourse, antisocial behavior, violence, school failure, and attempted suicide. Many of the high-risk behavior items are drawn from federally funded national research studies that have documented the validity of these measures.[3]

Each of the thirty assets is measured by one or more survey items, each with a minimum of five response options. Then each is converted into a binary variable. Generally, the criterion used to determine the presence of a particular asset is a mean of 4.0 or greater on the applicable items. For most cases, variable range is 1 to 5, with 3.0 a neutral midpoint. Some of the psychometric properties of the asset measures have been assessed in a longitudinal study of one thousand middle school students and their parents in Minneapolis and St. Paul, Minnesota. This project demonstrated strong internal consistency reliability for assets measured by multiple items (for example, family support, self-esteem), and strong test-retest reliability. As one validity check, parents' assessments of their child's developmental assets correlated significantly with child reports. Additional evidence for validity can be seen in the correlations of specific assets with specific risk behaviors, in directions that replicate the legacy of research studies listed in Appendix A.

To enhance the accuracy of these local school district studies, we take a number of precautionary actions to eliminate survey respondents whose responses indicate an intent to exaggerate or distort answers (for example, in each location, about 2 percent of students report frequent use of a fictitious drug).

Sample Characteristics

For this book, we have aggregated responses from the 460 school districts that assessed all or most grades in the 6–12 grade span and that conducted either a full census or a random sampling of its students. Though it includes surveys conducted from 1990 and 1991, most of the data was collected between 1992 and 1995. The resulting sample of 254,634 students (which we call the "1990–1995 assets sample") is diverse in geography, race and ethnicity, and community size. It represents one of the largest efforts ever undertaken to describe the life experience of American youth.

We do not claim that this is a purposeful, representative sample of public school districts. The decision to conduct the study is in the hands of local communities, not the research team.[4] They contact us, not vice versa. Furthermore, it does not include youth who have dropped out of school. Thus this sample is likely to slightly overestimate assets and underestimate risks among all youth. So we need to examine more closely the nature of this quarter-million sample.

States: The 460 school districts are located in thirty-two states. The largest numbers include Minnesota (60), Iowa (56), Wisconsin (55), and Michigan (38). Hence, there is a Great Plains tilt to the sample. But there is good representation from East Coast (for example, New York, 13), Western (Colorado, 13; Oregon, 11), and Mid-Atlantic (North Carolina, 42) states.

Race or ethnicity: As Table B.1 shows, the sample underrepresents students of color (85 percent white, compared to 68 percent white among U.S. youth ages twelve to eighteen).

Community size: The sample also slightly over-represents large communities and under-represents small communities. The 460 school districts are located as follows:

Community Size	Distribution of 460 School Districts	Distribution of All U.S. Communities
Less than 10,000	74 percent	88 percent
10,000–49,999	16 percent	10 percent
50,000–250,000	6 percent	2 percent
250,000+	4 percent	0.3 percent

TABLE B.1. THE 1990–1995 ASSETS SAMPLE
COMPARED TO U.S. YOUTH.

		Number	Percentage of Total	Percentage of U.S. Youth*
Total students		254,634	100	
Grade	6	20,431	8	15
	7	41,896	16	15
	8	41,969	17	15
	9	44,394	17	14
	10	40,065	16	14
	11	34,605	14	14
	12	30,874	12	13
Gender	Female	128,677	51	49
	Male	124,726	49	51
Race or Ethnicity	African American	20,470	8	15
	American Indian	7,869	3	1
	Asian American	3,393	1	4
	Hispanic American	7,259	3	12
	White American	213,025	85	68

Notes: Numbers within demographic categories may not sum to 254,634 because of missing data.

*Based on 1994 statistics in the *Statistical Abstract of the United States: 1995*. Percentages for each grade are based on ages twelve to eighteen.

Comparisons to other studies: In spite of these demographic nuances, our national sample closely approximates findings on key behavioral indicators from other large, representative studies of U.S. youth. As shown in Table B.2, rates for substance abuse, sexual intercourse, and related indicators are equal to, if not slightly higher than, those established in other major studies.

One final note about our sample: it is only a matter of methodological convenience that this study focuses on America's middle school and high school students (grades six to twelve). Because our efforts require portraits of developmental assets as they are perceived and experienced by youth in each participating community, by necessity we rely on the cost-effective methodology of in-depth survey instruments that require a reading comprehension at about the sixth-grade level. Developmental assets, of course, begin to be shaped in the first year of life, and could, with other research methodologies, be documented for preschool and elementary school-aged children.

TABLE B.2. COMPARISONS TO OTHER NATIONAL STUDIES ON KEY BEHAVIORAL INDICATORS.

	Other National Studies	1990–1995 Assets Sample
Percentage who live with a single parent	23[a]	21
Percentage who have tried alcohol		
• 8th graders	66[b]	71
• 12th graders	87[b]	90
Percentage who have had five or more drinks at one time in the past two weeks (binge drinkers)		
• 8th graders	14[c]	17
• 10th graders	23[c]	26
• 12th graders	28[c]	34
Percentage who smoked one or more cigarettes in the past month		
• 10th graders	25[d]	27
• 12th graders	30[d]	32
Percentage who have used marijuana one or more times in their lifetime		
• 8th graders	13[b]	14
• 10th graders	25[b]	24
• 12th graders	31[b]	32
Percentage who have had sexual intercourse one or more times in their lifetime		
• 10th graders	48[d]	44
• 12th graders	67[d]	66

[a] National Center for Children in Poverty. (1995). *News and Issues, 5* (Fall/Winter), 1990 census data.

[b] Johnston, L. D., et al. (1994). *National survey results on drug use from the Monitoring the Future study, 1975–1983. Vol. 1: Secondary school students.* Rockville, Md.: National Institute on Drug Abuse.

[c] University of Michigan Institute for Social Research. (1994). Unpublished data from Monitoring the Future, as reported in Carnegie Council on Adolescent Development. (1995). *Great transitions: Preparing adolescents for a new century.* New York: Carnegie Council of New York, p. 39.

[d] Kann, L., et al. (1993). Results from the national school-based 1991 youth risk behavior survey and progress toward achieving related health objectives for the nation. *Public Health Reports, 108,* 47–67.

Profile of Developmental Assets

Major findings on young people's experiences of developmental assets are included in Chapter Three. The following detailed charts are included in this section:

- Figure B.1 shows the average number of developmental assets among youth, by grade. The average falls from 17.8 in sixth grade to 16.1 in twelfth grade.
- Figure B.2 shows the percentages of communities with different average levels of assets. Of the communities surveyed, 96 percent have average levels of assets between 15 and 17.
- When comparing communities by community size, the average number of assets remains virtually the same, as shown in Figure B.3.
- Table B.4 draws together the larger challenge of asset development, showing average levels of assets by gender, grade, race, town size, and family composition.
- Finally, Table B.5 presents detailed findings on each developmental asset by gender, grade, race or ethnicity, and family composition.

FIGURE B.1. AVERAGE NUMBER OF
THIRTY DEVELOPMENTAL ASSETS, BY GRADE.

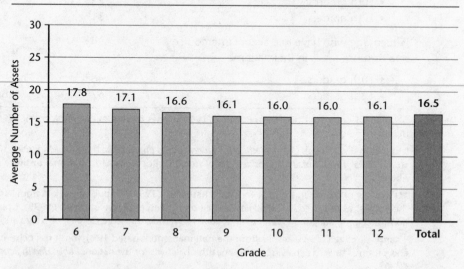

Note: See Table B.1 for sample sizes.

TABLE B.3. SEARCH INSTITUTE'S
THIRTY ORIGINAL DEVELOPMENTAL ASSETS.

External Assets

Asset Type	Asset Name	Asset Definition
Support	1. Family support	Family life provides high levels of love and support.
	2. Parent(s) as social resources	Young person views parent(s) as accessible resources for advice and support.
	3. Parent communication	Young person has frequent, in-depth conversations with parent(s).
	4. Other adult resources	Young person has access to nonparent adults for advice and support.
	5. Other adult communication	Young person has frequent, in-depth conversations with nonparent adults.
	6. Parent involvement in schooling	Parent(s) are involved in helping young person succeed in school.
	7. Positive school climate	School provides a caring, encouraging environment.
Boundaries	8. Parental standards	Parent(s) have standards for appropriate conduct.
	9. Parental discipline	Parent(s) discipline young person when a rule is violated.
	10. Parental monitoring	Parent(s) monitor "where I am going and with whom I will be."
	11. Time at home	Young person goes out for "fun and recreation" three nights or fewer per week.
	12. Positive peer influence	Young person's best friends model responsible behavior.
Structured time use	13. Involved in music	Young person spends three hours or more per week in music training or practice.
	14. Involved in school extracurricular activities	Young person spends one hour or more per week in school sports, clubs, or organizations.
	15. Involved in community organizations	Young person spends one hour or more per week in organizations or clubs outside of school.
	16. Involved in church or synagogue	Young person spends one hour or more per week attending programs or services.

TABLE B.3. SEARCH INSTITUTE'S
THIRTY ORIGINAL DEVELOPMENTAL ASSETS, cont'd.

Internal Assets

Asset Type	Asset Name	Asset Definition
Educational commitment	17. Achievement motivation	Young person is motivated to do well in school.
	18. Educational aspiration	Young person aspires to pursue post-high school education (e.g., trade school, college).
	19. School performance	Young person reports school performance is above average.
	20. Homework	Young person reports six hours or more of homework per week.
Positive values	21. Values helping people	Young person places high personal value on helping other people.
	22. Is concerned about world hunger	Young person reports interest in helping to reduce world hunger.
	23. Cares about people's feelings	Young person cares about other people's feelings.
	24. Values sexual restraint	Young person values postponing sexual activity.
Social competencies	25. Assertiveness skills	Young person reports ability to "stand up for what I believe."
	26. Decision-making skills	Young person reports that "I am good at making decisions."
	27. Friendship-making skills	Young person reports that "I am good at making friends."
	28. Planning skills	Young person reports that "I am good at planning ahead."
	29. Self-esteem	Young person reports high self-esteem.
	30. Positive view of personal future	Young person is optimistic about her or his personal future.

Note: This chart lists the thirty developmental assets that were measured in the 1990–1995 assets sample. This framework has since been expanded to forty developmental assets (see Chapter Two).

FIGURE B.2. PERCENTAGES OF COMMUNITIES,
BY AVERAGE NUMBER OF ASSETS.

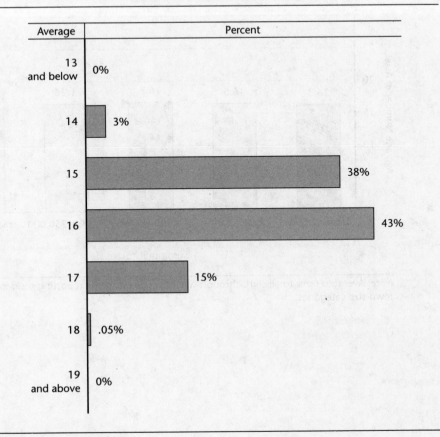

Note: N = 460 communities.

FIGURE B.3. AVERAGE NUMBER OF THIRTY ASSETS, BY COMMUNITY SIZE.

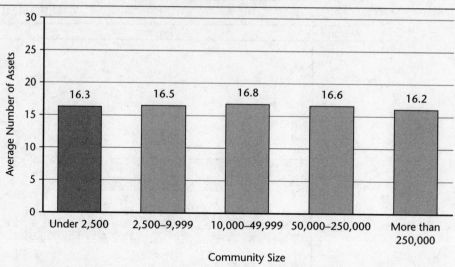

Note: Averages refer to all sixth-through-twelfth-grade students reporting residence in above town-size categories.

TABLE B.4. PERCENTAGES OF YOUTH WITH
LEVELS OF DEVELOPMENTAL ASSETS (0–10, 11–20, 21–25, 26–30)
BY GENDER, GRADE, RACE, TOWN SIZE, AND FAMILY COMPOSITION.

	Number of 30 Developmental Assets							
	0–5	6–10	0–10	11–15	16–20	11–20	21–25	26–30
Total National Asset Sample	2	12	**14**	29	34	**62**	**20**	**4**
Gender								
Male	3	15	**18**	32	33	**65**	**61**	**2**
Female	1	9	**10**	26	35	**61**	**24**	**5**
Grade								
6	1	8	**9**	23	36	**59**	**27**	**5**
7	1	10	**11**	26	34	**60**	**24**	**5**
8	2	12	**14**	28	34	**62**	**21**	**4**
9	2	13	**15**	30	33	**63**	**18**	**3**
10	2	13	**15**	31	33	**64**	**18**	**3**
11	2	14	**16**	31	33	**64**	**17**	**3**
12	2	13	**15**	31	35	**66**	**17**	**3**
Race or Ethnicity								
African American	1	10	**11**	29	38	**7**	**19**	**2**
American Indian	3	16	**19**	33	32	**65**	**14**	**2**
Asian	2	13	**15**	31	34	**65**	**18**	**3**
Hispanic	3	17	**20**	32	32	**64**	**15**	**2**
White	2	12	**14**	28	33	**61**	**20**	**4**
City Size								
Under 2,500	2	13	**15**	29	33	**62**	**19**	**3**
2,500–9,999	2	12	**14**	29	33	**62**	**20**	**4**
10,000–49,999	1	11	**12**	27	34	**61**	**22**	**4**
50,000–249,999	2	11	**13**	28	35	**63**	**20**	**8**
250,000 or more	2	12	**14**	30	35	**65**	**18**	**3**
Family Composition								
Lives with one parent	3	17	**20**	33	31	**64**	**14**	**2**
Lives with two parents	2	11	**13**	28	34	**62**	**21**	**4**

TABLE B.5. PERCENTAGES OF YOUTH WITH EACH DEVELOPMENTAL ASSET, BY GENDER, GRADE, AND RACE OR ETHNICITY.

Asset Types	Asset Name	All	Gender		Grade							Race or Ethnicity				
			M	F	6	7	8	9	10	11	12	African American	American Indian	Asian American	Hispanic American	White American
Support	Family support	57	56	58	73	65	58	54	52	50	52	59	53	49	55	57
	Parent(s) as social resources	46	48	45	59	51	46	43	43	43	45	53	44	42	48	46
	Parent communication	48	51	45	45	44	45	46	49	53	56	47	41	41	43	49
	Other adult resources	49	49	49	52	50	47	47	47	49	52	48	48	39	44	49
	Other adult communication	41	45	37	28	31	35	40	44	51	58	40	40	36	37	41
	Parent involvement in schooling	26	26	27	44	37	31	25	21	17	14	30	27	20	25	26
	Positive school climate	30	32	28	48	36	30	25	24	26	31	33	31	29	29	30
Boundaries	Parental standards	76	79	73	88	86	81	77	72	67	58	75	74	79	75	76
	Parental discipline	58	60	56	63	62	60	59	58	55	49	59	59	53	54	58
	Parental monitoring	76	81	72	71	73	75	78	81	79	74	71	68	74	74	77
	Time at home	68	72	63	69	69	68	68	68	66	65	58	63	74	66	69
	Positive peer influence	31	41	20	39	33	30	28	29	30	32	27	25	33	25	31
Structured Time Use	Involved in music	27	33	21	26	30	30	27	26	25	23	16	16	27	15	29
	Involved in school extra-curricular activities	61	61	62	57	62	62	61	62	62	61	57	54	61	54	62
	Involved in community organizations or activities	41	43	38	48	43	42	39	40	39	37	40	35	38	35	41

Educational Commitment	Involved in church or synagogue	57	61	53	63	61	59	57	55	52	50	58	46	44	46	58
	Achievement motivation	70	77	64	78	75	71	70	68	66	67	74	64	75	65	70
	Educational aspiration	89	92	86	89	88	88	89	89	91	92	88	80	92	83	90
	School performance	47	48	45	48	47	48	45	45	45	49	39	31	59	35	48
	Homework	23	28	19	18	23	22	24	26	27	22	16	17	36	17	24
Positive Values	Values helping people	52	62	42	70	62	55	50	46	44	44	68	62	60	61	50
	Is concerned about world hunger	47	61	32	53	50	46	45	45	45	45	45	49	53	48	47
	Cares about people's feelings	86	94	79	85	83	84	86	88	89	90	79	81	85	81	87
	Values sexual restraint	36	46	30	55	49	43	35	29	25	21	25	31	45	37	38
Social Competencies	Assertiveness skills	83	84	82	81	80	81	82	84	85	88	86	81	79	81	83
	Decision-making skills	69	68	71	69	68	69	69	70	70	73	72	66	60	62	70
	Friendship-making skills	75	77	73	74	74	74	75	77	74	80	81	75	69	74	75
	Planning skills	59	59	58	62	59	58	57	57	58	59	66	57	55	53	58
	Self-esteem	47	43	53	56	49	47	44	44	46	50	65	43	41	43	46
	Positive view of personal future	69	68	70	71	69	67	67	68	73	76	65	61	63	69	69

Notes: Based on the original framework of thirty developmental assets; all numbers are percentages.

For definitions of assets, see Table B.1. For sample sizes, see Table B.3.

Profile of Developmental Deficits

Also assessed were ten developmental deficits, as defined in Tables B.6 and B.7. Table B.6 presents the average number of ten deficits by grade and gender.

Table B.7 presents percentages for each deficit by gender, grade, and race or ethnicity.

Risk-Taking Behaviors

Dozens of studies have looked in depth at individual risk-taking behaviors among youth. Some, for example, focus on use of alcohol and other drugs, while others may focus on sexual activity or problems in school. These studies add important depth to our understanding of these issues. However, we wanted to step back and look at a broader range of behaviors to look for patterns and connections between these behaviors as well as with assets.

Our working definition is that risk-taking behaviors are choices that potentially limit psychological, physical, or economic well-being during adolescence or adulthood. Many of the behaviors can have negative, long-term consequences.

To some extent, our choice of these at-risk indicators is based on speculative and incomplete knowledge, for evidence about the actual long-term consequences of certain choices during the first eighteen years of life is not adequately documented. We rely, then, on informed hunches, choosing indicators that one could reasonably argue are possible precursors to later difficulties.

The issue is probability, which means in part that a risky choice (or even several) during adolescence does not guarantee negative, long-term consequences.

TABLE B.6. AVERAGE NUMBER OF TEN DEFICITS, BY GRADE AND GENDER.

	Average Number of Ten Deficits	
Grade	Male	Female
6	1.84	1.74
7	2.07	2.11
8	2.22	2.39
9	2.35	2.61
10	2.44	2.71
11	2.52	2.73
12	2.58	2.75

Note: See Table B.1 for sample sizes.

TABLE B.7. PERCENTAGES OF YOUTH WITH EACH DEVELOPMENTAL DEFICIT, BY GENDER, GRADE, AND RACE OR ETHNICITY.

Deficit and Definition	All	Gender		Grade							Race or Ethnicity				
		M	F	6	7	8	9	10	11	12	African American	American Indian	Asian American	Hispanic American	White American
1. Alone at home: Student spends two hours or more per day at home without an adult.	60	59	60	53	57	60	61	61	61	61	63	61	57	57	59
2. Hedonistic values: Student places high importance on self-serving values.	46	53	39	38	45	59	48	47	45	43	49	46	47	42	46
3. TV overexposure: Student watches television three hours or more per day.	38	41	36	43	47	44	41	35	29	28	70	51	33	47	35
4. Drinking parties: Student frequently attends parties where peers drink.	29	30	28	3	8	15	26	39	51	59	32	30	22	33	28
5. Stress: Student feels under stress or pressure "most" or "all" of the time.	21	15	27	12	15	19	22	25	28	28	22	24	25	21	21
6. Physical abuse: Student reports at least one incident of physical abuse by an adult.	18	15	21	13	16	18	20	20	19	18	20	28	21	20	17
7. Sexual abuse: Student reports at least one incident of sexual abuse.	11	3	19	6	8	10	12	13	13	14	13	16	11	13	11
8. Parental addiction: Student reports a parent "has a serious problem with alcohol or drugs."	7	6	8	5	6	7	8	8	8	7	8	11	4	8	7
9. Social isolation: Student feels a consistent lack of care, support, and understanding.	7	6	7	6	7	7	7	7	7	6	7	10	8	7	6
10. Negative peer pressure: Most close friends are involved in chemical use or are in frequent trouble at school.	3	3	2	<1	1	3	3	3	3	3	3	4	3	5	2

Notes: All numbers are percentages.

See Table B.1 for sample sizes.

But given the possibility of harm, we press the point that prevention of these risk-taking behaviors is the prudent approach to long-term well-being.

We look at twenty negative risk-taking behaviors from two perspectives. First, we examine the levels of youth involvement in individual acts of risk taking. Then we examine patterns of risk taking in which young people are involved in several acts of a particular behavior.

Individual Acts of Risk-Taking Behavior

Initially, we look at twenty behaviors, counting the percentage who engage in each behavior one or more times in a given period of time.

Figure B.4 shows that the average public school student (grades six to twelve) engages in 4.2 of the 20 risk behaviors, ranging from an average of 2.4 in grade six to an average of 5.3 in grade twelve. Males dominate. They average 4.9 of 20 behaviors; girls average 3.4. Thus, the average young person in our nation is involved in about one out of four of these risky activities.

In addition to identifying the percentage of youth involved in each of the twenty risk-taking behaviors, we also assess the percentage of youth involved in one or more of the twenty behaviors. As shown in Table B.8, four out of five (82 percent) young people in our communities are engaging in one or more of these behaviors. More than half (54 percent) are engaging in three or more of these behaviors.

Table B.9 shows the involvement in each risk-taking behavior by gender, grade, race or ethnicity, and family composition.

Patterns of Risk Taking

The portrait of risk taking deepens as we move to patterns of high-risk behavior. Figure B.5 displays percentages engaging in repeated health-compromising behaviors (for example, daily cigarette use, three or more experiences with sexual intercourse, three or more acts of violence in the last year). All rates increase with age, except for violence and antisocial behavior, which stabilizes after grade eight.

Some key findings follow:

1. On the average, youth average nearly 2 (1.8) of these patterns. Sixth graders, on the average, are engaged in 1 pattern of risk taking. The average rises to 2.6 for high school seniors.
2. As shown in Figure B.6, 64 percent of all youth engage in at least one of the patterns, ranging from 46 percent of sixth graders to 81 percent of twelfth graders. For boys, the rate is 68 percent; for girls, 61 percent.

FIGURE B.4. AVERAGE NUMBER OF TWENTY RISK-TAKING BEHAVIORS.

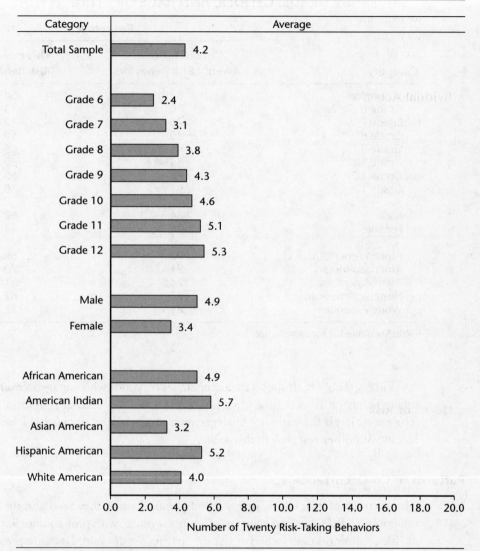

Note: See Table B.1 for sample sizes.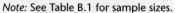

TABLE B.8. PERCENTAGES REPORTING ONE OR MORE AND THREE OR MORE OF TWENTY RISK BEHAVIORS, BY GRADE, GENDER, AND RACE OR ETHNICITY.

	Percentage	
Category	One or More of Twenty Risk Behaviors	Three or More Risk Behaviors
Total Sample	82	54
Grade 6	70	33
Grade 7	76	42
Grade 8	80	50
Grade 9	83	65
Grade 10	84	60
Grade 11	88	65
Grade 12	91	70
Male	84	62
Female	78	47
African American	92	69
American Indian	91	70
Asian American	74	51
Hispanic American	87	62
White American	81	52

Note: See Table B.1 for sample sizes.

Finally, Table B.10 shows the percentages of youth who engage in each risk-taking behavior. Boys demonstrate higher pattern rates than girls in most areas. The exception is the category of depression or attempted suicide, which is consistent with other research in this area.

Patterns of Co-Occurrence

The patterns of risk taking rarely travel alone. Rather, they feed and fuel each other.[5] Table B.11 presents patterns of co-occurrence, with probabilities for being at risk in other domains when at risk in a particular domain. Data are presented for high school students only, grades nine to twelve ($N = 150,001$).

For example, if a high school student engages in a pattern of alcohol use, then the probability that he is at risk in the area of tobacco use rises exponentially (to 45 percent). Other drug use has a particularly strong predictive power. If he is *not* at risk in this area, for example, then there is a 30 percent chance that he engages in a pattern of sexual intercourse (three or more times). But when he *is* at risk in the other drug category, then the probability jumps to 74 percent.

TABLE B.9. PERCENTAGES OF YOUTH INVOLVED IN SINGLE INCIDENTS OF SELECTED RISK-TAKING BEHAVIORS, BY GENDER, GRADE, AND RACE OR ETHNICITY.

Risk Behavior	Definition	All	Gender		Grade							Race or Ethnicity				
			M	F	6	7	8	9	10	11	12	African American	American Indian	Asian American	Hispanic American	White American
Alcohol	Used alcohol one or more times in the past month	34	36	32	10	18	28	36	42	48	53	29	37	22	36	35
	Got drunk one or more times in the past two weeks	21	25	18	8	12	17	21	26	30	34	20	28	15	28	21
Tobacco	Smoked cigarettes one or more times in the past month	22	23	22	7	14	19	24	27	30	32	14	35	15	23	23
	Used smokeless tobacco one or more times in the past twelve months	16	28	5	7	10	14	17	20	22	22	4	20	9	11	18
Marijuana	Used marijuana one or more times in the past twelve months	14	15	12	2	5	10	14	18	21	23	17	21	10	20	13
Other Drug Use	Used other illicit drugs one or more times in the past twelve months*	6	7	5	1	3	5	6	8	8	8	3	10	6	9	6
Sexual Activity	Had intercourse one or more times in lifetime	36	40	32	11	20	26	35	43	54	65	64	49	24	39	33

TABLE B.9. PERCENTAGES OF YOUTH INVOLVED IN SINGLE INCIDENTS OF SELECTED RISK-TAKING BEHAVIORS, BY GENDER, GRADE, AND RACE OR ETHNICITY, cont'd.

Risk Behavior	Definition	All	Gender		Grade							Race or Ethnicity				
			M	F	6	7	8	9	10	11	12	African American	American Indian	Asian American	Hispanic American	White American
	Is sexually active; did not use contraception at first intercourse	17	19	15	7	11	14	18	19	22	26	36	29	12	21	15
Antisocial Behavior	Shoplifted one or more times in the past twelve months	21	26	16	13	18	23	23	23	21	19	25	28	21	30	20
	Committed vandalism one or more times in the past twelve months	20	29	11	13	18	22	23	22	21	19	21	26	18	25	20
	Got into trouble with police one or more times in the past twelve months	19	26	12	11	13	18	19	21	24	23	19	25	16	26	18
Violence	Hit someone one or more times in the past twelve months	37	48	26	41	44	44	39	34	30	26	55	51	30	45	35
	Physically hurt someone one or more times in the past twelve months	14	22	7	13	15	17	15	14	12	11	25	26	12	22	12

Used a weapon to "get something from someone else" one or more in the past twelve months	**5**	8	2	4	6	7	6	5	4	4	13	11	6	10	4
Involved in group fighting one or more times in the past twelve months	**29**	33	25	31	32	33	30	27	25	23	39	41	26	40	27
School Problems — Skipped school one or more times in the past month	**21**	23	29	13	14	17	20	23	28	34	24	28	22	29	20
Has below a C grade average	**11**	14	8	7	11	12	13	12	10	7	16	20	6	17	10
Driving and Alcohol — Drove after drinking one or more times in the past twelve months	**15**	17	12	2	4	6	9	16	31	40	12	16	9	16	15
Rode with a driver who had been drinking one or more times in the past twelve months	**44**	43	45	28	35	40	46	48	51	54	47	52	29	49	43
Attempted Suicide — Attempted suicide one or more times in lifetime	**13**	9	17	8	11	13	15	15	14	14	13	21	14	18	12

Notes: All numbers are percentages.

*Includes cocaine, LSD, PCP or angel dust, heroin, or amphetamines.

See Table B.1 for sample sizes.

FIGURE B.5. AVERAGE NUMBER OF
NINE HIGH-RISK PATTERNS OF BEHAVIOR.

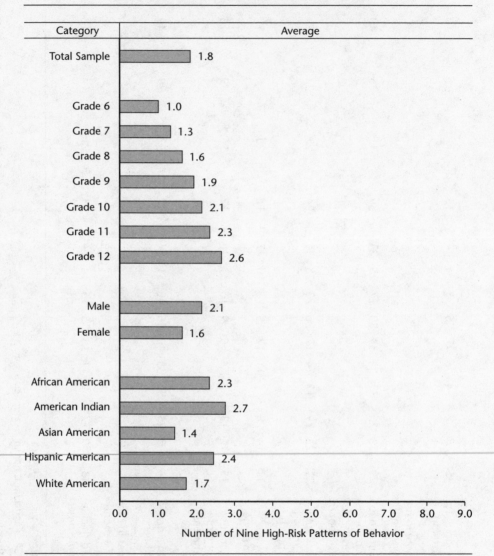

Note: See Table B.1 for sample sizes.

FIGURE B.6. PERCENTAGES OF YOUTH ENGAGING IN ONE OR MORE HIGH-RISK PATTERNS OF BEHAVIOR.

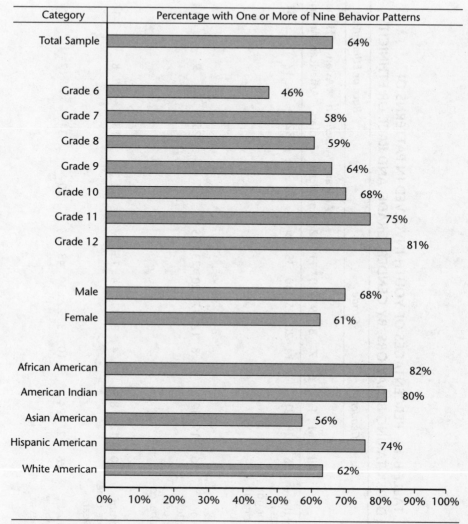

Category	Percentage with One or More of Nine Behavior Patterns
Total Sample	64%
Grade 6	46%
Grade 7	58%
Grade 8	59%
Grade 9	64%
Grade 10	68%
Grade 11	75%
Grade 12	81%
Male	68%
Female	61%
African American	82%
American Indian	80%
Asian American	56%
Hispanic American	74%
White American	62%

Note: See Table B.1 for sample sizes.

TABLE B.10. PERCENTAGES OF YOUTH INVOLVED IN PATTERNS OF SELECTED RISK-TAKING BEHAVIORS, BY GENDER, GRADE, AND RACE OR ETHNICITY.

Risk Behavior	Definition	All	Gender		Grade							Race or Ethnicity				
			M	F	6	7	8	9	10	11	12	African American	American Indian	Asian American	Hispanic American	White American
Alcohol	Used alcohol three or more times in past month or got drunk one or more times in last two weeks.	25	28	21	9	14	20	25	30	35	39	24	32	17	31	25
Tobacco	Smokes one or more cigarettes every day or uses smokeless tobacco frequently.	16	19	12	3	8	12	17	20	23	25	7	25	9	14	16
Other Drugs	Used illicit drugs three or more times in the past year.	10	12	8	1	4	8	11	14	15	17	12	16	8	16	9
Sexual Intercourse	Has had sexual intercourse three or more times in lifetime.	26	27	24	5	10	13	22	30	43	56	50	34	17	27	23

Category	Description														
Depression/ Suicide	Is frequently depressed or has attempted suicide.	**23**	17	29	17	20	23	26	26	25	24	29	35	27	31	22
Antisocial Behavior	Was involved in three or more acts of shoplifting, trouble with police, or vandalism in the past year.	**18**	26	11	9	14	19	20	20	18	21	25	18	26	17
Violence	Was involved in three or more acts of fighting, hitting, injuring a person, or using a weapon in the past year.	**24**	32	16	26	28	29	25	22	19	16	40	39	19	33	21
School Problems	Skipped school two or more days in the last month or has below C average.	**20**	24	16	13	17	19	21	21	22	24	28	33	17	31	18
Driving and Alcohol	Drove after drinking or rode with a drinking driver three or more times in the past year.	**23**	24	22	11	15	18	22	25	31	37	24	28	12	27	22

Note: See Table B.1 for sample sizes.

TABLE B.11. CO-OCCURRENCE RATES AMONG HIGH-RISK PATTERNS OF BEHAVIOR.

High-Risk Patterns of Behavior		At Risk, Alcohol Use	At Risk, Tobacco Use	At Risk, Illicit Drug Use	At Risk, Sexual Activity	At Risk, Depression/ Suicide	At Risk, Antisocial Behavior	At Risk, Violence	At Risk, School Problems	At Risk, Driving and Alcohol
Alcohol	If not at risk, then	—	10	5	26	22	11	14	14	15
	If at risk, then	—	45	32	58	33	38	36	38	56
Tobacco	If not at risk, then	22	—	7	28	21	14	16	16	22
	If at risk, then	68	—	41	65	38	42	39	45	52
Other Drugs	If not at risk, then	25	14	—	30	23	15	17	17	23
	If at risk, then	73	62	—	74	41	51	45	49	60
Sexual Activity	If not at risk, then	21	11	6	—	20	14	14	15	19
	If at risk, then	51	7	29	—	35	30	33	35	45
Depression/ Suicide	If not at risk, then	28	17	11	31	—	17	18	18	25
	If at risk, then	41	31	23	50	—	27	30	33	37
Antisocial Behavior	If not at risk, then	24	15	8	31	23	—	14	17	22
	If at risk, then	60	43	36	55	35	—	36	43	51
Violence	If not at risk, then	25	16	10	31	22	13	—	17	23
	If at risk, then	54	39	30	56	36	46	—	40	46
School Problems	If not at risk, then	25	15	9	30	22	14	16	—	23
	If at risk, then	55	42	31	37	38	39	38	—	45
Driving and Alcohol	If not at risk, then	19	14	8	28	22	13	16	17	—
	If at risk, then	63	39	30	58	34	36	35	35	—

Notes: All numbers are percentages.

For definitions of high-risk patterns of behavior, see Table B.10.

N = 150,001.

Relationships Between Developmental Assets and Risk-Taking Behaviors

This final section of the appendix focuses on the relationships between developmental assets and risk-taking behavior, showing that higher levels of developmental assets are consistently associated with lower levels of risk-taking behaviors. We include the following detailed findings:

1. Table B.12 shows the relationship between levels of developmental assets (0–10, 11–20, 21–25, 26–30) and percentage engaging in single incidents of risk taking. In each case, higher levels of assets are associated with lower levels of involvement in risk-taking behaviors.
2. Tables B.13 to B.21 show the relationship between levels of developmental assets (0–10, 11–20, 21–25, 26–30) and *patterns* of high-risk behavior, by gender, grade, and race or ethnicity.

TABLE B.12. DEVELOPMENTAL ASSETS AND INDIVIDUAL RISK-TAKING BEHAVIORS.

Risk-Taking Behaviors			Percentage of Youth Involved in Risk-Taking Behavior			
Category	Definition	All	If 0–0 Assets	If 11–20 Assets	If 21–25 Assets	If 26–30 Assets
Alcohol	Used alcohol one or more times in the past month	34	56	36	18	8
	Got drunk one or more times in the past two weeks	21	42	22	8	3
Tobacco	Smoked cigarettes one or more times in the past month	22	44	23	9	3
	Used smokeless tobacco one or more times in the past twelve months	16	28	17	8	3
Marijuana	Used marijuana one or more times in the past twelve months	14	31	14	4	<1
Other Drug Use	Used other illicit drugs one or more times in the past twelve months*	6	16	5	1	<1
Sexual Activity	Had intercourse one or more times in lifetime	36	56	39	20	9
	Is sexually active; did not use contraception at first intercourse	17	31	18	7	3
Antisocial Behavior	Shoplifted one or more times in the past twelve months	21	39	21	9	3
	Committed vandalism one or more times in the past twelve months	20	40	20	8	3
	Got into trouble with police one or more times in the past twelve months	19	39	19	7	3

TABLE B.12. DEVELOPMENTAL ASSETS
AND INDIVIDUAL RISK-TAKING BEHAVIORS, cont'd.

			Percentage of Youth Involved in Risk-Taking Behavior			
	Risk-Taking Behaviors					
Category	Definition	All	If 0–0 Assets	If 11–20 Assets	If 21–25 Assets	If 26–30 Assets
Violence	Hit someone one or more times in the past twelve months	**37**	55	39	24	13
	Physically hurt someone one or more times in the past twelve months	**14**	27	14	7	3
	Used a weapon to "get something from someone else" one or more times in the past twelve months	**5**	14	5	1	<1
	Involved in group fighting one or more times in the past twelve months	**28**	42	30	20	12
School Problems	Skipped school one or more times in the past month	**21**	40	22	9	5
	Has below a C grade average	**11**	30	10	2	<1
Driving and Alcohol	Drove after drinking one or more times in the past twelve months	**15**	28	15	6	2
	Rode with a driver who had been drinking one or more times in the past twelve months	**44**	61	46	30	19
Attempted Suicide	Attempted suicide one or more times in lifetime	**13**	25	13	6	3

*Includes cocaine, LSD, PCP or angel dust, heroin, or amphetamines.

N = 254,634.

TABLE B.13. PERCENTAGES REPORTING ALCOHOL RISK PATTERN,* BY LEVEL OF THIRTY DEVELOPMENTAL ASSETS.

	If 0–10 Assets	If 11–20 Assets	If 21–25 Assets	If 26–30 Assets
Total Sample	47	26	10	4
Males	48	28	11	4
Females	45	24	9	3
Grade 6	22	10	3	1
Grade 7	34	14	5	2
Grade 8	43	20	7	3
Grade 9	47	25	10	3
Grade 10	52	30	13	4
Grade 11	56	36	17	6
Grade 12	59	451	22	8
African American	44	25	12	4
American Indian	50	31	15	5
Asian American	32	17	9	3
Hispanic American	50	29	14	5
White American	47	26	10	3

*Used alcohol three or more times in past month or binge drank once or more in the last two weeks. See Table B.1 for sample sizes.

TABLE B.14. PERCENTAGES REPORTING ANTISOCIAL RISK PATTERN,* BY LEVEL OF THIRTY DEVELOPMENTAL ASSETS.

	If 0–10 Assets	If 11–20 Assets	If 21–25 Assets	If 26–30 Assets
Total Sample	40	18	5	1
Males	46	24	9	3
Females	30	11	3	<1
Grade 6	27	11	3	<1
Grade 7	37	14	4	<1
Grade 8	44	19	5	2
Grade 9	43	20	6	1
Grade 10	42	20	6	2
Grade 11	41	20	7	2
Grade 12	36	18	6	2
African American	42	21	9	2
American Indian	47	24	7	1
Asian American	39	17	7	2
Hispanic American	49	24	9	3
White American	39	17	5	1

*Involved in three or more acts of shoplifting, trouble with police, or vandalism in the last year. See Table B.1 for sample sizes.

TABLE B.15. PERCENTAGES REPORTING DRIVING AND DRINKING RISK PATTERN,* BY LEVEL OF THIRTY DEVELOPMENTAL ASSETS.

	If 0–10 Assets	If 11–20 Assets	If 21–25 Assets	If 26–30 Assets
Total Sample	40	24	11	5
Males	40	23	11	4
Females	41	24	11	5
Grade 6	23	12	6	3
Grade 7	29	15	8	4
Grade 8	33	19	9	5
Grade 9	39	22	11	5
Grade 10	41	25	12	5
Grade 11	50	32	16	6
Grade 12	55	38	20	8
African American	39	25	15	7
American Indian	42	28	15	4
Asian American	22	12	6	2
Hispanic American	41	27	15	11
White American	40	23	11	5

*Drove after drinking or rode with a drinking driver three or more times in the past year. See Table B.1 for sample sizes.

TABLE B.16. PERCENTAGES REPORTING DEPRESSION OR SUICIDE RISK PATTERN,* BY LEVEL OF THIRTY DEVELOPMENTAL ASSETS.

	If 0–10 Assets	If 11–20 Assets	If 21–25 Assets	If 26–30 Assets
Total Sample	42	24	11	5
Males	33	16	6	4
Females	58	33	14	6
Grade 6	38	20	7	3
Grade 7	41	22	9	3
Grade 8	43	24	9	5
Grade 9	44	26	12	6
Grade 10	43	26	13	6
Grade 11	40	25	14	8
Grade 12	39	25	14	7
African American	43	31	18	12
American Indian	51	36	19	6
Asian American	41	29	12	7
Hispanic American	43	31	19	4
White American	41	23	10	5

*Is "frequently" depressed or has attempted suicide one or more times. See Table B.1 for sample sizes.

TABLE B.17. PERCENTAGES REPORTING ILLICIT DRUG RISK PATTERN,* BY LEVEL OF THIRTY DEVELOPMENTAL ASSETS.

	If 0–10 Assets	If 11–20 Assets	If 21–25 Assets	If 26–30 Assets
Total Sample	25	10	3	<1
Males	26	11	3	<1
Females	24	9	2	<1
Grade 6	6	1	1	<1
Grade 7	13	3	<1	<1
Grade 8	22	7	2	<1
Grade 9	27	10	2	<1
Grade 10	31	13	4	<1
Grade 11	33	15	5	<1
Grade 12	32	17	5	<1
African American	28	12	5	<1
American Indian	30	15	5	0
Asian American	19	7	3	0
Hispanic American	33	14	4	0
White American	24	9	2	<1

*Three or more uses of an illicit drug (marijuana, cocaine, LSD, PCP or angel dust, heroin, or amphetamines) in the past year. See Table B.1 for sample sizes.

TABLE B.18. PERCENTAGES REPORTING SCHOOL RISK PATTERN,* BY LEVEL OF THIRTY DEVELOPMENTAL ASSETS.

	If 0–10 Assets	If 11–20 Assets	If 21–25 Assets	If 26–30 Assets
Total Sample	46	20	6	2
Males	48	22	7	2
Females	44	18	5	2
Grade 6	33	14	5	2
Grade 7	43	18	5	1
Grade 8	47	19	5	2
Grade 9	49	19	5	2
Grade 10	48	20	6	1
Grade 11	47	21	7	2
Grade 12	47	24	9	3
African American	54	28	12	6
American Indian	58	31	12	1
Asian American	37	17	7	3
Hispanic American	57	29	11	1
White American	45	18	5	1

*Skipped school two or more days in the past month or has below C average. See Table B.1 for sample sizes.

TABLE B.19. PERCENTAGES REPORTING SEXUAL ACTIVITY RISK PATTERN,* BY LEVEL OF THIRTY DEVELOPMENTAL ASSETS.

	If 0–10 Assets	If 11–20 Assets	If 21–25 Assets	If 26–30 Assets
Total Sample	41	27	14	5
Males	40	27	14	6
Females	43	27	13	5
Grade 6	10	5	2	<1
Grade 7	20	10	5	1
Grade 8	27	14	6	1
Grade 9	38	22	9	4
Grade 10	47	32	17	7
Grade 11	58	45	27	13
Grade 12	68	59	41	20
African American	66	52	38	23
American Indian	47	34	23	13
Asian American	26	17	9	5
Hispanic American	40	26	15	4
White American	39	25	11	4

*Has had sexual intercourse three or more times. See Table B.1 for sample sizes.

TABLE B.20. PERCENTAGES REPORTING TOBACCO RISK PATTERN,* BY LEVEL OF THIRTY DEVELOPMENTAL ASSETS.

	If 0–10 Assets	If 11–20 Assets	If 21–25 Assets	If 26–30 Assets
Total Sample	36	16	4	1
Males	36	28	6	2
Females	34	13	3	<1
Grade 6	11	4	1	<1
Grade 7	23	8	2	<1
Grade 8	31	11	3	<1
Grade 9	38	16	5	1
Grade 10	41	19	6	2
Grade 11	42	23	8	2
Grade 12	45	26	9	3
African American	16	7	2	<1
American Indian	43	24	11	4
Asian American	22	8	3	1
Hispanic American	29	12	4	2
White American	37	17	5	1

*Smokes one or more cigarettes every day or has used tobacco twenty or more times in the last year. See Table B.1 for sample sizes.

TABLE B.21. PERCENTAGES REPORTING VIOLENCE RISK PATTERN,* BY LEVEL OF THIRTY DEVELOPMENTAL ASSETS.

	If 0–10 Assets	If 11–20 Assets	If 21–25 Assets	If 26–30 Assets
Total Sample	41	25	13	6
Males	47	31	19	10
Females	32	18	9	5
Grade 6	45	30	16	8
Grade 7	50	31	16	8
Grade 8	50	31	16	8
Grade 9	44	26	13	5
Grade 10	39	22	10	5
Grade 11	35	19	8	3
Grade 12	29	16	7	2
African American	56	42	29	16
American Indian	54	39	23	7
Asian American	35	19	11	2
Hispanic American	50	32	18	10
White American	39	22	11	5

*Three or more acts of fighting, hitting, injury to a person, or using a weapon in the last year. See Table B.1 for sample sizes.

APPENDIX C

THE PROGRESSION OF DEVELOPMENTAL ASSETS FROM BIRTH TO AGE 18

Asset Type	Infants and Toddlers (Birth to age 2)	Preschoolers (Ages 3 to 5)	Elementary-Age Children (Ages 6 to 11)	Adolescents (Ages 12 to 18)
E X T E R N A L A S S E T S				
Support				
1.	Family support			
2.	Positive family communication			
3.	Other adult resources		Other adult relationships	
4.	Caring neighborhood			
5.	Caring out-of-home climate		Caring school climate	
6.	Parent involvement in out-of-home situations		Parent involvement in schooling	
Empowerment				
7.	Children valued		Community values children	Community values youth
8.	Children have roles in family life	Children given useful roles		Youth as resources
9.	Service to others			
10.	Safety			
Boundaries and Expectations				
11.	Family boundaries			
12.	Out-of-home boundaries		School boundaries	
13.	Neighborhood boundaries			
14.	Adult role models			
15.	Positive peer observation	Positive peer interactions		Positive peer influence
16.	Expectations for growth			High expectations
Constructive Use of Time				
17.	Creative activities			
18.	Out-of home activities		Child programs	Youth programs
19.	Religious community			
20.	Positive, supervised time at home			Time at home

Source: Excerpted with permission from *Starting Out Right: Developmental Assets for Children,* by Nancy Leffert, Peter L. Benson, and Jolene L. Roehlkepartain. Copyright © 1997 by Search Institute. All rights reserved.

The complete report includes definitions of each asset for each age group.

Asset Type	Infants and Toddlers (Birth to age 2)	Preschoolers (Ages 3 to 5)	Elementary-Age Children (Ages 6 to 11)	Adolescents (Ages 12 to 18)
	I N T E R N A L A S S E T S			

Commitment to Learning

21.	Achievement expectation		Achievement motivation	
22.	Engagement expectation		School engagement	
23.	Stimulating activity		Homework	
24.	Enjoyment of learning		Bonding to school	
25.	Reading for pleasure			

Positive Values

26.	Family values caring		Caring	
27.	Family values equality and social justice		Equality and social justice	
28.	Family values integrity		Integrity	
29.	Family values honesty		Honesty	
30.	Family values responsibility		Responsibility	
31.	Family values healthy lifestyle and sexual attitudes		Healthy lifestyle and sexual attitudes	Restraint

Social Competencies

32.	Planning and decision-making observation	Planning and decision-making practice	Planning and decision-making	
33.	Interpersonal observation	Interpersonal interactions	Interpersonal competence	
34.	Cultural observation	Cultural interactions	Cultural competence	
35.	Resistance observation	Resistance practice	Resistance skills	
36.	Peaceful conflict-resolution observation	Peaceful conflict-resolution practice	Peaceful conflict resolution	

Positive Identity

37.	Family has personal power		Personal power	
38.	Family models high self-esteem		Self-esteem	
39.	Family has a sense of purpose		Sense of purpose	
40.	Family has a positive view of the future		Positive view of personal future	

NOTES

Chapter One

1. The original framework introduced in 1989 included six categories. It was expanded in 1996. See Chapter Two and Appendix B for more information.
2. National Commission on the Role of the School and the Community in Improving Adolescent Health (1990). *Code blue: Uniting for healthier youth.* Chicago: American Medical Association; Alexandria, Va.: National Association of State Boards of Education.
3. Wiig, J. K., and Lahti-Johnson, K. (1995). Delinquents under 10 in Hennepin County. Minneapolis: Hennepin County Attorney's Office.
4. Dryfoos, J. G. (1990). *Adolescents at risk: Prevalence and prevention.* New York: Oxford University Press.
5. Moore, K. A,. and Glei, D. (1995). Taking the plunge: An examination of positive youth development. *Journal of Adolescent Research, 10,* 15–40.
6. Lerner, R. M. (1995). *America's youth in crisis: Challenges and options for programs and policies.* Thousand Oaks, Calif.: Sage; Bennett, W. J. (1993). *The index of leading cultural indicators.* Washington, D.C.: Heritage Foundation; Carnegie Council on Adolescent Development (1995). *Great transitions: Preparing adolescents for a new century.* New York: Carnegie Corporation of New York, chapter three; Children's Defense Fund (1994). *Wasting America's future: The Children's Defense Fund report on the costs of child poverty.* Boston: Beacon Press.
7. Goetting, A. (1994). Do Americans really like children? *The Journal of Primary Prevention, 15,* 81–92.
8. Carnegie Council on Adolescent Development. (1995). *Great transitions: Preparing adolescents for a new century.* New York: Carnegie Corporation of New York.

9. Bureau of the Census. (1997). *Current population reports: Poverty in the United States 1995.* Washington, D.C.: U.S. Department of Commerce.

10. Rainwater, L., and Smeeding, T. M. (1995). U.S. doing poorly—compared to others. *News and Issues, 5,* 4–5 (National Center for Children in Poverty).

11. Goetting, A. (1994).

12. Leffert, N., and Petersen, A. C. (1995). Patterns of development during adolescence. In M. Rutter and D. J. Smith (eds.), *Psychosocial disorders in young people.* New York: Wiley, 67–103.

13. U. S. Department of Education. (1995). Community service performed by high school seniors. *Education Policy Issues: Statistical Perspective* (National Center for Education Studies).

14. Benson, P. L. (1994). Changing families: National patterns and their implications. *Education Digest, 60*(6), 47–50; Zill, N., and Nord, C. W. (1994). *Running in place: How American families are faring in a changing economy and an individual society.* Washington, D.C.: Child Trends.

15. Elkind, D. (1994). *Ties that stress: The new family imbalance.* Cambridge, Mass.: Harvard University Press.

16. Furstenburg, F. (1993). How families manage risk and opportunity in dangerous neighborhoods. In W. J. Wilson (ed.), *Sociology and the public agenda.* Thousand Oaks, Calif.: Sage.

17. Putnam, R. D. (1996). The strange disappearance of civic America. *The American Prospect, 24,* Winter, 34–50.

18. McKnight, J. (1995). *The careless society: Community and its counterfeits.* New York: Basic Books, ix–x.

19. See Modell, J., and Goodman, M. (1990). Historical perspectives. In S. S. Feldman and G. R. Elliott (eds.), *At the threshold: The developing adolescent.* Cambridge, Mass.: Harvard University Press, 93–122; Leffert, N., and Petersen, A. C. (1995). Patterns of development during adolescence. In M. Rutter and D. J. Smith (eds.), *Psychosocial disorders in young people: Time trends and their causes.* New York: Wiley.

20. Hess, L. E., and Petersen, A. C. (1991). *Narrowing the margins: Adolescent unemployment and the lack of a social role.* Manuscript prepared for Academia Europaea and the World Scout Bureau; Petersen, A. C., Richmond, J. B., and Leffert, N. (1993). Social changes among youth: The United States experience. *Journal of Adolescent Health,* 14, 33–41.

21. Benson, P. L. (1996). *Developmental assets among Minneapolis youth: The urgency of promoting healthy communities.* Minneapolis: Search Institute.

22. See, for example, Comstock, G. (1991). *Television and the American child.* San Diego: Academic Press. In our analysis, the correlation between the amount of daily television viewing and an index of violence is .13 (p <.0001).

23. See the important perspective on risk reduction articulated in Hawkins, J. D., and Catalano, R. F. (1992). *Communities that care: Action for drug abuse prevention.* San Francisco: Jossey-Bass.

24. Annie E. Casey Foundation. (1995). *The path of most resistance: Reflections on lessons learned from New Futures.* Baltimore: author.

25. Washington, V., and Bailey, U.J.O. (1995). *Project Head Start: Models and strategies for the twenty-first century.* New York: Garland.

26. Goleman, D. (1995). *Emotional intelligence.* New York: Bantam Books, 256.

27. Annie E. Casey Foundation. (1996). *Kids Count data book: State profiles of well-being.* Baltimore: author.

28. Klite, P., Bardwell, R., and Salzman, J. (1996). *Pavlov's TV dogs: A snapshot of local TV news in America,* 9/20/95. Denver: Rocky Mountain Media Watch.

29. Kretzmann, J. P., and McKnight, J. L. (1993) *Building communities from the inside out: A path toward finding and mobilizing a community's assets.* Evanston, Ill.: Center for Urban Affairs and Policy Research, 5. Note that Kretzmann and McKnight use the term *assets* to focus on the

resources and capacities within the community, not the developmental assets identified by Search Institute. Though the overlapping language can be confusing, the two frameworks are highly compatible.

30. Hawkins, J. D., and Catalano, R. F. (1992). *Communities that care: Action for drug abuse prevention*. San Francisco: Jossey-Bass.

31. Pittman, K. J., and Cahill, M. (1991). *A new vision: Promoting youth development*. Washington, D.C.: Center for Youth Development and Policy Research, 3.

32. Covey, S. R. (1990). *The seven habits of highly effective people*. New York: Fireside, 31.

33. Personal interview, Feb. 27, 1996.

34. A current listing of communities involved in asset building can be found in Search Institute's Web site at http://www.search-institute.org/communities/

35. For a particularly astute review of the concept of community, see Selznick, P. (1992). *The moral commonwealth: Social theory and the promise of community*. Berkeley: University of California Press.

36. One of the wiser portrayals of healthy community is presented by John Gardner in *Building Community* (Washington, D.C.: Independent Sector). He calls attention to the defining characteristics of community as well as some of the dangers found in historical examples of community.

37. National League of Cities. (1996). *The state of America's cities*. Annapolis, Md.: author.

Chapter Two

1. Pivotal sources for the construction of the asset framework include the works of Diana Baumrind, B. B. Brown, James Coleman, William Damon, Joy Dryfoos, Norm Garmezy, Carol Gilligan, Francis Ianni, W. W. Hartup, Richard Jessor, Richard Lerner, Ann Masten, Michael Rutter, and Emmy Werner.

2. The Search Institute team contributing to the framework of forty developmental assets includes Thomas Berkas, Dale A. Blyth, Craig DeVille, Nancy Leffert, Eugene C. Roehlkepartain, Rebecca N. Saito, Peter C. Scales, and Jean L. Wachs.

3. Benson, P. L. (1990, 1993). *The troubled journey: A portrait of 6th–12th grade youth*. Minneapolis: Search Institute.

4. Benson, P. L. (1996). *Developmental assets among Minneapolis youth*. Minneapolis: Search Institute; Benson, P. L. (1996). *Developmental assets among Albuquerque youth*. Minneapolis: Search Institute.

5. For a review of the literature on nonparent adult support for youth, see Scales, P. C., and Gibbons, J. L. (1996). Extended family members and unrelated adults in the lives of young adolescents: A research agenda. *Journal of Early Adolescence, 16* (Nov.), 365–389.

6. See, for example, Rice, K. G., and Mulkeen, P. (1995). Relationships with parents and peers: A longitudinal study of adolescent intimacy. *Journal of Adolescent Research, 10*(3), 338–357; Werner, E. E. (1993). Risk, resilience, and recovery: Perspectives from the Kauai longitudinal study. Special issue: Milestones in the development of resilience. *Development and Psychopathology, 5*(4), 503–515.

7. See, for example, Carnegie Council on Adolescent Development (1989). *Turning points: Preparing American youth for the 21st century*. Washington, D.C.: author.

8. Significance tests show that the increase from three or four adults to five or more is associated with a decrease in alcohol use, depression and attempted suicide, illicit drug use, and sexual activity.

9. For a deeper discussion of mentoring programs, see Saito, R. N., and Blyth, D. A. (1994). *Understanding mentoring relationships*. Minneapolis: Search Institute; Freedman, M. (1993). *The kindness of strangers: Adult mentors, urban youth, and the new volunteerism*. San Francisco: Jossey-Bass.

10. Tierney, J. P., Grossman, J. B., and Resch, N. L. (1995). *Making a difference: An impact study of Big Brothers/Big Sisters*. Philadelphia: Public/Private Ventures.

11. See, for example, Noddings, N. (1995). A morally defensible mission for schools in the 21st century. *Phi Delta Kappan, 76,* 365–368.

12. See Eccles, J. S., and Midgley, C. (1989). Stage/environment fit: Developmentally appropriate classrooms for early adolescents. In R. E. Ames and C. Ames (eds.), *Research on motivation in education (vol. 3)*. New York: Academic Press; Carnegie Council on Adolescent Development. (1989). *Turning points: Preparing American youth for the 21st century*. Washington, D.C.: author.

13. Noblit, G. W., Rogers, D. L., and McCadden, B. M. (1995). In the meantime: The possibilities of caring. *Phi Delta Kappan, 76,* 386–693.

14. Scales, P. C. (1996). *Boxed in and bored: How middle schools continue to fail adolescents—and what good middle schools do right*. Minneapolis: Search Institute.

15. For an important review of this area, see Epstein, J. L. (1995). School/family/community partnerships: Caring for the children we share. *Phi Delta Kappa, 76,* 701–712.

16. Hersch, P. (1990). The resounding silence. *Family Therapy Networker* (July/Aug.), 19–29.

17. See Moore, C. W., and Allen, J. P. (1996). The effects of volunteering on the young volunteer. *Journal of Primary Prevention, 17,* 2.

18. Fick, A. C., and Thomas, S. M. (1995). Growing up in a violent environment: Relationship to health-related beliefs and behaviors. *Youth & Society, 27,* 2, 136–147.

19. Bly, R. (1996). *The sibling society*. Reading, Mass.: Addison-Wesley.

20. Ianni, F.A.J. (1989). *The search for structure: A report on American youth today*. New York: Free Press.

21. Damon, W. (1995). *Greater expectations: Overcoming the culture of indulgence in America's home and schools*. New York: The Free Press.

22. Carnegie Council on Adolescent Development (1992). *A matter of time: Risk and opportunity in the nonschool hours*. New York: Carnegie Council of New York, 28.

23. Ibid., 33.

24. Benson (1993).

25. McLaughlin, M. W., and Irby, M. I. (1994). *Urban sanctuaries: Neighborhood organizations in the lives and futures of inner-city youth*. San Francisco: Jossey-Bass.

26. Your child's brain. (1996). *Newsweek* (Feb. 10), 54ff.

27. Leffert, N., Saito, R. N., Blyth, D. A., and Kroenke, C. H. (1996). *Making the case: Measuring the impact of youth development programs*. Minneapolis: Search Institute.

28. Carnegie Council on Adolescent Development (1992), 77.

29. National Commission on Children. (1991). *Speaking of kids: A national survey of children and parents*. Washington, D.C.: author.

30. Saito, R. N., and Roehlkepartain, E. C. (1995). *Places to grow: Youth development opportunities for seven-to-fourteen-year-olds in Minneapolis*. Minneapolis: Search Institute.

31. Living in "lockdown." (1995). *Newsweek* (Jan. 23), 56–57.

32. Donahue, M. J., and Benson, P. L. (1995). Religion and the well-being of adolescents. *Journal of Social Issues, 51,* 145–160.

33. See Roehlkepartain, E. C., and Scales, P. C. (1995). *Youth development in congregations: An exploration of the potential and barriers*. Minneapolis: Search Institute; Roehlkepartain, E. C. (1997). *Building assets in congregations*. Minneapolis: Search Institute.

34. Also see Greenberger, E., and Steinberg, L. (1986). *When teenagers work: The psychological and social costs of adolescent employment.* New York: Basic Books.
35. See Scales (1996).
36. Cernkovich, S. A., and Giordano, P. C. (1992). School bonding, race, and delinquency. *Criminology, 30*(2), 261–291.
37. An excellent survey of the issues related to caring among youth is Chaskin, R. J., and Hawley, T. (1994). *Youth and caring: Developing a field of inquiry and practice.* Chicago: Chapin Hall Center for Children, University of Chicago.
38. In the Minneapolis study, for example, antisocial behavior correlates-.22 with responsibility and-.20 with honesty. Each of the added values (integrity, honesty, responsibility) correlates above .27 with the affirmation of diversity.
39. Carter, S. L. (1996). *Integrity.* New York: Basic Books.
40. See, for example, Dryfoos, J. G. (1990). *Adolescents at risk: Prevalence and prevention.* New York: Oxford Press; Benson, P. L., Griffin, T., and Svendsen, R. (1992). *Promising prevention strategies: A look at what works.* St. Paul: Minnesota Department of Education.
41. See, for example, Botvin, G. J., et al. (1990). A cognitive-behavioral approach to substance use prevention: One-year follow-up. *Addictive Behaviors, 15,* 47–63.
42. Peaceful conflict resolution correlates as follows: violence (-.32), sexual activity (-.31), illicit drug use (-.21), alcohol use (-.20).
43. r = .44.
44. See, for example, Simmons, R. G., and Blyth, D. A. (1987). *Moving into adolescence: The impact of pubertal change and school context.* New York: Aldine deGruyter; Petersen, A. C. (1988). Adolescent development. *Annual Review of Psychology, 39,* 583–607; Stattin, H., and Magnusson, D. (1990). *Pubertal maturation in female development, vol. 2, Paths through life.* Hillsdale, N.J.: Erlbaum.
45. Seligman, M.E.P. (1995). *The optimistic child.* New York: Houghton Mifflin, 7.
46. Father Flanagan's Boys Town in Nebraska has developed a comprehensive body of research and technologies for teaching basic social skills to young people, based on the organization's work with highly vulnerable and high-risk youth in their residential homes. See, for example, Dowd, T., and Tierney, J. (1992). *Teaching social skills to youth: A curriculum for child care providers.* Boys Town, Nebr.: Boys Town Press.

Chapter Three

1. Benson, P. L. (1996). *Developmental assets among Albuquerque youth.* Minneapolis: Search Institute; Benson, P. L. (1996). *Developmental assets among Minneapolis youth.* Minneapolis: Search Institute.
2. The definitions of the behavior patterns have been altered from those in several earlier publications (for example, *What Kids Need to Succeed, Uniting Communities for Youth*). For this book, the antisocial behavior and violence domains have been split into separate patterns, and the criterion in most cases has been moved to three acts.
3. For example, "spending time helping people who are poor, hungry, or sick."
4. See Seligman (1995).
5. For review of this literature, see Egeland, B., Jacobvitz, D., and Sroufe, L. A. Breaking the cycle of child abuse. *Child Development, 59,* 1080–1088; Garmezy, N. (1991). Resiliency and vulnerability to adverse developmental outcomes associated with poverty. *American Behavioral*

Scientist, 34, 416–430; Masten, A. S., Best, K. M., and Garmezy, N. (1991). Resilience and development: Contributions from the study of children who overcome diversity. *Development and Psychology, 2,* 425–444; Werner, E. E., and Smith, R. S. (1992). *Overcoming the odds: High-risk children from birth to adulthood.* Ithaca, N.Y.: Cornell University Press.

6. Two other factors in the literature that are not part of the forty-asset framework are problem-solving skills and intelligence.

7. Werner and Smith (1992).

8. Schorr, L. (1988). *Within our reach: Breaking the cycle of disadvantage.* New York: Anchor Press. Thanks to Emmy Werner for pointing out this connection.

9. Benson, P. L. (1993). *The troubled journey: A portrait of 6th–12th grade youth.* Minneapolis: Search Institute.

10. For more detailed statistics supporting these conclusions, see Appendix B.

11. Each of the thirty assets is measured by one or more survey items, each with a minimum of five response options. Then each is converted into a binary variable. Generally, the criterion used to determine the presence of a particular asset is a mean of 4.0 or greater on the applicable items. The psychometric properties of the asset measures have been assessed in a longitudinal study of one thousand middle school students and their parents in Minneapolis and St. Paul, Minnesota. This project demonstrated strong internal consistency reliability for assets measured by multiple items (for example, family support, self-esteem) and test-retest reliability. As one validity check, parents' assessments of their child's developmental assets correlated significantly with child self-reports.

12. According to Current Population Reports (P20–479), U.S. Bureau of the Census, approximately 12.7 percent of eighteen-to-twenty-four-year-olds dropped out of school before completing high school (1993). See *Statistical Abstract of the United States* (1995), table 267.

13. This analysis is delimited to the school districts surveying students (either a complete census or a purposeful random sample) on all grades between six and twelve.

14. The four types of assets by grades look like this:

Type	Grades 6–8	Grades 9–12
Low on both	78 percent	84 percent
Low External, High Internal	13 percent	9 percent
High External, Low Internal	4 percent	3 percent
High on both	5 percent	3 percent

15. See, for example, Wellesley College Center for Research on Women (1992). *How schools short-change girls.* Washington, D.C.: AAUW Educational Foundation.

16. See, for example, Simmons, R. G., and Blyth, D. A. (1987). *Moving into adolescence: The impact of pubertal change and school context.* New York: Aldine deGruyter; Petersen, A. C. (1988). Adolescent development. *Annual Review of Psychology, 39,* 583–607; Stattin, H., and Magnusson, D. (1990). *Pubertal maturation in female development, vol. 2, Paths through life.* Hillsdale, N.J.: Erlbaum. For a less academic discussion of this issue, Pipher, M. (1994). *Reviving Ophelia: Saving the selves of adolescent girls.* New York: Ballantine.

17. de Beauvoir, S. (1952). *The second sex.* New York: Knopf.

18. Benson, P. L., William, D. L., and Johnson, A. L. (1987). *The quicksilver years: The hopes and fears of early adolescence.* San Francisco: Harper San Francisco.

19. Benson, P. L., and Donahue, M. D. (1989). Ten-year trends in at-risk behaviors: A national study of black adolescents. *Journal of Adolescent Research, 4,* 125–139.

20. Bureau of Census. (1992). *Statistical abstract of the United States (112th ed.).* Washington, D.C.: author, 55.

21. Whitehead, B. D. (1993). Dan Quayle was right. *Atlantic Monthly* (Apr.), 47–84.

22. In a multivariate analysis of variance, F for family structure is 160.77 ($p <.0001$) after the effects for grade, race, gender, and maternal employment were extracted.

23. Benson, P. L., and Roehlkepartain, E. C. (1993). *Youth in single-parent families: Risk and resiliency.* Minneapolis: Search Institute. The analysis is based on the first forty-seven thousand students captured in the national study.

24. Benson, P. L. (1996). *Developmental assets among Minneapolis youth.* Minneapolis: Search Institute.

25. The correlation between self-esteem and depression/suicide is −.30. With other risk patterns: alcohol use (−.11), violence (−.08), illicit drugs (−.07), and sexual intercourse (−.04).

26. The correlation of the behavioral restraint value is −.36 with sexual activity, −.24 with tobacco use, −.19 with violence, and −.29 with alcohol use.

27. Correlations with risk patterns are as follows:

	Family Support	Parental Standards
Alcohol use	−.17	−.30
Tobacco use	−.15	−.22
Illicit drug use	−.14	−.22
Depression/suicide	−.26	−.10

28. This analysis aggregated data in 112 communities conducting the Search Institute attitude and behavior study: see Blyth, D. A., and Leffert, N. (1995). Communities and contexts for adolescent development: An empirical analysis. *Journal of Adolescent Research, 10*(1), 64–87; and Blyth, D. A., and Roehlkepartain, E. C. (1993). *Healthy communities, healthy youth: How communities contribute to positive youth development.* Minneapolis: Search Institute.

29. Goetting, A. (1994) Do Americans really like children? *Journal of Primary Prevention, 15,* 81–92.

Chapter Four

1. See Bowlby, J. (1980). *Attachment and loss,* vol. 3. New York: Basic Books; Rutter, M. (1983). Continuities and discontinuities in socio-emotional development. In Emde, R. N., and Harmon, R. J. (eds.), *Continuities and discontinuities in development.* New York: Plenum.

2. Leffert, N., Benson, P. L., and Roehlkepartain, J. L. (1997). *Starting out right: Developmental assets for children.* Minneapolis: Search Institute. The material in this section was adapted from the report.

3. Cited in Higgins, G. O. (1994). *Resilient adults: Overcoming a cruel past.* San Francisco: Jossey-Bass, 15. A helpful resource for parents designed to help them address gaps in their upbringing is Clarke, J. I., and Dawson, C. (1989). *Growing up again: Parenting ourselves, parenting our children.* San Francisco: Harper San Francisco.

4. Bly, R. (1996). *The sibling society.* Reading, Mass.: Addison-Wesley.

5. Goleman, D. (1995). *Emotional intelligence: Why it can matter more than IQ.* New York: Bantam Books, chapter nine.
6. Ibid., 161.
7. Ibid., 170.
8. Shaffer, C. R., and Anundsen, K. (1993). *Creating community anywhere: Finding support and connection in a fragmented world.* New York: Putnam, 22.
9. Parks Daloz, L. A., Keen, C. H., Keen, J. A., and Parks, S. D. (1996). *Common fire: Lives of commitment in a complex world.* Boston: Beacon Press.

Chapter Five

1. Scales, P. C. (1991). *A portrait of young adolescents in the 1990s: Implications for promoting healthy growth and development.* Minneapolis: Search Institute, 7.
2. Immerwahr, J. (1995). *Talking about children: A focus group report from Public Agenda.* Washington, D.C.: Public Agenda, 1.
3. Pittman, K. J., and Cahill, M. (1991). *A new vision: Promoting youth development.* Washington, D.C.: Center for Youth Development and Policy Research, 7.
4. Benson, P. L. (1996). *Developmental assets among Minneapolis youth: The urgency of promoting healthy community.* Minneapolis: Search Institute, 8; Benson, P. L. (1996). *Developmental assets among Albuquerque youth: The urgency of promoting healthy community.* Minneapolis: Search Institute, 8.
5. Minow, M., and Weissbourd, R. (1993). Social movements for children. *Daedalus: Journal of the American Academy of Arts and Sciences* (Winter), 14.
6. Fost, D. (1996). Child-free with attitude. *American Demographics* (Apr.), 15–16.
7. *Great expectations: How American voters view children's issues* (1997). Washington, D.C.: Coalition for America's Children.
8. McKnight, J. L. (1989). Regenerating community. *Kettering Review* (Fall), 50.
9. National Commission on Children. (1991). *Beyond rhetoric: A new American agenda for children and families.* Washington, D.C.: author, 233.
10. Ibid., 372.
11. This story is based on Tyler, K. (1996). Collaboration: One community's story. *Assets: The Magazine of Ideas for Healthy Communities & Healthy Youth* (Fall), 8–9.
12. Gardner, J. W. (1994). National renewal. *National Civic Review, 83* (Fall/Winter), 374–382.
13. Ianni, F.A.J. (1989). *The search for structure: A report on American youth today.* New York: Free Press.
14. Coleman, J. S., and Hoffer, T. (1987). *Public and private high schools: The impact of communities.* New York: Basic Books.
15. Gardner, J. W. (1991). *Building Community.* Washington, D.C.: Independent Sector, 14–15.
16. Bellah, R. N. (1995/1996). Community properly understood. *The responsive community: Rights and responsibilities, 6*(1), 49–54.
17. Blackwell, A. G. (1994). Investing in youth in urban America. *National Civic Review, 83* (Fall/Winter), 405–412.
18. Kretzmann, J. P., and Schmitz, P. H. (1995). It takes a child to raise a whole village. *Wingspread, 17*(4), 8–10.
19. Lappé, F. M., and DuBois, P. M. (1994). *The quickening of America: Rebuilding our nation, remaking our lives.* San Francisco: Jossey-Bass, 13.

20. Blyth, D. (1994). *Healthy communities, healthy youth*. Minneapolis: Search Institute; Blyth, D. A., and Leffert, N. (1995). Communities as contexts for adolescent development: An empirical analysis. *Journal of Adolescent Research, 10*(1), 64–87.

21. A current listing of communities involved in asset building can be found in Search Institute's Web site at http://www.search-institute.org/communities/

Chapter Six

1. For an important synthesis on community building, see Stone, R. (1996). *Core issues in comprehensive community-building initiatives*. Chicago: Chapin Hall Center for Children.

2. Chaskin, R. J. (1992). *The Ford Foundation's neighborhood and family initiative: Toward a model of comprehensive, neighborhood-based development*. Chicago: Chapin Hall Center for Children.

3. U.S. General Accounting Office. (1995). *Community development: Comprehensive approaches address multiple needs but are challenging to implement*. Washington, D.C.: author.

4. Center for the Study of Social Policy. (1995). *Building new futures for at-risk youth. Findings from a five-year, multisite evaluation*. Washington, D.C.: author.

5. Norris, T. (1993). *The healthy communities handbook*. Denver: National Civic League.

6. Sustainable Seattle (1995). *Indicators of sustainable community*. Seattle: author.

7. Kellogg Youth Initiative Project, W. K. Kellogg Foundation, One Michigan Ave. East, Battle Creek, MI 49017; (616) 968–1611.

8. Public/Private Ventures, 2005 Commerce Square, Philadelphia, PA 19103; (215) 557–4400.

9. Center for Youth Development and Policy Research, Academy for Educational Development, 1875 Connecticut Ave., N. W., Washington, DC 20009; (202) 884–8273.

10. Indiana Youth Institute, 333 N. Alabama Street, Suite 200, Indianapolis, IN 46204; (317) 634–4222.

11. Stone (1996), viii–ix.

12. This project was one of the four pilot sites in the initiative by the Center for Youth Development and Policy Research called YouthMapping. It involves young people in identifying youth development opportunities in their own community. For information, call (202) 884–8273.

13. Gitlin, T. (1995). *The twilight of common dreams: Why America is wracked by culture wars*. New York: Metropolitan Books.

14. Andress, I. S., and Strommen, M. P. (1990). *Change takes time: A conceptual model for planned change*. Minneapolis: Search Institute.

15. Scales, P. C. (1996). A responsive ecology for positive young adolescent development. *Clearing House: A Journal of Educational Research, Controversy and Practices, 69*(4), 226–230.

16. Saito, R. N., et al. (1995). *Places to grow: Youth development opportunities for seven-to-fourteen-year-olds in Minneapolis*. Minneapolis: Search Institute.

17. A helpful, in-depth exploration of issues related to training across cultures is Landis, D., and Bhagat, S. (eds.). (1996). *Handbook of intercultural training (2nd ed.)*. Thousand Oaks, Calif.: Sage.

18. Dryfoos, J. G. (1994). *Full-service schools: A revolution in health and social services for children, youth, and families*. San Francisco: Jossey-Bass.

19. Louv, R. (1990). *Childhood's future*. Boston: Houghton Mifflin, p. 173.

20. Hawkins, J. D., and Catalano, R. F. (1992). *Communities that care: Action for drug abuse prevention*. San Francisco: Jossey-Bass.

21. Kretzmann, J. P., and McKnight, J. L. (1993). *Building communities from the inside out: A path toward finding and mobilizing a community's assets.* Evanston, Ill.: Center for Urban Affairs and Policy Research, Northwestern University.

Chapter Seven

1. This information is based on our initial experiences in communities, models from other efforts, and literature on community change and collaboration. As more communities move further into implementation with the asset-building concepts, this framework will be updated and adapted to reflect our growing understanding.
2. Covey, S. R. (1989). *The seven habits of highly effective people.* New York, Fireside, 98.
3. Kretzmann, J. P., and McKnight, J. L. (1993). *Building community from the inside out: A path toward finding and mobilizing a community's assets.* Evanston, Ill.: Center for Urban Affairs and Policy Research, 351–352.
4. Kurth-Schai, R. (1994). Young people as resources: The challenge of transforming dreams into reality. *New Designs for Youth Development* (Fall), 5–11.
5. Ibid.
6. Kretzmann, J. P., and Schmitz, P. H. (1995). It takes a child to raise a whole village. *Wingspread Journal* (Fall), 8–10. Reprinted with permission of the author.
7. This material draws on Winer, M. B., and Ray, K. L. (1994). *Collaboration handbook: Creating, sustaining, and enjoying the journey.* St. Paul, Minn.: Amherst H. Wilder Foundation, 45–59.
8. *Profiles of student life: Attitudes and behaviors.* For an information packet, call (800) 888–7828.
9. Briand, M. K. (1995). *Building deliberative communities.* Charlottesville, Va.: Pew Partnership for Civic Change, 9.
10. Ibid., 13.
11. Cited in Broholm, R. R. (1990). *The power and purpose of vision: A study of the role of vision in exemplary organizations.* Indianapolis: Robert K. Greenleaf Center, 6.
12. Ibid., 12–13.
13. Search Institute has developed a model and process called Vision-to-Action Planning, which integrates interpretation of survey results on young people's developmental assets. Call (800) 888–7828 for information. Other useful models are found in Grossman, W., and Norris, T. (1993). *Healthier communities action kit: A guide for leaders embracing change.* San Francisco, Calif.: The Healthcare Forum Leadership Center; Weisbord, M. R., et al. (1992) *Discovering common ground: How Future Search Conferences bring people together to achieve breakthrough innovation, empowerment, shared vision, and collaborative action.* San Francisco: Berrett-Koehler.
14. Harwood Group (1993). *Making community coalitions work.* Charlottesville, Va.: Pew Partnership for Civic Change, 5.
15. Pew Partnership for Civic Change and Communities of the Future. (1994). *Creating change in American communities.* Charlottesville, Va.: author, 11.
16. Briand (1995), 8.
17. The Institute for Educational Leadership has an extensive curriculum for training facilitative leaders, titled *Preparing Collaborative Leaders.* For information, call the institute at (202) 822–8405.
18. Harwood Group (1993), 4.
19. Based on a personal interview with Barb Maher, Feb. 27, 1996.

20. It can be very effective to provide detailed information in bite-sized pieces. For example, Search Institute has prepared a set of newsletter masters called *Ideas for Parents* that organizations and community groups can customize and send out regularly to parents.

21. See, for example, Schwartz, E. (1996). *Net activism: How citizens use the Internet.* Sebastopol, Calif.: O'Reilly.

22. Millenium Communications Group. (1994). *Communications as engagement: A communications strategy for revitalization.* Washington, D.C.: author, 20.

23. See, for example, Gitlin, T. (1995). *The twilight of common dreams: Why America is wracked by culture wars.* New York: Metropolitan Books.

24. Schwartz, E. (1992). *To promote the general welfare: A discussion guide for developing community social contracts.* Philadelphia: Institute for the Study of Civic Values.

25. Ibid.

26. Hamner, C. J. (1994). *Neighborhood revitalization: Building civic infrastructure.* Charlottesville, Va.: Pew Partnership for Civic Change, 5.

27. Study Circles Resource Center, Box 203, Pomfret, CT 06258; (860) 928–2616.

28. Community Self-Leadership Project, Campus Box 308 (Davis 144), Trinidad State Junior College, Trinidad, CO 81082; (719) 846–5240.

29. National Issues Forum, 100 Commons Road, Dayton, OH 45459; (800) 433–7834.

30. National Association of State Units on Aging (1984). *Intergenerational programs: A synthesis of findings, research, and demonstration projects.* Washington, D.C.: author, 17.

31. Excerpted from Roehlkepartain, J. L. (1996). *Creating intergenerational community: 75 ideas for building relationships between youth and adults.* Minneapolis: Search Institute.

32. See Newman, S., and Brummel, S. W. (eds.). (1989). *Intergenerational programs: Imperatives, strategies, impacts, trends.* Binghamton, N.Y.: Haworth Press.

33. Saito, R. N., and Blyth, D. A. (1992). *Understanding mentoring relationships.* Minneapolis: Search Institute, 6–8.

34. See Coles, R. (1993). *The call of service: A witness to idealism.* Boston: Houghton Mifflin.

35. See Roehlkepartain, E. C. (1995). *A practical guide for developing agency/school partnerships for service-learning.* Washington, D.C.: Points of Light Foundation.

36. For a congregational perspective, see Benson, P. L., and Roehlkepartain, E. C. (1993). *Beyond leaf raking: Learning to serve/serving to learn.* Nashville, Tenn.: Abingdon Press.

37. Elkind, D. (1994). *Ties that stress: The new family imbalance.* Cambridge, Mass.: Harvard University Press, 199.

38. Oldenburg, R. (1989). *The great good place: Cafes, coffee shops, community centers, beauty parlors, general stores, bars, hangouts, and how they get you through the day.* New York: Paragon House, xvi.

39. For more information, see Carnegie Council on Adolescent Development (1992). *A matter of time: Risk and opportunity in the nonschool hours.* New York: Carnegie Corporation of New York; Saito, R. N., and Roehlkepartain, E. C. (1995). *Places to grow: Youth development opportunities for seven-to-fourteen-year-olds in Minneapolis.* Minneapolis: Search Institute.

40. For information, contact MOST, School-Age Child Care Project, Center for Research on Women, Wellesley College, 106 Central Street, Wellesley, MA 02181; (612) 283–2556.

41. Oldenburg, 20–42.

42. Based on Brown, P. (1995). The role of the evaluator in comprehensive community initiatives. In J. P. Connell, A. C. Kubisch, L. B. Schorr, and C. H. Weiss. *New approaches to evaluating community initiatives: Concepts, methods, and contexts.* Washington, D.C.: Aspen Institute, 201–225.

43. A helpful exploration of the barriers faced by community coalitions is found in Wolff, T. (1995). Barriers to coalition building and strategies to overcome them. In G. Kaye and T. Wolff, *From the ground up: A workbook on coalition building and community development.* Amherst, Mass.: AHEC/Community Partners, 40–50.

Chapter Eight

1. Hedin, D., Hannes, K., and Saito, R. (1985). *Minnesota youth poll: Youth look at themselves and the world.* Minneapolis: Center for Youth Development and Research, University of Minnesota, 4.
2. Immerwahr, J. (1995). *Talking about children: A focus group report from Public Agenda.* Washington, D.C.: Public Agenda, 6.
3. Edelman, M. W. (1995.) *Guide my feet: Prayers and meditations on loving and working for children.* Boston: Beacon Press, 189.
4. Youth and America's Future (William T. Grant Foundation Commission on Work, Family, and Citizenship). (1988). *The forgotten half: Pathways to success for America's youth and young families: Final report.* Washington, D.C.: William T. Grant Foundation, 44.
5. Ibid., 51.
6. Andreasen, A. R. (1995). *Marketing social change.* San Francisco: Jossey-Bass, 3. His model builds on the extensive research and testing by Prochaska and DiClemente in a "transtheoretical model" of behavioral change. See Prochaska, J. O., and DiClemente, C. C. (1984, 1994). *The transtheoretical approach: Crossing the traditional boundaries of therapy.* Malabar, Fla.: Krieger.
7. Andreasen (1995), 149.
8. Ibid., 223.
9. Ibid., 223.
10. Ibid., 224.
11. Ibid., 263.
12. Ibid., 264.
13. Personal interview, March 5, 1996.
14. Prochaska and DiClemente (1984, 1994), 28–29.
15. Andreasen (1995), 283–286.
16. Ibid., 281.
17. Ibid., 285–286.
18. Tindall, J. A. (1995). *Peer programs: An in-depth look at peer helping.* Bristol, Pa.: Accelerated Development, 7.
19. See, for example, Varenhorst, B. V. (1978) *Curriculum guide for student peer counseling training.* Palo Alto, Calif.: author.
20. This information is adapted from Roehlkepartain, E. C. (1996). Rebuilding community: A vision for peer helping. *Peer Facilitator Quarterly, 13*(3), 12–19.
21. Personal interviews with Deon Richardson and Tom Bardal, March 19, 1996.

Chapter Nine

1. Scarf, M. (1995). *Intimate worlds: Life inside the family.* New York: Random House, xxxiv–xxxv.
2. See, for example, Furstenberg, F. (1993). How families manage risk and opportunity in dangerous neighborhoods. In W. J. Wilson (ed.), *Sociology and the public agenda.* Thousand Oaks, Calif.: Sage, 231–258.

3. Blyth, D. A., with Roehlkepartain, E. C. (1993). *Healthy communities, healthy youth: How communities contribute to positive youth development.* Minneapolis: Search Institute; Blyth, D. A., and Leffert, N. (1995). Communities as contexts for adolescent development: An empirical analysis. *Journal of Adolescent Research, 10*(1), 64–87.

4. Blyth, D. A., with Roehlkepartain, E. C. (1992) Working together: A new study highlights what youth need from communities. *Source* (May), 2.

5. Immerwahr, J., and Kamrin, J. (1995). *Talking about children: A focus group report from Public Agenda.* Washington, D.C.: Public Agenda, 7.

6. Hewlett, S. A. (1991). *When the bough breaks: The cost of neglecting our children.* New York: Basic Books, 27.

7. Bronfenbrenner, U. (1979). Beyond the deficit model in child and family policy. *Teachers College Record, 81*(1), 95–104.

8. Furstenberg (1993), 253.

9. This isn't just an issue with government assistance programs. For example, how many insurance companies will pay for family counseling without a diagnosis of some sort of serious problem?

10. Elkind, D. (1994). *Ties that stress: The new family imbalance.* Cambridge, Mass.: Harvard University Press, 8.

11. Ibid., 38.

12. For more information on asset building in families, see Feldmeyer, D., and Roehlkepartain, E. C. (1995) *Parenting with a purpose: A positive approach for raising confident, caring youth.* Minneapolis: Search Institute.

13. Scales, P. C. (1996). *Working with families with young adolescents.* Minneapolis: Search Institute.

14. Dunst, D. J., and Trivette, C. M. (1987). Enabling and empowering families: Conceptual and intervention issues. *School Psychology Review, 16*(4), 443–456.

15. Allen, M. L., Brown, P., and Finlay, B. (1992). *Helping children by strengthening families: A look at family support programs.* Washington, D.C.: Children's Defense Fund, 6–12.

16. Dunst and Trivette (1987).

17. Allen, Brown, and Finlay (1992), 13.

18. Search Institute has developed a set of newsletter masters called *Ideas for Parents* that are designed for local organizations to customize and send to parents on a regular basis. For information, call (800) 888–7828.

19. Roehlkepartain, E. C. (1997). *Building assets in congregations.* Minneapolis: Search Institute.

20. See LeFevre, D. N. (1988). *New games for the whole family.* New York: Perigee Books.

Chapter Ten

1. For a resource filled with more than five hundred ideas for how different sectors can build each individual asset, see Benson, P. L., Galbraith, J., and Espeland, P. (1995). *What kids need to succeed.* Minneapolis: Free Spirit. It includes ideas for how to build assets at home, at school, in communities, and in congregations.

2. See Roehlkepartain, E. C. (1996). *A practical guide to developing agency-school partnerships for service-learning.* Washington, D.C.: Points of Light Foundation; Cairn, R. W., and Kielsmeier, J. C. (eds.). (1991). *Growing hope: A sourcebook on integrating youth service into the school curriculum.* St. Paul, Minn.: National Youth Leadership Council.

3. Dorman, G., and Pulver, R. (1995). *Middle grades assessment program: user's manual (rev. ed.).* Minneapolis: Search Institute, 33–47.

4. Scales, P. C. (1996). *Boxed in and bored: How middle schools continue to fail young adolescents—and what good middle schools do right.* Minneapolis: Search Institute.

5. For more information on asset building in schools, see Scales, P. C. (1996); Draayer, D., and Roehlkepartain, E. C. (1995). *Learning and living: How asset building for youth can unify a school's mission.* Minneapolis: Search Institute.

6. See, for example, Carnegie Council on Adolescent Development (1993). *A matter of time: Risk and opportunity in the nonschool hours.* New York: Carnegie Corporation of New York.

7. Pittman, K. J., and Cahill, M. (1991). *A new vision: Promoting youth development.* Washington, D.C.: Center for Youth Development and Policy Research, 10.

8. Based on the 1990–1995 assets sample.

9. Carnegie Council on Adolescent Development (1993), 66–67.

10. See Leffert, N., et al. (1996). *Making the case: Measuring the impact of youth development programs.* Minneapolis: Search Institute.

11. Carnegie Council on Adolescent Development (1993), 114.

12. See Leffert, N., et al. (1996).

13. Carnegie Council on Adolescent Development (1993), 52.

14. Cisneros, H. G. (1996). *Higher ground: Faith communities and community building.* Washington, D.C.: U. S. Department of Housing and Urban Development, 3–5.

15. Roehlkepartain, E. C., and Scales, P. C. (1995). *Youth development in congregations: An exploration of the potential and barriers.* Minneapolis: Search Institute, 59–74.

16. For example, LOGOS Systems, which helps congregations develop midweek programs in Christian congregations, has made asset building part of the foundation and training for its work. In promotional literature, program leaders suggest that their program has the potential of building most of the developmental assets identified by Search Institute.

17. Roehlkepartain, E. C. (1997). *Building assets in congregations.* Minneapolis: Search Institute.

18. Ibid.

19. Ibid., chapter seven.

20. For more suggestions on congregations' role in asset building, see Seefeldt, G. A., and Roehlkepartain, E. C. (1995). *Tapping the potential: Discovering congregations' role in building assets in youth.* Minneapolis: Search Institute.

21. Institute for the Study of Civic Values (1994). *Block club social contract: "To secure the blessings of liberty."* Philadelphia: author.

22. Community Partnerships with Youth (1997). Growing caring neighborhoods. *Empowerment News,* 3(1), 1–2.

Chapter Eleven

1. Grossman, W., and Norris, T. (1993). *Healthier communities action kit—module 1: Getting started.* San Francisco: Healthcare Forum Leadership Center, 4.

2. Tyler, K. (1996). Collaboration: One community's story. *Assets: The Magazine of Ideas for Healthy Communities & Healthy Youth,* Autumn, 8–9.

3. See Roehlkepartain, E. C. (1996). *A practical guide for developing agency/school partnerships for service-learning.* Washington, D.C.: Points of Light Foundation.

4. See also Geraghty, L.L.G., and Roehlkepartain, E. C. (1995). *Renewing hope: Strengthening community-based organizations' role in helping youth thrive.* Minneapolis: Search Institute.

5. For information, see Kunstler, J. H. (1993). *The geography of nowhere: The rise and decline of America's man-made landscape.* New York: Simon & Schuster (especially chapter thirteen).

6. A useful resource on reexamining the physical features in a community for their impact on relationships and community health is Morris, W. R., and Brown, C. R. (1994). *Planning to stay: Learning to see the physical features of your neighborhood.* Minneapolis: Milkweed Editions.

7. For additional exploration of the role of local government in asset building, see Melton, H., and Roehlkepartain, E. C. (1995). *Finding a focus: Rethinking the public sector's role in building assets in youth.* Minneapolis: Search Institute.

8. State Legislative Leaders Foundation. (1995). *State legislative leaders: Keys to effective legislation for children and families.* Centerville, Mass.: author, 15–17.

9. Texas Commission on Children and Youth. (1994). *Safeguarding our future: Children and families first.* Austin: author, 7.

10. See American Youth Policy Forum et al. (1995). *Contract with America's youth: Toward a national youth development agenda.* Washington, D.C.: author.

11. Ibid.

12. An interesting model is the Student Service and Philanthropy Project, a partnership between the New York City Schools and the Surdna Foundation, which trained and supported youth to establish student-run foundations. For information, contact the Student Service and Philanthropy Project at (212) 877–1775.

13. ICR Survey Research Group. (1995). *Youth problems study.* New York: AUS Consultants.

14. Millennium Communications Group. (n.d.). *Communications as engagement: A communications strategy for revitalization.* Washington, D.C.: author, 17.

15. At least three prominent national organizations work to promote civic journalism: The Pew Center for Civic Journalism (Washington, D.C.); Project on Public Life and the Press, New York University (New York City); and Poynter Institute for Media Studies (St. Petersburg, Fla.).

16. Millennium Communications Group (n.d.), 38.

Postscript

1. Bly, R. (1996). *The sibling society.* Reading, Mass.: Addison-Wesley, 28.

2. Carson, E. D. (1996). We need to build circles of care around our children. *Minneapolis Star Tribune* (May 11), A19.

3. Lerner, M. (1996). *The politics of meaning: Restoring hope and possibility in an age of cynicism.* Reading, Mass.: Addison-Wesley, 4.

4. Damon, W. (1995). *Greater expectations: Overcoming the culture of indulgence in America's homes and schools.* New York: Free Press.

5. Putnam, R. D. (1996). The strange disappearance of civic America. *The American Prospect* (Winter), 34–49.

Appendix B

1. In addition to public schools, the survey has been administered in a number of private schools, both independent and parochial. A national study of students in Lutheran Church—Missouri Synod schools was completed in 1995. See Benson, P. L. (1995). *A portrait of students in Lutheran schools: Students in grades 6–12 in Lutheran Church—Missouri Synod Schools.* Minneapolis: Lutheran Brotherhood.

2. Blyth, D. A., with Roehlkepartain, E. C. (1993). *Healthy Communities, Healthy Youth.* Minneapolis: Search Institute.

3. A case in point is the Monitoring the Future project, conducted annually by the University of Michigan under contract to the National Institute on Drug Abuse.

4. For information on conducting the survey in your community, call (800) 888–7828 and ask for the information packet *Profiles of Student Life: Attitudes and Behaviors.*

5. See Elliott, D. S. (1993). Health enhancing and health compromising lifestyles. In S. G. Millstein, A. C. Petersen, and E. O. Nightingale (eds.), *Promoting the health of adolescents: New directions for the twenty-first century.* New York: Oxford University Press; Jessor, R., and Jessor, S. (1977). *Problem behavior and psychosocial development: A longitudinal study of youth.* New York: Academic Press.

INDEX

A

Abuse, prevalence of, 14. *See also* Violence

Academic achievement: developmental assets correlation with, 59, 60, 74; shared values and, 95; in United States versus other countries, 7

Academy for Educational Development, 172

Achievement motivation (asset #21), 47; academic achievement and, 74; as internal asset, 33. *See also* Commitment-to-learning assets

Action plans, developing initial, 135–136

Action stage of social marketing, 167–169. *See also* Social marketing

Action tasks for community change initiatives, 126, 128. *See also* Implementation phase; Individual engagement; Maintenance; Networking; Organizations; Renewal

Adolescents: American adults as, 41, 83; developmental assets among, state of, 54–76, 250–257; developmental assets framework and, 28; developmental needs of, versus children, 89; disconnection of, 13; discretionary time of, 43; as modern invention, 13; parent education about, 182–183; relationship building with, 161–162; relationships of, with children, 91, 149; sources of development of, 75; viewed as objects versus actors, 96–97, 108–109, 172–173; viewed as problems versus resources, 39–40, 88. *See also* Children; *Youth headings*

Adolescents at Risk (Dryfoos), 5

Adult relationships with youth: characteristics of asset-building, 160, 161–162; in community-based asset building, 114–115; proactive, 161–162. *See also* Individual engagement; Intergenerational community/relationships; Other adult relationships; Support assets

Adult role models (asset #14), 41, 42; for children, 80; and development of caring, 49; as external asset, 32; shortage of, 64. *See also* Boundaries-and-expectations assets; Individual engagement; Intergenerational community/relationships

Adults: as adolescents, 41, 83; asset-building characteristics of, 159–163; asset-building lifestyle for, 169–172; attitudes of, toward youth, 132, 160; "being" characteristics of, 160; character of, 160, 161; competencies of, 132, 160, 161; concrete actions for, 164, 169; developmental assets for, 83–85; differences among, in perception of youth problems, 158–159; discomfort of, with youth, 158; disempowerment/empowerment of, 11, 158, 167; distrust of, 159; "doing" characteristics of, 160; emotional competencies of, 84; emotional needs of, versus of children, 180; engaging, in asset building,

157–172; extrinsic rewards for, 171; hidden benefits to, 170; influencers of, 166–167, 171; monitoring satisfaction of, 170; physical health of, 84; proactive relationship-building of, 161–162; realistic expectations for, 170; relational skills of, 161; skills building for, 171; social marketing to, 163–172; stereotypes about, 162–163; youth advocacy activities of, 162. *See also* Families; Individual engagement; Intergenerational community/relationships; Other adult relationships; Parents/parenting; Social marketing

Advocacy: of community youth organizations, 200; for families, 188–189; of secondary socializing systems, 209; for youth, 162

African American youth: developmental assets prevalence in, 69–70; self-esteem in, 69–70

American Indian youth, developmental assets prevalence in, 69

Age segregation, 11, 49, 147; culture shift from, to intergenerational community, 89–91. *See also* Intergenerational community/relationships; Intergenerational support

Agendas, fragmented, versus unifying vision, 93–94, 228–229. *See also* Problem focus

Alaska, 125

Albuquerque, 31, 56; developmental assets and high-risk behavior in, 56, 57

Albuquerque Assets, 113–114

Alcohol use/abuse, 5, 7; developmental assets as protection against, 56, 57, 58. *See also* Driving and alcohol; High-risk behaviors; Substance abuse

Allen, B., 180

American Express Financial Advisors, 210

American Medical Association, 4

AmeriCorps, 114

Andreasen, A. R., 163–172

Andress, I. S., 112

Annie E. Casey Foundation, 16, 17, 104

Antisocial behavior, developmental assets as protection against, 58, 74. *See also* High-risk behaviors

Anundsen, K., 84

Arrests, prevalence of, 6

Asian American youth, developmental assets prevalence in, 69

Asset building, community-based: adult characteristics useful for, 159–163; audits for, 119, 132; in business sector, 209–210; in community-based organizations, 211–213; community change for, 103–123, 124–156; in community youth organizations, 199–201; connections across socializing systems in, 113–114, 141; costs of, 229; countercultural approach of, 115; economic infrastructure and, 110, 111, 120–121; everyday spontaneous acts of, 114–116; families and, 176–189; formal programs of, 118; in foundations, 219–220; goals for, 110–120; in government, 213–216; growing healthy communities for, 124–156; in health care systems, 210–211; images of, 226; individual action for, 114–116, 157–175; in juvenile justice system, 217–219; in the media, 220–222; in neighborhoods, 204–206; new initiative introduction in, 111, 119–120; organizations and, 116–118, 190–206, 207–223; process of change to, 121–123; in religious congregations, 201–204; in schools, 197–198; of secondary socializing systems, 207–224; service infrastructure and, 110, 111, 120–121; shared norms and beliefs in, 111, 112–113; shared vision for, 18–20, 103–104, 111, 112, 134–135; signs of progress in, 152–153. *See also* Community change; Developmental assets; Developmental assets framework; Families; Family support; Healthy communities; Individual engagement; Initiatives; Organizations; Youth development; Youth engagement

Asset-building programs, 118; expanding the reach of, 118–119. *See also* Youth programs

Asset-promotion paradigm, 18–20, 85, 225–231; culture shift toward, 86–88; versus deficit-reduction paradigm, 18–20, 86–88; development of developmental assets framework and, 28–31; educating residents about, 141–144; for families, 180–181; impact of, 227–228; versus prevention, 230; versus resiliency, 230; terms for, 230; and vision of healthy community, 20–23; versus youth development, 230. *See also* Asset building, community-based; Developmental assets; Developmental assets framework

Assets. *See* Developmental assets; Developmental assets framework

Assets: The Magazine of Ideas for Healthy Communities & Healthy Youth, 116

Assets for Colorado Youth, 125

At-risk youth, labeling of, 88. *See also* High-risk behavior

Atkinson, K., 198

Atlantic Monthly, 70

Attachment, 79, 83

Attitudes toward youth, 160; gathering information about, 132

B

Bardal, T., 174

Battle Creek, Michigan, 105

Beauvoir, S. de, 66

Behavioral choices: developmental assets influence on, 55–62, 73–75; factors in, 62. *See also* High-risk behaviors

Beliefs, shared, 111, 112–113